Religious Diversity in Australia

Also Available from Bloomsbury

The Covid Pandemic and the World's Religions,
Edited by George D. Chryssides and Dan Cohn-Sherbok
Religion and Inequality in Africa, Edited by Ezra Chitando,
Loreen Maseno and Joram Tarusarira
Beyond Religion in India and Pakistan, Virinder S. Kalra and
Navtej K. Purewal

Religious Diversity in Australia

Living Well with Difference

Edited by
Douglas Ezzy, Anna Halafoff, Greg Barton
and Rebecca Banham

BLOOMSBURY ACADEMIC
LONDON • NEW YORK • OXFORD • NEW DELHI • SYDNEY

BLOOMSBURY ACADEMIC
Bloomsbury Publishing Plc, 50 Bedford Square, London, WC1B 3DP, UK
Bloomsbury Publishing Inc, 1359 Broadway, New York, NY 10018, USA
Bloomsbury Publishing Ireland, 29 Earlsfort Terrace, Dublin 2, D02 AY28, Ireland

BLOOMSBURY, BLOOMSBURY ACADEMIC and the Diana logo are trademarks of
Bloomsbury Publishing Plc

First published in Great Britain 2024
Paperback edition published 2025

Cover design: Rebecca Heselton
Cover image © Attila Csaszar

A catalogue record for this book is available from the British Library.

A catalog record for this book is available from the Library of Congress.
Names: Ezzy, Douglas, editor.
Title: Religious diversity in Australia : living well with difference /
edited by Douglas Ezzy, Anna Halafoff, Greg Barton, and Rebecca Banham.
Description: London; New York : Bloomsbury Academic, 2025. |
Includes bibliographical references and index.
Identifiers: LCCN 2023036372 | ISBN 9781350334441 (hb) | ISBN 9781350334489 (pb) |
ISBN 9781350334458 (epdf) | ISBN 9781350334465 (ebook)
Subjects: LCSH: Australia–Religion. | Religious pluralism–Australia. |
Cultural pluralism–Australia.
Classification: LCC BL2610 .R485 2025 | DDC 200.994–dc23/eng/20230929
LC record available at https://lccn.loc.gov/2023036372

ISBN: HB: 978-1-3503-3444-1
PB: 978-1-3503-3448-9
ePDF: 978-1-3503-3445-8
eBook: 978-1-3503-3446-5

Typeset by Newgen KnowledgeWorks Pvt. Ltd., Chennai, India

For product safety related questions contact productsafety@bloomsbury.com.

To find out more about our authors and books visit www.bloomsbury.com
and sign up for our newsletters.

In memory and appreciation of Emeritus Prof. Gary D. Bouma

Contents

Tables

Maps

Contributors

Dharma Arunachalam is a social demographer at School of Social Sciences, Monash University. His current research focuses on cultural diversity and immigrant integration, including intermarriage, in Australia and population dynamics in Australia and India.

Rebecca Banham is a research fellow at the University of Tasmania, where she completed her PhD in environmental sociology in 2019. Her current work focuses on religious diversity in Australia and the sociology of (non)religion.

Greg Barton is Research Professor in Global Islamic Politics in the Alfred Deakin Institute for Citizenship and Globalisation. He is an adjunct professor at the School of Strategic and Global Studies, University of Indonesia. His most recent book (with Matteo Vergani) is *Countering Violent and Hateful Extremism in Indonesia: Islam, Gender and Civil Society* (2022). His current research includes an ARC project, 'Appropriate International Development Intervention Responses to Address Violent and Hateful Extremism in Asia'; a second ARC 'Religious Populism, Emotions and Political Mobilisation in Turkey, Indonesia and Pakistan' and another ARC 'Religious Diversity in Australia'.

Lori G. Beaman is the Canada Research Chair in Religious Diversity and Social Change, professor in the Department of Classics and Religious Studies at the University of Ottawa and the director and principal investigator of the 'Nonreligion in a Complex Future' project. Recent publications include 'Towards Equality: Including Non-human Animals in Studies of Lived Religion and Nonreligion', (with Lauren Strumos) *Social Compass* 70(2) (June 2023), *The Transition of Religion to Culture in Law and Public Discourse* (2020) and *Deep Equality in an Era of Religious Diversity* (2017).

Gary Bouma AM was the UNESCO Chair in Intercultural and Interreligious Relations – Asia Pacific, Emeritus Professor of Sociology at Monash University. His research in the sociology of religion examines the management of religious diversity in plural multicultural societies. His books include *Australian Soul: Religion and Spirituality in the Twenty-First Century* (2006) and *Being Faithful in Diversity: Religions and Social Policy in Multifaith Societies* (2011).

Danielle Campbell is currently an independent social researcher who undertakes collaborations with the University of Tasmania, Australia. Her research focuses on trauma, transition and vulnerability. She currently works primarily in the emergency management and in leadership. Her PhD focused on understanding police and newly arrived refugee interactions and relationships in a regional Australian setting.

Angela Dwyer is Associate Professor in Policing and Emergency Management, School of Social Sciences, University of Tasmania, and the deputy director of the Tasmanian Institute of Law Enforcement Studies. Angela conducts research on the intersection between sexuality, gender diversity and criminal justice and is the lead editor of *Queering Criminology*, edited with Matthew Ball and Thomas Crofts, and published with Palgrave.

Douglas Ezzy is Professor of Sociology at the University of Tasmania, Australia. He is the lead investigator of the Australian Research Council Discovery Projects 'Religious Diversity in Australia: Strategies to Maintain Social Cohesion' and 'Religious Freedom, LGBT+ Employees, and the Right to Discriminate'. He is a co-investigator on the Canadian 'Nonreligion in a Complex Future' project led by Professor Lori Beaman. His books include *LGBT Christians* (2017, with Bronwyn Fielder), *Sex, Death, and Witchcraft* (2014) and *Teenage Witches* (2007, with Helen Berger).

Ruth Fitzpatrick is a research fellow with Deakin University and has served on a range of projects relating to religion, spirituality and contemplative traditions and their relationship to young people, death and dying, conspiracy movements, religious diversity and education. Her earlier research specialised on how cultural narratives shape what Australian Buddhists conceive Buddhist social engagement to be.

Alan Gamlen is Associate Professor of Geography at Monash University in Melbourne, Research Associate at Oxford University's Centre on Migration, Policy and Society, and a High-Level Advisor to the United Nations Migration Agency (IOM). He was formerly founding editor-in-chief of the journal *Migration Studies* (Oxford University Press) and director of the Australian Population and Migration Research Centre. He is the author of *Human Geopolitics: States, Emigrants and the Rise of Diaspora Institutions* (2019), winner of the Distinguished Book Award for Best Book on Ethnicity and Migration, from the International Studies Association.

Anna Halafoff is Associate Professor in Sociology of Religion in the School of Humanities and Social Sciences at Deakin University, Australia. She is a chief investigator on three Australian Research Council Discovery Projects on the Worldviews of Generation Z Australians, Religious Diversity in Australia and on Australian Spirituality. Her research interests include worldview diversity, contemporary spirituality, interreligious relations, religion and education, preventing violent extremism, and Buddhism in Australia. Anna is the author of *The Multifaith Movement: Global Risks and Cosmopolitan Solutions* and co-author (with Andrew Singleton, Mary Lou Rasmussen and Gary Bouma) of *Freedoms, Faiths and Futures: Teenage Australians on Religion, Sexuality and Diversity*.

Ernest Healy is a research affiliate with the School of Social Sciences, Monash University. His research focuses on immigration trends, geography of migrant settlement and social cohesion in Australia. He co-edited *Creating Social Cohesion in an Interdependent World* (2016).

Emily Marriott is currently working as a consultant and social researcher with a focus on health, mental health and the social services sectors. Previous to this Emily was a PhD candidate in sociology at Deakin University, where she was exploring women's participation and involvement in the Men's Rights Movement. While undertaking her PhD studies, Emily was employed as a research assistant, including on a project funded by the International Research Network for Science and Belief in Society, on (Con)spirituality, Science and the COVID-19 pandemic in Australia.

Geraldine Smith is a researcher in the School of Social Sciences, the University of Tasmania, Australia. Her PhD examined the multifaith movement in Australia and the ways in which multifaith organisations facilitate respectful relations between diverse religious individuals and communities. She currently works on a range of projects such as the Australian Research Council Discovery projects 'Religious Diversity in Australia: Strategies to Maintain Social Cohesion', and the 'Religious Freedom, LGBT+ Employees, and the Right to Discriminate' as well as the Canadian 'Nonreligion in a Complex Future' project led by Professor Lori Beaman.

Enqi Weng is a research fellow at the Alfred Deakin Institute for Citizenship and Globalisation (ADI) at Deakin University. She is a sociologist with research interests in migration and multiculturalism, religion and decoloniality. She has published on media representations of religion, race and religion, religious/ cultural diversity, religious literacy and decolonial ways of thinking about 'religion'. She is vice president of the Australian Association for the Study of Religion (AASR), co-convenor for the Religion Thematic Group at TASA and reviews editor for the *Journal of Religion, Media and Digital Culture*. She is the author of *Media Perceptions of Religious Changes in Australia: Of Dominance and Diversity* (Routledge, 2020).

Acknowledgements

Chapter 1 was originally published as 'Religious Diversity through a Super-Diversity Lens: National, Sub-regional and Socio-economic Religious Diversities in Melbourne' in the *Journal of Sociology* 58(1) (2022): 7–25. We are grateful to the authors and publisher for permission to reprint it here.

The research in this book was funded by the Australian Research Council Discovery Project entitled 'Religious Diversity in Australia: Strategies to Maintain Social Cohesion' (Project ID: DP180101664).

Introduction

Douglas Ezzy, Rebecca Banham, Anna Halafoff and Greg Barton

Highly diverse, multicultural and multifaith societies, shaped by migration, provide many benefits and opportunities as well as creating numerous challenges. But, as this study of Australian society shows, these challenges can be met through transformative, community-led programmes and the development of appropriate policy responses. This book documents some of the accomplishments and unpacks key challenges in the negotiation of religious diversity in Australia. We describe the dimensions of religious diversity in Australia, paying particular attention to issues of shifting power and privilege, and the discourses and assumptions that mask the reality and practice of diversity. We also highlight examples of the practice of living well with diversity.

This book is distinctive because of the range of social contexts within which we examine religious diversity: migration, education, policing, legislation, media, countering violent extremism and interfaith practices. We consider the perspectives of individuals, organisations and social policy. Our aim is to provide a broad understanding of effective, respectful *and* problematic negotiations of religious diversity in Australia. These negotiations are formal and informal, legislated and everyday practices, symbolic and concrete and often all of these things at once. It is this breadth of perspective that makes this book unique. It is important to identify tensions, barriers and inequalities in the negotiation of religious diversity. These contribute to significant harms, some of which are examined in the following chapters. We also seek out important positive responses to religious diversity, identifying constructive experiences and successful strategies.

Encouraging respectful practices and constraining harm is a theme that runs through our analyses. Members of religious minorities experience significant discrimination, vilification and harassment in Australia, as has been extensively documented elsewhere (Iner 2019, Markus 2021) and in the chapters of this book. In several key areas, our analyses extend Ghassan Hage's (1998: 237) insightful notion of multiculturalism as a policy. Multiculturalism emerged as a result of ethnically diverse Australians fighting hard for representation and for an active role in governance, with policies of multiculturalism created from below and above, 'precisely because diversity had already become an entrenched part of social reality' (Hage 1998: 237). In a similar way, Australia's religious diversity is 'an entrenched part of social reality' (see Weng and Halafoff 2021). The policies and practices that embrace and respond constructively to the reality of religious diversity are often a product of the hard work of religiously diverse Australians.

Global crises, such as the post-11 September 2001 threat of terrorism (amplified by the unintended consequences of lengthy military campaigns in Afghanistan, Iraq and beyond) and the rise of white supremacist violent extremism (shockingly brought home by an Australian far-right terrorist shooting fifty-one people dead in two Christchurch mosques in March 2019) have had significant impacts on multifaith relations in Australia. Many communities, the Muslim community in particular, have been subjected to new forms of discrimination and securitization as a result of geopolitical tensions. In the face of such events, diaspora communities have partnered with state actors to counter their negative impacts, and these well-established networks have therefore been in place to deal with new crises as they occur (Bouma et al. 2007; Halafoff 2013). In this book we examine such constructive policies and practices as implemented in a wide range of social contexts.

The diversity of religious diversity is another key theme (Bouma, Halafoff and Barton 2022). Both the Christian and Muslim communities in Australia, for example, are becoming increasingly ethnically diverse, with complex inter-group and demographic characteristics driven by migration and residential mobility. Here we extend Inger Furseth's (2017) analysis of religious complexity and Gary Bouma and Anna Halafoff's (2017) analysis of Australia's religious super-diversity. Religion and nonreligion run as themes across and throughout the various chapters. Religious diversity is interwoven with diversities of languages, ethnicities, histories, geographies, migration and media representations.

Another key theme that runs through the book is that of power and privilege, and the challenges and constraints on funding and resources, including how resources are unevenly or inconsistently distributed in Australia. White Christian Australians have considerable resources, access to power and privileges. Here our arguments build on critical responses to Australia's 1901 Immigration Restriction Act, known as the White Australia Policy (Hage 1998;

Bouma and Halafoff 2017; Reynolds 2003). The large numbers and successes of (particularly) the Chinese and Japanese diaspora in the far north of Australia led to the introduction of this racist policy, which then socially engineered the myth of a white, Christian nation (Hage 1998; Halafoff et al. 2022; Reynolds 2003). The 1901 Immigration Restriction Act stemmed the flow of non-white migration to Australia (although non-white Australians who had already settled in Australia, some with their families, were permitted to stay). In the 1970s, this began to change when policies of multiculturalism began to be introduced. Consequently, Australia during the White Australia Policy years was never actually as white as it was imagined to be, particularly across the far north (Ganter 2005; Halafoff et al. 2022; Reynolds 2003). In a similar way, we note throughout this volume how Christian privilege, consciously and unconsciously, shapes policies and practices to exclude, and facilitate marginalisation of, and discrimination towards, diverse religiosities and spiritualities in Australia.

Alongside this, we explore how belonging – and the visibility of belonging – are important expressions of the social inclusion of diverse religiosities. Examples of this include the use of non-English languages, Indigenous place names, public expressions of ethnic and cultural identity and the processes surrounding the approval and construction of religious buildings. This develops and extends previous analyses of how a sense of belonging is an affective, multilayered, dynamic process comprising complex 'everyday practices' (Yuval-Davis 2006; Anthius 2013; Antonsich 2010). As Nira Yuval-Davis (2006: 205) pointedly notes, the 'politics of belonging involves not only the maintenance and reproduction of the boundaries of the community of belonging by the hegemonic political powers but also their contestation and challenge by other political agents'. Migration has generated a diversity of religiosities in Australia that is 'strategically interruptive, decentring the boundaries and borders of place and identity' (Davidson 2008: 15–16). It is precisely this process, and the responses of people with diverse religiosities to this process, that we examine in this volume.

This book arose out of the Australian Research Council Discovery Project entitled 'Religious Diversity in Australia: Strategies to Maintain Social Cohesion' (Project ID: DP180101664). The chief investigators on this project were Douglas Ezzy, Anna Halafoff, Greg Barton and Gary Bouma. The partner investigators were Lori Beaman and Robert Jackson, whose participation was more limited by their international locations. Rebecca Banham, Enqi Weng and Ruth Fitzpatrick were employed as postdoctoral fellows on the project. Geraldine Smith was a PhD student on the project, and Smith, Danielle Campbell and Emily Marriott worked as research assistants on the project. We met regularly as a team as we designed and conducted our respective research streams. The book is very much a collective endeavour, as the varied and shared authorship of each chapter shows. Our focus is on Victoria and Tasmania, although other parts of Australia are often discussed. Ethics approval for all the research projects was obtained through the University of Tasmania Human Research Ethics Committee. We also note our deep gratitude to all the participants who agreed to talk to us as part of the various research projects that form the foundation of this book.

This volume is centred predominantly on religious diversity in Australia. It also examines the growing significance of nonreligious and spiritual worldviews in this country (Halafoff, Singleton and Fitzpatrick 2023). As none of the editors or chief investigators of the research project is Indigenous it is inappropriate for us to represent Indigenous knowledge and culture (Walter et al. 2021). However, wherever appropriate we have sought to acknowledge First Nations perspectives where they intersect with the themes of the book.

Chapter summaries

In Chapter 1 Gary Bouma, Dharma Arunachalam, Alan Gamlen and Ernest Healy provide a detailed analysis of the demography of religious diversity in Melbourne as influenced by migration and residential mobility. Drawing on Vertovec's (2010) concept of super-diversity, they emphasise the way religious diversity is interwoven with other diversities of nationality, language and ethnicity. They describe how some areas of Melbourne are characterised by high religious diversity, whereas others have much lower levels of diversity. And this diversity is itself diverse, with areas of high religious diversity being overlaid with diversities of nationality, residential mobility, suburb location and length of establishment. The cosmopolitan residential churn of the inner suburbs is quite different from residential turnover in the mid-range suburbs where ageing populations are being replaced by arrivals from East and Southeast Asia. Similarly, the Muslims and Christians from the Eastern Mediterranean region who are establishing themselves in the outer metropolitan areas are quite different South Asians in these suburbs. They highlight that these different types of diversities have very different policy implications, emphasising the inter- and intra-group diversity of religion and ethnicity in Australia.

In Chapter 2, Douglas Ezzy, Anna Halafoff, Greg Barton and Rebecca Banham examine Australian attitudes towards religious diversity and the impact of Christian nationalism. It highlights the variation in attitudes towards diversity, with approximately one-third of survey respondents supportive of religious diversity and one-third antagonistic to religious diversity. Younger people and people with more education are more likely to be supportive of diversity. One striking finding of the chapter is that it is Christian nationalist ideas, rather than Christian practice, that are most associated with antagonism to religious diversity. Christian nationalists are sometimes also practising Christians, but often they are not practising Christians. Rather, they are people who want Christian prayers in Parliament, and Christian values to guide all Australians, even Australians who are nonreligious or who follow other religions. It is not surprising that such people are antagonistic to religious diversity. Significantly, these findings introduce the complex background of privilege, discrimination and concerns about freedom in Australian religious diversity.

Similar themes of privilege are developed in Chapter 3 on the media, where Anna Halafoff, Emily Marriot, Geraldine Smith and Enqi Weng examine the reporting of spirituality, religion, nonreligion and related terms in mainstream newspapers in Melbourne and Hobart. They demonstrate that Abrahamic institutional religions are treated more seriously and given more respect than other forms of religion, such as Buddhism or Hinduism, and forms of spirituality. Furthermore, while the authors report that discussion of nonreligion or secularity is widespread, it is often represented in more negative ways than Christianity. They also make the point that conservative news media is more likely to represent non-Christian forms of religion and spirituality negatively. Because of the monopoly of Murdoch/News Corp owned newspapers in many Australian cities, this means that the privileging of Christianity and negative views of other religions, spirituality and nonreligion are reinforced in these parts of Australia. At the same time the authors note a growing interest in and respect for First Nations spirituality and culture in Australian media.

Chapter 4 examines the interweaving of religion and the diaspora communities of Chinese, Indian, Russian and Afghan Australians. In this chapter, Anna Halafoff, Rebecca Banham, Enqi Weng, Greg Barton and Gary Bouma examine the history of these communities in Australia, their experiences of racism, belonging and resistance, and the impact of Covid-19. Religion and ethnic identity are related in complex and changing ways, reflecting the dynamics of the treatment of these communities by their host nation, their relationships with their countries of origin and geopolitical relations.

In Chapter 5, Anna Halafoff and Ruth Fitzpatrick analyse Australian and Victorian curricula for their discussion of diverse worldviews, spiritual, religious and nonreligious. They argue that Christianity and Abrahamic faiths are privileged in these, and particularly the Australian curricula, and that religious diversity, including First Nations spirituality, so-called minority faiths, and nonreligious worldviews receive far less serious attention. This is important because recent research, conducted by Halafoff and her colleagues, has demonstrated that students who are provided with more inclusive educational material about diverse religions are more accepting and respectful of people from diverse religious backgrounds (Singleton et al. 2021).

Geraldine Smith and Anna Halafoff's Chapter (6) on the multifaith movement in Australia documents that while the early forms of the multifaith movement focused on dialogue between representatives of religious traditions, this is changing with reductions in government funding and as younger people are increasingly adopting complex and hybrid forms of religiosity. They emphasise the performed and relational aspects of multifaith that facilitate the development of respectful relationships between people of diverse religiosities. The chapter illustrates the important link between practitioners, policymakers and religious representatives than can be made by the multifaith movement in their account of the Faith Communities Council of Victoria, the Common Statement and yearly renewal of this by the Interfaith Network of the City of Greater Dandenong. Multifaith plays an important role in both individual and collective practices of respect, and this chapter emphasises both formal and informal frameworks in the negotiation of religious diversity.

The legislation Chapter (7) from Douglas Ezzy, Rebecca Banham, Lori Beaman and Geraldine Smith highlights how the desire to protect Christian privilege drives much of the opposition to religious anti-discrimination legislation. Religious minorities in Australia – including Muslims, Buddhists, Hindus, Sikhs and Pagans – report disturbing and distressing forms of discrimination and vilification. A mosque is set on fire, a Sikh is prevented from enrolling in a school and a Pagan is physically assaulted. In contrast, the harms reported by Christian conservatives largely focus on their inability to engage in conduct that would harm others. This chapter argues that religious anti-discrimination and anti-vilification legislation can be an effective mechanism as one part of a broader set of policies and practices to encourage the respectful negotiation of religious difference.

The Policing Chapter (8) by Rebecca Banham, Douglas Ezzy, Greg Barton, Danielle Campbell and Angela Dwyer describes the challenges of policing in an increasingly religiously diverse society. In particular, the chapter highlights the tensions between proactive forms of policing, also referred to as community policing, and the more standard 'call and response' model of policing. Tasmania and Victoria have very different types and experiences of religious diversity, which in turn impacts policing practices. Victoria Police's greater size and diversity has resulted in a more proactive engagement with diversity and more resources. Tasmania Police's smaller size has created particular challenges and creative forms of engagement. Both underline the strength and value of community policing and community partnerships for effective police engagement with a religiously diverse community. Concerns about extremism remain typically focused on minority religions, although this may be changing.

Chapter 9, by Greg Barton and Anna Halafoff, charts the development and impact of preventing and countering violent extremism (P/CVE) programmes in Australia, with a particular focus on Victoria, critically setting out the historical development of CVE in a manner never done before. P/CVE programmes, done well, can be a vital complement to counterterrorism (CT), when they involve community-led initiatives to build social cohesion and resilience, engage with individuals and groups at risk and work to effect rehabilitation. The chapter examines the emerging evidence that cooperative P/CVE programmes are the most effective and beneficial. Much of the critical work of P/CVE requires trustful cooperation with police. Without the leadership of community groups, police are incapable of developing and running effective P/CVE programmes. Similarly, without the support of police, community groups are severely constrained in terms of what they can accomplish, particularly with respect to engaging with at-risk individuals and facilitating rehabilitation. Earlier CT and CVE programmes left the Muslim community in particular feeling stigmatised and undermined from all sides. But the rise of the Islamic State caliphate, so-called, in June 2014, and the awareness of the widescale impact of grooming and recruitment that saw hundreds of young Australians travel, or attempt to travel, to Syria via Turkey to join violent extremist groups, precipitated a new level of cooperation between community groups and government agencies.

In Chapter 10 Lori Beaman contextualises the findings of the book through international comparisons. She highlights Bouma et al.'s (Chapter 1) analysis of super-diversity and the geography of diversity. A key comparison made here is with Dejean and Germain's (2022) study of the role of urban policies in the regulation of religious diversity in Montreal. Next Beaman considers the themes of nationalism and belonging (referencing Halafoff et al.'s Chapter 4 on migration). Nationalism can reinforce privilege and result in exclusion for religious diversities. It can, however, also be a moment of inclusion, referencing Modood's (2010: 6) conception of multiculturalism as 'based not just on the equal dignity of individuals but also on the political accommodation of group identities as a means of challenging exclusionary racisms and practices and fostering respect and inclusion for demeaned groups'. Finally, she compares Ezzy et al's (Chapter 7) analysis of legislation in Australia with similar legal developments in Canada and elsewhere. At the heart of Beaman's chapter is an argument for conceptualising '"we" as diverse and equal'.

Australia has a complex history of the treatment of diverse religions. Christianity has often, and continues to be, privileged. Evidence of this privilege is found in a range of places, including the media, education, the law and the treatment of migrant communities. Respectful ways of living well with religious diversity are encouraged when members of diverse religions see themselves represented in the media and educational materials and treated fairly in government policies and the law. Such respectful practices are facilitated by the interfaith movement, critical worldviews education and are the foundation of effective policing and the prevention of violent extremism. As Australia, and the world, moves into an increasingly challenging future, we hope that the insights provided in this book can contribute to respectful and creative ways of living well with religious diversity, cognisant that religious freedom does not impinge upon the rights and freedoms of others.

References

Anthias, F. 2013. 'Moving beyond the Janus Face of Integration and Diversity Discourses: Towards an Intersectional Framing'. *Sociological Review* 61: 323–43.

Antonsich, M. 2010. 'Searching for Belonging – An Analytical Framework'. *Geography Compass* 4(6): 644–59.

Bouma, G., and Halafoff, A. 2017. 'Australia's Changing Religious Profile – Rising Nones and Pentecostals, Declining British Protestants in Superdiversity: Views from the 2016 Census'. *Journal for the Academic Study of Religion* 30(2): 129–43.

Bouma, G., Halafoff, A., and Barton, G. 2022. 'Worldview Complexity: The Challenge of Intersecting Diversities for Conceptualising Diversity'. *Social Compass* 69(2): 186–204.

Bouma, G. D., Pickering, S., Dellal, H., and Halafoff, A. 2007. *Managing the Impact of Global Crisis Events on Community Relations in Multicultural Australia*. City East, Queensland: Multicultural Affairs Queensland and the Victorian Office of Multicultural Affairs.

Davidson, A. P. 2008. 'The Play of Identity, Memory and Belonging: Chinese Migrants in Sydney'. In K.-P. Khun Eng and A. P. Davidson (eds), *At Home in the Chinese Diaspora*. London: Palgrave Macmillan, 12–32.

Dejean, F., and Germain, A. 2022. *Se faire une place dans la cite: la participation des groupes religieux à la vie urbaine*. Montréal: Les Presses de l'Université de Montréal.

Furseth, I., ed. 2017. *Religious Complexity in the Public Sphere: Comparing Nordic Countries*. London: Springer.

Ganter, R. 2005. 'Turning the Map Upside Down'. *Griffith Review* 9. https://www.griffith review.com/articles/turning-the-map-upside-down/. Accessed 12 April 2021.

Hage, G. 1998. *White Nation: Fantasies of White Supremacy in a Multicultural Society*. Annandale: Pluto Press.

Halafoff, A. 2013. *The Multifaith Movement, Global Risks and Cosmopolitan Solutions*. Dordrecht: Springer.

Halafoff, A., Lam, K., Weng, E., and Smith, S. 2022. 'Buddhism in the Far North of Australia Pre-WWII: (In)visibility, Post-Colonialism and Materiality'. *Journal of Global Buddhism* 23(2): 105–28.

Halafoff, A., Singleton, A., and Fitzpatrick, R. 2023. 'Spiritual Complexity in Australia: Wellbeing and Risks'. *Social Compass* 70(3): 003776862311620.

Iner, D. 2019. *Islamophobia in Australia* (2016–17). https://www.islamophobia.com. au/wp-content/uploads/2019/12/Islamophobia-Report-2019-2.pdf. Accessed 1 August 2022.

Markus, A. 2021. 'Mapping Social Cohesion. Scanlon Foundation Research Institute'. Scanlon Institute. https://scanloninstitute.org.au/sites/default/files/2021-12/ Mapping_Social_Cohesion_2021_Report_0.pdf. Accessed 1 August 2022.

Modood, T. 2010. *Multiculturalism*. Chichester: John Wiley.

Reynolds, H. 2003. *North of Capricorn: The Untold Story of Australia's North*. Crows Nest, New South Wales: Allen & Unwin.

Walter, M., Lovett, R., Maher, B., Williamson, B., Prehn, J., Bodkin-Andrews, G., and Lee, V. 2021. 'Indigenous Data Sovereignty in the Era of Big Data and Open Data'. *Australian Journal of Social Issues* 56(2): 143–56.

Weng, E., and Halafoff, A. 2021. 'Religion on an Ordinary News Day in Australia: Hidden Christianity and the Pervasiveness of Lived Religion, Spirituality and the Secular Sacred'. *Religion, Media and Digital Culture* 10: 225–49.

Yuval-Davis, N. 2006. 'Belonging and the Politics of Belonging'. *Patterns of Prejudice* 40(3): 197–214.

Religious Diversity through a Super-Diversity Lens: National, Sub-regional and Socio-economic Religious Diversities in Melbourne

Gary Bouma, Dharma Arunachalam, Alan Gamlen and Ernest Healy

Introduction

Religious diversity is becoming more diverse – as new waves of immigrants and residential relocators compound and complicate existing patterns of religious difference in different parts of major cities. This new 'super-diversification' explodes previous ideas of the components of a multicultural society and thus has implications for how we conceptualise, theorise and analyse the demography of cities. Moreover, measuring and mapping religious diversity is important for social policy and planning purposes, not least because religious organisations and people play persistent, albeit changing, roles in public life (Casanova 1994; Gryzmala-Busse 2015). We address the challenge of deciding what to measure and at what spatial and denominational levels of detail. Our analyses reveal how patterns of religious diversity in Melbourne vary by urban location and have been the product of both immigration and intra-urban mobility over time.

Prior studies often examine migration and diversity at the national scale, overlooking diversities that matter crucially within cities and even more so within suburbs (Gamlen 2010). Our analysis thus focuses not on nation-states but on neighbourhoods, revealing the dimensions of diversity that persons and families are negotiating in daily life within major cities (Beaman 2017; Cloke and Beaumont 2012). Our approach parallels the growing interest in the governance of religious diversity in urban settings (Burchardt 2019; Martinez-Ariño 2019) and diversity within religious categories (Becci 2018; Burchardt and Becci 2016; Stringer 2014). Moreover, while most examinations of the governance of religious diversity examine Muslim and Christian interactions, we discover a substantially richer and more dynamic diversity of local religious diversities intersecting in one richly diverse major metropolitan area: Melbourne, Australia.

This chapter reveals the diversities within what were previously considered single-colour elements in a spatial mosaic of urban religious diversity. Our analyses focus on the key processes of human mobility that are driving these changes. One is continuing immigration from countries outside Australia, which is increasing the range of national groups within existing religious communities, and vice versa. Another is residential mobility between our focal suburbs and other parts of Melbourne and Australia. This often leads to spatial concentrations of particular religious and national groups. These dynamics are complicating the older religious diversities in different parts of cities and leading to distinctive new intersections of national and ethnic identity in specific urban neighbourhoods.

The layering of these cross-cutting and intersecting axes of social difference is leading to what has been called 'super-diversity', a term designed to draw attention to the increasingly multidimensional nature of urban diversity (Vertovec 2007). The key dimensions of our analyses include nationality, residential background, length of settlement, urban location and income level – factors which are themselves diverging in large cities like Melbourne. We present data showing how different combinations of these dimensions of social difference are leading to increasing levels and types of diversity in self-identified religious affiliation. Thus, we show how a diversification of religious diversities is contributing to Melbourne's emerging super-diversity (Davern et al. 2015; Sharifian and Musgrave 2013; Williams and Mikola 2018).

We outline our conceptual understanding of 'religious diversity' and 'super-diversity' and explain how we operationalise the concept. We then delineate five key dimensions of urban change that we have found to be crucial in the diversification of religious diversities that now characterise Melbourne: religious dissimilarity, immigrant nationality, residential mobility, suburb location and suburb length of establishment. After describing overarching changes in each of these dimensions between the 2011 and 2016 censuses, we analyse how these cross-cutting dimensions of diversity are intersecting to generate distinctive configurations of religious diversity in Melbourne. Through our analyses, we derive a working typology of urban religious diversity in what we refer to as 'Cosmopolitan Hipster Villages', 'East Asian Turnover Settlements', 'Levantine Gateway Enclaves' and 'South Asian Growth Corridors', so named to reflect emerging shared characteristics of diversity rather than the dominant religion or ethnicity – there being none. We discuss the challenges of religious super-diversification and re-homogenisation for policy, planning and service provision in Melbourne.

Our analyses reveal that, in Melbourne, combinations of existing patterns of religious difference, compounded by successive waves of immigration, residential mobility and socio-economic change, are producing fundamentally new compounds of religious and national diversity. The emergence of these new urban social compounds presents national immigration and settlement policymakers and urban planners with a challenging 'diversity of diversities', as both established and more recently settled groups welcome new members who come from different national, neighbourhood and class backgrounds. Furthermore, these new combinations of urban diversity present scholars of religion, ethnicity, nationality and migration with challenges regarding how to conceptualise, analyse and theorise the nature of social diversity in twenty-first-century cities.

Religious super-diversification and re-homogenisation

The diversification of religious diversities in Melbourne is leading to what Steven Vertovec has called super-diversity, 'a term intended to capture a level and kind of complexity surpassing anything many migrant-receiving countries have previously experienced' (Vertovec 2010: 1024). The concept has taken root in disciplines including 'sociology, anthropology, geography, political science, migration and ethnic studies ... linguistics, history, education, law, business studies, management, literature, media studies, public health, social work, urban planning and landscape studies' (Vertovec 2014: 92; cf. Becci 2018; Davern et al. 2015; Sharifian and Musgrave 2013; Stringer 2014; Vertovec 2006; Williams and Mikola 2018). In this section we detail our conceptual approach to urban super-diversity, identify a need for greater attention to what we refer to as re-homogenisation in contexts of urban super-diversification and outline the research methodology underlying this article.

Conceptual framework

Super-diversity draws attention to the increasingly multidimensional nature of urban diversity, which is the result of the layering of cross-cutting and intersecting axes of social difference (Vertovec 2007). For Sigona, the 'super-diversity lens' provides new 'ways of looking at a society getting increasingly complex, composite, layered and unequal' (Sigona 2013). The lens of super-diversity draws our attention to increased differences among migrants' 'nationality, ethnicity, language, and religion, but also ... motives, patterns and itineraries of migration, processes of insertion into the labour and housing markets of the host societies, and so on' (Blommaert and Rampton 2016: 21).

A key purpose of the super-diversity lens is to break down the black boxes of reified, binary social categories and assert the emergence of social 'complexity' as the new baseline for social analysis (Meissner 2015). As well as addressing the problem of 'culturalism in multiculturalism' – and its arrangement of political representation and service provision around the reified boundaries of 'cultural communities' – thinking in terms of super-diversity resists the tendency to collapse all categories of social difference (e.g. race, culture, income, education) into ethnicity, which can exacerbate problems of segregation, stigma and stereotyping (Vertovec 1996, 2010). Super-diversity calls for analyses that disaggregate morality-play-like social caricatures into their constituent layers and dimensions, and in this sense it is related to the concept of 'intersectionality', which studies 'the complexity that arises when the subject of analysis expands to include multiple dimensions of social life and categories of analysis' (McCall 2005: 1772). As Vertovec (2014: 92) puts it

> it is not enough to see 'diversity' only in terms of ethnicity, as is regularly the case both in social science and the wider public sphere. In order to understand and more fully address the complex nature of contemporary, migration-driven diversity, additional variables need to be better recognized by social scientists, policy-makers, practitioners and the public.

Although the reification of culture is a central target of the term, super-diversity also takes issue with a range of homogenising categories of difference and calls for the recognition that these categories are breaking down and no longer capable of describing or explaining how social difference is now organised in major cities (Vertovec 2021). Formerly majority groups may become minorities, the children of migrants may integrate into many social groups rather than one, and we see both a proliferation of groups and of differences within those groups – to the point where 'grand theories like segmented and new assimilation theory no longer suffice in tackling that new reality of large cities' (Crul 2016: 54). As a result, 'the predictability of the category of "migrant" and of his/her sociocultural features has disappeared' (Blommaert and Rampton 2016: 21).

Far from being an abstraction, the concept of super-diversity has direct relevance for issues of migration governance at multiple scales (Gamlen and Marsh 2011), including for challenges of national immigration and settlement policy, and for urban planning in increasingly complex city neighbourhoods. For example, super-diversity studies often address the shortcomings of culturally oriented forms of welfare and service provision. They highlight the complexity of perspectives, political positions and service needs that multiculturalism does not address – and indeed conceals. Unlike multicultural places, which may be characterised by large spatial concentrations of purportedly homogeneous ethno-religious groups that are represented in politics and policy, super-diverse places are characterised by a kaleidoscope of small groups, where new diversity interacts with old, creating new configurations of social difference and thus new challenges for service providers (Berg 2019; Phillimore 2011: 7).

Excellent work has already been done in Australia relevant to the emergence of urban super-diversity, and some pioneering work has recently emerged on Melbourne. Fincher et al. (2014: 1) investigate how 'multicultural urban planning simultaneously celebrates diversity and reinforces difference'. Wise and Noble (2016, 2018) explore how migrants negotiate 'shared life' in super-diverse urban locations, focusing on novel expressions of 'conviviality' – roughly defined as 'the capacity to live together'. Martin (2018) uses the super-diversity lens to analyse recurring moral panics about ethnic gangs in Australian cities. Davern et al. (2015: 5) note that 'Melbourne is ... one of the world's most superdiverse cities'. Moving beyond the notion of a 'multicultural' city, with large concentrations of ethnic communities located in particular areas, they highlight the emergence of high levels of 'population fragmentation' in parts of Melbourne and argue that the concept of super-diversity can 'help policy makers and practitioners respond in a more nuanced way to the ever changing and diversifying populations whom they serve' (Davern et al. 2015: 6). Here we build on such studies, highlighting how recent immigration and residential mobility patterns are interacting with earlier rural and regional settlement patterns, spreading new levels and types of diversity into new fringe suburbs, edge cities and rural areas around the Australian state of Victoria, presenting new challenges for social and health service delivery and planning.

Moreover, in this article we seek to highlight a relatively under-examined aspect of the super-diversification process, which we refer to as re-homogenisation. In our view, super-diversity researchers have focused predominantly on the disintegration of old group boundaries and less on the integration of diverse populations into new forms of social groups. We note that more could be done to delineate how emerging combinations of social variables are forming into new group categories with relatively stable boundaries in super-diverse urban contexts. Super-diversity has been a very useful concept for highlighting the disintegration of the old social categories under conditions of late-modern capitalist globalisation and 'planetary urbanisation' (Brenner 2018). But it has been less interested in what comes next: in the recombination of multiple characteristics into relatively stable, spatially co-located groups among which labour is divided and around which politics is organised as they seek to live well together. In short, we argue for the need to examine not only processes of diversification within super-diverse places but also processes of re-homogenisation.

We focus on this knowledge gap, asking: What are the important new boundaries in the new social organisation of difference in major cities like Melbourne? And how are these new groups and categories formed in specific contexts? In this article we address these questions by first identifying the new diversities and then examining the emergence of new, relatively stable and coherent types of group in suburbs characterised by a diversity of religious differences.

Methodology

Because immigration is regulated by national governments, studies of immigration have tended to focus on who crosses national borders. But a national-scale view obscures the rich intersections that diversity of national origin leads to when it is diffracted in specific localities by other facets of identity, such as class, time of arrival and intra-urban trajectory. It is when the range of combinations and permutations of these kinds of identities proliferate that we can point to the emergence of super-diversity. A key aspect of super-diversity is that it is most evident in local social life, where each distinctive neighbourhood deserves attention because it reveals distinctive contexts in which people from very different backgrounds work out and negotiate what it means to belong and to live well together (Beaman 2017; Selby et al. 2018). It is in the daily lives of residents that the intersections of diversity are played out, either towards cooperation or towards conflict.

While Sydney, currently Australia's largest city and known globally as the location of the 2000 Olympics, is usually the focus of international attention, Melbourne in many ways warrants greater attention. In the period from 2011 to 2016, it had a higher rate of internal in-migration from other states than any other Australian city, partly due to its celebrated status as 'the world's most liveable city' from 2010 to 2017, as judged by the Economist Intelligence Unit's annual survey. Melbourne is also growing through international migration, and it is predicted to overtake Sydney as Australia's largest city in the next five to ten years. Melbourne, as the clear Australian destination of choice for both inter-state and international migration in recent years, is therefore an excellent city in which to explore the diversification of religious diversity at a fine-grained geographical scale. At Australia's most recent census, in 2016, Melbourne had a population of 4,485,211 – making it similar in size to cities like Boston (4.3m) and Qingdao (4.7m), smaller than Singapore (5.6m) or Washington, DC (5m), but larger than San Francisco-Oakland (3.3m), Berlin (3.6m) or Tel Aviv (3.7m).

Religious diversity can be understood in various ways, such as 'the absolute number of separate religious organisations'; or 'the individuals that associate with … religious groups'; or 'the number of distinct faith traditions'; or 'the number of individuals who combine different religious outlooks in their own identity'; or 'internal differentiation' of faith traditions into sects, schools, denominations (Beckford 2005: 74–5; see also Becci 2018; Burchardt and Becci 2016; Stringer 2014). In this chapter, we focus on self-identified religious affiliation, which is measured in terms of the different answers people have given when asked, in the five-yearly Australian Census, a consistent but increasingly fraught question: 'What is your religion?' (ABS 2005).

Australia's unmatched data resources enable fine-grained urban studies. The country's five-yearly census includes questions not only about religious identification, but also geo-coded information about housing, country of birth and place of residence five years ago. These data are available at national, state, urban and much smaller units of analysis, enabling the production of transition tables for regions at various levels of inclusion. We have opted to analyse census data at the SA2 level (Statistical Areas Level 2), because intersections of diversity are very much negotiated and governed at the local level (Beaman 2017; Cloke and Beaumont 2012). According to the Australian Bureau of Statistics (ABS) SA2s represent 'a community that interacts together socially and economically', with population size ranging from 3,000 to 25,000, and averaging around 10,000 (ABS 2016). In 2016, ABS divided Australia into 2310 SA2 areas (ABS 2016). For this chapter, we constructed and examined hundreds of religious composition and transition tables for all 309 Melbourne SA2s and for each religious group in Melbourne. The particular SA2s selected (see Map 1.1) were identified as particularly diverse both in this analysis and by the state government (Victoria 2018b).

Map 1.1 Melbourne suburbs (SA2s) selected for analysis
Source: Authors' analysis.

To trace residential mobility from 2011 to 2016, we tabulated responses to Question 10 of the Australian Census, which asks where respondents were living five years ago. Using SA2 regions, we constructed a matrix with 2011 usual residence on one axis and 2016 usual residence on the other. We selectively aggregated SA2 regions beyond Greater Melbourne. This matrix allowed us to identify large-scale residential movements between Greater Melbourne, the remainder of Victoria and elsewhere within Australia, and to identify smaller-scale movements at the SA2 level within Greater Melbourne between 2011 and 2016. The data also show how many people did not move between SA2s in the period from 2011 to 2016 and how many 2016 Melbourne residents lived overseas in 2011. We then used this matrix as a template to identify the residential concentrations and movements of people with specific religious affiliations, using ABS religious affiliation classifications at the broad one-digit level and comparing groups on that basis. We use ABS TableBuilder data to compare the religious composition of selected SA2s in 2011 and 2016, but we use the 2016 Australian Census database to analyse the religious affiliation of people who arrived in Australia from 2011 to 2016. Based on these spatial analyses of religious identification, immigration and residential mobility, we derived a working typology of different types of religious diversity that have emerged in parts of the city.

Towards a typology of Melbourne's new religious diversities

In this section we describe the main dimensions of our analyses, namely religious dissimilarity, immigrant nationality, residential mobility, suburb location and suburb length of establishment. We begin by describing trends in each dimension and then outline an original typology of new socio-religious composites that we observe emerging through the intersection of these different axes of social difference in specific urban locations within Melbourne.

Religious dissimilarity

Until quite recently, Australia was a very different country in terms of religion (Bouma 1995, 2016). Protestant groups, formerly in the majority, only began serious decline from around 1966. Catholics only assumed the lead in 1986 but, with quickening pace, other immigrant religions are making their mark. Religious diversity is distributed unevenly among Australian cities (Bouma and Hughes 2014). Christian groups and those declaring 'no religion' are the most widely and generally distributed in the population. Adelaide has the most even distribution of religious groups, except for Hindus and Sikhs, the most recent to arrive in large numbers. Melbourne has the most spatially concentrated single religious group (Jews), but Sydney generally has the highest rates of dissimilarity. Religious diversity also varies spatially within Melbourne (Map 1.2). Some suburbs report 55–68 religious identities, while others report just 20–40. Most suburbs report 45–55 religious identities.

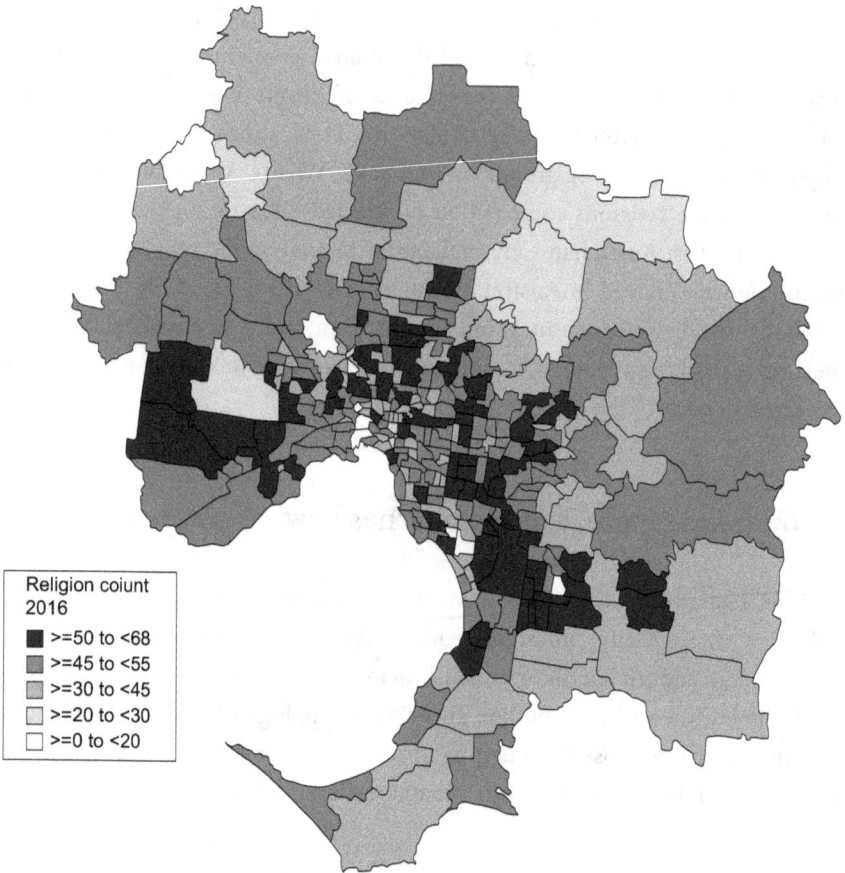

Map 1.2 Count of religious identities in Melbourne SA2 areas, 2016
Source: ABS, 2016 Census. Authors' analysis.

Immigrant nationality

Religious diversification in Australia has resulted from increasingly diverse immigration for two centuries (Bouma 1995, 1997a, 1997b, 2006). Following 50,000+ years of indigenous diversity, Australia has been an immigrant society since 1788, and particularly since its 'White Australia' immigration regulations were dismantled from the 1970s (Koleth 2010; Pascoe 2018; Wooden et al. 1990). By 2016, successive waves of immigration had made Australia far more religiously diverse than most other developed Western countries (Bouma 2016).

In 2016 Christians remained dominant (52.1 per cent at the national level vs 46.3 per cent in Melbourne), but Anglicans, who comprised 39 per cent of the population in 1947, accounted for just 13.3 per cent versus 7.6 per cent.

Catholics were more numerous (22.6 per cent vs 23.4 per cent), being sustained by immigration not from Ireland, as in the nineteenth and early twentieth centuries, but from Southeast Asia and the Middle East. Immigration had also brought increasing numbers of Pentecostals (3.7 per cent vs 3.5 per cent), Uniting (those who identify with Uniting Church) (3.7 per cent vs 2.3 per cent), Muslims (2.6 per cent vs 4.2 per cent), Buddhists (2.4 per cent vs 3.8 per cent), Hindus (1.9 per cent vs 2.9 per cent), Sikhs (0.5 per cent vs 1.1 per cent) and Jews (0.4 per cent vs 0.9 per cent) (Bouma and Halafoff 2017). Moreover, immigration was creating internal differentiation within religious categories: by 2016 Muslims in Australia traced their origins to over sixty different countries. While most Hindus had still immigrated directly from the Indian subcontinent, an increasing number were drawn from the multi-generational Indian diaspora, spread across 135+ countries. Meanwhile, those declaring 'no religion' had risen to 30.1 per cent of Australia and 31.0 per cent of Melbourne, partly through substantial Chinese immigration.

Residential mobility

At the national level religious diversification is driven by immigration, but at the local level it is driven by the interaction of immigration and residential mobility among states and suburbs. The latter have been overlooked in studies of diversity in Australia. Greater Melbourne grew by 485,230 persons between 2011 and 2016: in the average week, the city gained 1,800 people. This growth was not spread evenly across the city. In addition to the development of new suburbs in deliberate 'growth corridors' on the urban fringes, existing suburbs also grew and diversified in different ways. Importantly, Melbourne's varying rates of residential mobility appear to have been shaped partly by patterns of religious identification, as people have sought to move towards or through neighbourhoods where significant number of people share their religion.

Suburb location and length of establishment

Patterns of religious dissimilarity and residential mobility vary according to where suburbs are within the city and how long they have been established. Like many cities, Melbourne has generally expanded outwards over time, so that the inner suburbs tend to be longer established, followed by mid-range suburbs – some of which used to be in the outer ring of the city. The 'Established Inner Suburbs' in our analysis are Brunswick and surrounds, lying a few minutes' drive to the north of the CBD (central business district). Among Melbourne's 'Established Mid-Range Suburbs', we focus on Blackburn and Box Hill, which lie approximately 20 km east of Melbourne's CBD. Our 'Established Former Outer Suburbs' include Broadmeadows, Campbellfield-Coolaroo, Gladstone Park-Westmeadows, Greenvale-Bulla and Meadow Heights, which lie some 20–30 km north of the CBD. The 'New Outer Suburbs' that we focus on include Hopper's Crossing South, Laverton, Tarneit and Truganina, located around 20–30 km west of the CBD. Each of these groupings showed different levels of different types of diversity in terms of religion, nationality and residential mobility. Figures depicting the complex transitions in each suburb were produced but were too complex to include.

New socio-religious composites

Each of the dimensions of urban diversification identified earlier has shaped the dynamics of self-identified religious affiliation that we observe in Melbourne. High levels of immigration and residential mobility from other parts of the city, state and wider country are creating a settlement dynamic whereby distinct cultural and religious communities can quickly form and dissipate. Next, we analyse this process in the target suburbs and derive four emerging types of suburban religious diversities in Melbourne, which we call 'Cosmopolitan Hipster Villages', 'East Asian Turnover Settlements', 'Levantine Gateway Enclaves' and 'South Asian Growth Corridors'.

Type 1: Cosmopolitan Hipster Villages

'Cosmopolitan Hipster Villages' are Established Inner Suburbs with high rates of temporary immigration, permanent immigration, residential churn and very high and dynamic levels of religious diversity. These include the Brunswick area – a few minutes' drive or a 25-minute bike ride north of the CBD – which is characterised by a gentrifying, young professional and university student population. Residential turnover rates are very high. Inflows have been drawn to a plethora of new apartment blocks and the associated emergence of a vibrant, round-the-clock inner-city lifestyle. Outflows are driven partly by the high and rising costs of housing. In 2016, Christian-identifying residents were still a significant minority (30–40 per cent). Meanwhile, the growing proportion of 'no religion' (42–52 per cent) reflects both large and increasing immigration of Asian international students, and the general tendency for young people, who are prevalent in these suburbs, is to identify with 'no religion' (Singleton et al. 2020). In Brunswick, Brunswick East and (to a lesser extent) Brunswick West, 'no religion' was prevalent among overseas settler arrivals, which reinforced the existing predominance of this group. The shares of Hindus and Muslims arriving were significant – but they paled in comparison to the proportions of such arrivals in other regions.

Type 2: East Asian Turnover Settlements

'East Asian Turnover Settlements' are Established Mid-Range Suburbs with substantial but ageing 'traditional' populations, which are being replaced by East Asian new arrivals. These include Box Hill, Blackburn, Blackburn South and Box Hill North. The two predominant religious affiliations in these suburbs are Christianity (under 50 per cent) and 'no religion' (34–44 per cent). There were small increases among Muslims and Buddhists. This reflects significant change as older, predominantly Anglo-Christian residents pass away. Some 21 per cent of Box Hill residents arrived between 2011 and 2016, compared to 5–11 per cent of neighbouring suburbs such as Blackburn, Blackburn South and Box Hill North.

Christians comprise just 14–23 per cent of new overseas arrivals to these suburbs; many are Chinese immigrants declaring 'no religion', reinforced by residential movers with a similar demographic profile. The area has appealed to some Chinese based on its favourable feng shui, with the tail of the Dandenong Mountain ranges rising from them to the west of the CBD (Michell 2013), and it offers a mid-range commute of 30–40 minutes to the CBD. To others, the area's appeal lies in its older homes on larger blocks, which can be demolished, subdivided and redeveloped as what non-Asian residents sometimes derisively call 'McMansions'. By 2016 more than 60 per cent of Box Hill residents were either born in China or had Chinese ancestry.

Type 3: Levantine Gateway Enclaves

'Levantine Gateway Enclaves' are established suburbs with large and growing populations of Muslims and Christians from the Levant (the Eastern Mediterranean region), where new immigrants either settle into low-income areas or move 'out and up' from them. These suburbs were once outer metropolitan areas, but they are no longer on the fringe. In the decades prior to 2011 they had already attracted substantial migrations of Muslims and Christians from conflict-afflicted countries, who have established schools, shops and places of worship suited to their needs. This infrastructure has attracted subsequent migrants from similar areas, in this case, from the Levant and Eastern Europe. The proportion of Melbournians who were Muslim was 4.2 per cent in 2016, but the proportion of people in Broadmeadows, Campbellfield-Coolaroo and Meadow Heights who were Muslims was up around 31 per cent, 41 per cent and 41 per cent, respectively. These suburbs had significant shares of Christians but relatively few Hindus and comparatively few declaring 'no religion' (about 10 per cent). All these areas are situated about 30–60 minutes' drive north of the CBD.

These suburbs are welcoming substantial numbers of Muslims and Christians from overseas destinations. The Christians are often Eastern Orthodox from Syria, Lebanon and other places in the Middle East. In Broadmeadows, 13 per cent of the 2016 residents arrived in the previous five years, 44 per cent of whom were Muslim – joining a suburb population that was already 25 per cent Muslim in 2011. In the high-Muslim areas, residential mobility outflows equalled or outweighed inflows in the period 2011–16. As these areas have comparatively low incomes, this common pattern of 'residential churning' (Birrell et al. 1999) may reflect Muslims experiencing upward social mobility moving to better-off areas within Greater Melbourne.

Type 4: South Asian Growth Corridors

'South Asian Growth Corridors' are New Outer Suburbs with large, recent and fast-growing settlements of upwardly mobile Muslim and Hindu South Asians, boosted by both internal in-migration and international immigration. They include Hoppers Crossing, Laverton, Tarneit and Truganina, 45 minutes' drive west of the CBD. Immigration has helped consolidate pre-existing patterns of residential concentration. In these areas, between 8 per cent and 17 per cent of people were recent overseas arrivals in 2016. In only one of the four areas did Christianity account for more than half of the population, although it remained the largest single religious identification category. Those with 'no religion' were a significant presence in all areas but, like Christians, comprised a smaller share in Hindu- and Muslim-dominant areas such as Tarneit and Truganina.

These outer suburbs are new and less expensive and attracted sizeable shares of growing South Asian immigration to Australia from 2011 to 2016. Tarneit and Truganina also drew large net Hindu inflows through residential mobility from other parts of Metropolitan Melbourne. A small, but noticeable net inflow to these areas is also discernible from other Australian states. The existing presence of substantial numbers of South Asians in these suburbs seems to be attracting further South Asian immigrants and internal in-migrants from Hindu and Muslim backgrounds. Our analyses showed that, for most of these South Asian Growth Corridor suburbs, the 2016 population included many persons who had moved in from nearby suburbs. It is possible that relatively stable local religious communities are characterised by a relatively high level of residential churning at a sub-regional level, especially as those who age choose to downsize their housing but stay nearby, or those who have children move to accommodate them. Part of this may reflect the rising rates of home rental rather than ownership.

Super-diversification, re-homogenisation and service provision

The patterns of super-diversification and re-homogenisation that we discovered raise significant questions for policy, planning and service provision at both the national and the urban scale. First, while immigration is regulated at the national level in response to macro-economic, political and foreign policy goals, diversification is managed by local, municipal and state governments in response to implications of demographic trends for the provision of infrastructure, schools, hospitals, policing and other essential services (Koleth 2010; Modood 2018). These two scales of policy formation, with their different implementation concerns, are difficult to reconcile because Australian diversity looks fundamentally different at the national and local levels. For example, at the national level, Australia is demographically 'Christian' (52.1 per cent identify with a Christian group). But the only Australian states with Christian majorities are New South Wales and Queensland. Also, new dynamics of income inequality, multiplication of migration arrival waves and periodic cycles of residential mobility have all been radically changing previous configurations of religious life at the local level, leading to increased diversity among lived religious diversities. One clear takeaway is that national-scale migration policies must be increasingly attentive to dynamics at the local level.

Second, policy and service provision have been locked into 'ghetto thinking', which sees cities as patchworks of cohesive if not homogeneous 'communities', each with suburb territories, defined by conventional social science variables that approximate 'culture' (Vertovec et al. Forthcoming). Exemplifying this spirit, Australian institutions nominally welcome and celebrate 'multiculturalism', understood as the harmonious coexistence of multiple, cohesive ethno-religious groups. Multiculturalism is particularly strong as a framework for service provision in Melbourne and the wider state of Victoria (Victoria 2018a). However, realities on the ground revealed in this article show that each ethno-religious group splinters into many sub-groups based not just on religious denomination but also on nationality, prior residential location and length of settlement. Moreover, these sub-groups are coalescing into new socio-spatial groups that do not fit conventional social science categories. Thus, while official discourses continue to reify ethno-religiously defined ideas of culture and multiculturalism, lived realities in cities like Melbourne increasingly involve super-diversification and the emergence of new composite forms of group identity without precedent. In this chapter we have delineated some of the more prominent of these social compounds emerging in some notable areas of religious super-diversification.

Each of these new intersectional compounds comes with its own distinctive policy and planning issues for those involved in urban governance. The dynamic profile of Cosmopolitan Hipster Villages presents unique challenges to community building and city planning because the student populations of these areas are transient and hard to engage in long-term community building, while the longer-term residents tend to be very open to diversity, but unlikely to be engaged religiously. As a result, traditional civil society sources of community, including organised religion, are conspicuously thin in these inner suburbs – a fact that no amount of vegan dieting, beer brewing, community-garden tending or animal-print-legging-wearing has quite managed to compensate for. The vibrant urban fashions and fetishes that can be seen in these locations ape the working-class artisanal cultures and religious communities which used to exist there – but increasingly it is only the rich who can afford to 'slum it' in these kinds of places.

Meanwhile, East Asian Turnover Settlements also pose their own policy, planning and service provision challenges. Some long-term inhabitants are displeased with immigration-driven changes to their neighbourhoods, while others are delighted with the way immigration has massively driven up the values of their properties; prices have increased in excess of 10 per cent per year for over a decade. Meanwhile, there is plenty of existing religious, civic and other infrastructure in place – but it often caters to an ageing Anglo-Irish Christian population and is ill-suited to the young, new Asian inhabitants of these areas, most of whom identify with 'no religion'.

In the other suburb types we identify, the main religious distinctions are between Muslims on the one hand and either Christians or Hindus on the other. In the Muslim-Christian areas in our study (the Levantine Gateway Enclaves), policymakers and settlement practitioners have been deeply concerned about the potential spillover into Australia of violence between Muslim and Christian groups in the source countries from which immigrants to these areas come. Consequently, they have focused on supporting civic and other organisations that promote harmonious inter-religious relations. Community building has involved care, commitment and substantial attention to programmes including 'bridge building', interfaith cooperation and 'countering violent extremism' – many of which are, in their own ways, controversial.

By contrast, South Asian Growth Corridors, with their large Hindu and Muslim populations, present scholars and policymakers with particularly interesting and unique issues of settlement and community building. These suburbs did not exist ten years ago, some not even five years ago: many residents in these locations are new to Australia and to each other. Because their suburbs are new and distant from the CBD, there is little or no local civic or religious organisation to assist new arrivals to settle and promote incorporation. Victoria Police indicate that community organisations like Rotary, Lions and Neighbourhood Watch that help bring communities together and foster intercultural interactions are active and appreciated by the local communities. And Victoria Police (n.d.) itself plays a major role in promoting harmonious, healthy and respectful inter-religious interactions.

Given the incipient nature of organised community in these locations, alongside the current tensions playing out between Hindus and Muslims in South Asia (Gamlen 2019), the fact that religious disagreements have not been a feature of communal life in Melbourne's South Asian Growth Corridors indicates that Melbourne's history and culture of interfaith cooperation and mutual respect may be prevailing. The evolution of community in these suburbs seems to be happening mostly at the personal level, as families and children find their way, ask neighbours for help and give assistance themselves.

Discussion and conclusions

Using the lens of super-diversity, this article has examined the diversification of religious diversity in Melbourne, Australia, through analyses of residential movement and immigrant settlement patterns at a fine spatial scale, derived from 2011 and 2016 Australian Census data. These analyses reveal how intersecting of patterns of religious diversity across Melbourne vary by region and have been the product of both immigration inter- and intra-urban mobility over time. We have observed and recorded new patterns of super-diversification and the re-homogenisation of groups based on new, multidimensional combinations of characteristics. These emergent social configurations may evolve into new categories, into which future scholars and policymakers may compartmentalise their observations about urban social life. In some cases, the patterns of suburban community we observe are producing what Beaman (2017) calls 'deep equality'. Selby et al. (2018) present examples of this happening in Canada – telling stories of ordinary people negotiating religious diversity with occasional mistakes but general dignity and grace. Such 'commonplace diversity' and 'conviviality' have also been noted by scholars focused on other diversifying Australian and British cities (see Wessendorf 2014; Wise and Noble 2018). Our findings are summarised in Table 1.1.

Our analyses enable us to make some wider comments about the dynamics, drivers and implications of religious change in Melbourne – which may also have relevance to cities elsewhere in Australia and beyond. For example, we observed that the distinctive local religious composition of some areas is subject to a degree of sub-regional residential 'shuffling', whereby persons from a particular religious group shift residence within a relatively contiguous sub-region. Further research is required to more fully understand the dynamic behind such sub-regional relocation. Preliminary observations suggest that upward social mobility may be a factor and that members of a particular religious group may be making decisions about the social status of localities in a familiar sub-regional context, without necessarily leaving the comfort zone of their community's distinctive religious character.

Furthermore, our analyses suggest a dynamic picture of the various challenges facing families, governments and local organisations as a result of new and emerging combinations and compounds of different types of diversity. Such challenges are particularly apparent in the new suburbs which have grown up on the fringes of Melbourne where literally everyone is 'new' and there are virtually no existing structures of support – schools, shops and the like. But 'new' diversity is also found in middle and inner suburbs. Taken together, our analyses demonstrate both the scholarly and practical value of examining urban religious diversity at the local level, rather than through national level, or macro-urban studies which have tended to predominate in the existing literature. We

Table 1.1 Working typology of religious diversity in Melbourne in 2020

	Cosmopolitan Hipster Villages	East Asian Turnover Settlements	Levantine Gateway Enclaves	South Asian Growth Corridors
Summary of type	Established inner suburbs with high temporary and permanent immigration, residential churn and religious diversity	Established suburbs with ageing 'traditional' populations being replaced by East Asian and particularly Chinese new arrivals	Established suburbs with stable enclaves of Muslims and Christians from the Levant, where new immigrants either settle into low incomes or move 'out and up'	New-build suburbs with large, recent and fast-growing settlements of upwardly mobile Muslim and Hindu South Asians, boosted by both internal in-migration and international immigration
Suburb distance from CBD	Inner	Mid-range	Former outer	Outer
Religious dissimilarity	High and growing	Medium and shrinking	Medium and shrinking	High and growing
Main religions before	Christian, No Religion	Christian, No Religion	Christian, No Religion	Christian, No Religion
Main religions now	No Religion, Christian	No Religion, Christian	Muslim, Christian	Hindu, Muslim, Christian, No Religion
Immigration rate	High	High	High	High
Main new national backgrounds	Highly diverse	Chinese	The Levant	South Asia
Residential churn	High	High	High	Low
Length of establishment	Established	Established but transitioning	Established	New
Income profile	Gentrifying	High	Low	Upwardly mobile

Source: Authors' analyses.

hope to see similar studies emerge in other cities that utilise and build upon our approach in this chapter.

All of this points to a rich and growing diversity of diversities in the dimension of religious diversity in Melbourne. Given intersections of this diversity with other diversities, including immigrant nationality, residential mobility, suburb location and length of establishment, these patterns radically complexify Melbourne, making it super-diverse. Since processes of super-diversification are now common across many major world cities, we anticipate that by analysing multiple dimensions of diversification and processes of re-homogenisation in new ways, this chapter will prove useful to scholars of diversity well beyond Melbourne.

Acknowledgements

This chapter was originally published as Bouma, G., Arunachalam, D., Gamlen, A., and Healy, E., 2022. 'Religious Diversity through a Super-Diversity Lens: National, Sub-Regional and Socio-Economic Religious Diversities in Melbourne'. *Journal of Sociology* 58(1): 7–25. We are grateful to the publisher and the authors for permission to reprint it here.

References

ABS (Australian Bureau of Statistics). 2005. 'Australian Standard Classification of Religious Groups', Cat. No. 1266.0. URL (consulted 16 April 2021). https://www.abs.gov.au/ausstats/abs@.nsf/mf/1266.0.

ABS (Australian Bureau of Statistics). 2016. 'Australian Statistical Geography Standard (ASGS): vol. 1 – Main Structure and Greater Capital City Statistical Areas, Statistical Area Level 2 (SA2)', Cat. No. 1270.0.55.001. URL (consulted 16 April 2021). https://www.abs.gov.au/ausstats/abs@.nsf/mf/1270.0.55.001.

Beaman, L. 2017. *Deep Equality in an Era of Religious Diversity*. Oxford: Oxford University Press.

Becci, I. 2018. 'Religious Superdiversity and Gray Zones in Public Total Institutions'. *Journal of Religion in Europe* 11(2–3): 123–37.

Beckford, J. 2005. *Social Theory and Religion*. Cambridge: Cambridge University Press.

Berg, M. L. 2019. 'Super-Diversity, Austerity, and the Production of Precarity: Latin Americans in London'. *Critical Social Policy* 39(2): 184–204.

Birrell, B., O'Connor, K., and Rapson, V. 1999. 'Explaining Concentrations of the Poor in Metropolitan Melbourne'. *People and Place* 7(1): 53–64.

Blommaert, J., and Rampton, B. 2016. 'Language and Superdiversity'. In K. Arnaut, J. Blommaert and B. Rampton (eds), *Language and Superdiversity*. Abingdon: Routledge, 21–48.

Bouma, G. 1995. 'The Emergence of Religious Plurality in Australia: A Multicultural Society'. *Sociology of Religion* 56: 285–302.

Bouma, G. 1997a. *Many Religions All Australian: Religious Settlement, Identity and Cultural Diversity*. Melbourne: Christian Research Association.

Bouma, G. 1997b. 'The Settlement of Islam in Australia'. *Social Compass* 44(1): 71–82.

Bouma, G. 2006. *Australian Soul*. Cambridge: Cambridge University Press.

Bouma, G. 2016. 'The Role of Demographic and Socio-Cultural Factors in Australia's Successful Multicultural Society: How Australia Is Not Europe'. *Journal of Sociology* 52: 750–71.

Bouma, G., and Halafoff, A. 2017. 'Australia's Changing Religious Profile – Rising Nones and Pentecostals, Declining British Protestants in Superdiversity: Views from the 2016 Census'. *Journal for the Academic Study of Religion* 30(2): 129–43.

Bouma, G., and Hughes, P. (2014) 'Using Census Data in the Management of Religious Diversity: An Australian Case Study'. *Religion* 44: 434–52.

Brenner, N. 2018. 'Debating Planetary Urbanization: For an Engaged Pluralism'. *Environment and Planning D: Society and Space* 36(3): 570–90.

Burchardt, M. 2019. 'Religion in Urban Assemblages: Space, Law, and Power'. *Religion, State and Society* 47: 374–89.

Burchardt, M., and Becci, I. 2016. 'Religion and Super-Diversity: An Introduction'. *New Diversities* 1(18): 1–8.

Casanova, J. 1994. *Public Religions in the Modern World*. Chicago: University of Chicago Press.

Cloke, P., and Beaumont, J. 2012. 'Geographies of Postsecular Rapprochement in the City'. *Progress in Human Geography* 37: 27–51.

Crul, M. 2016. 'Super-Diversity vs. Assimilation: How Complex Diversity in Majority-minority Cities Challenges the Assumptions of Assimilation'. *Journal of Ethnic and Migration Studies* 42(1): 54–68.

Davern, M., Warr, D., Higgs, C., Dickinson, H., and Phillimore, J. 2015. *Superdiversity in Melbourne*. Melbourne: University of Melbourne.

Fincher, R., Iveson, K., Leitner, H., Preston, V. 2014. 'Planning in the Multicultural City: Celebrating Diversity or Reinforcing Difference?'. *Progress in Planning* 92: 1–55.

Gamlen, A. 2010. *International Migration Data and the Study of Super-Diversity, Working Paper 10–05*. Göttingen: Max Planck Institute for the Study of Religious and Ethnic Diversity.

Gamlen, A. 2019. *Human Geopolitics: States, Emigrants, and the Rise of Diaspora Institutions*. Oxford: Oxford University Press.

Gamlen, A., and Marsh, K. 2011. *Migration and Global Governance*. Cheltenham: Edward Elgar.

Gryzmala-Busse, M. 2015. *Nations under God: How Churches Use Moral Authority to Influence Policy*. Princeton, NJ: Princeton University Press.

Koleth, E. 2010. 'Multiculturalism: A Review of Australian Policy Statements and Recent Debates in Australia and Overseas', Parliamentary Library, Research Paper No. 6, 2010–11, Canberra.

Martin, F. 2018. 'Iphones and "African Gangs": Everyday Racism and Ethno-transnational Media in Melbourne's Chinese Student World'. *Ethnic and Racial Studies* 43(5): 892–910.

Martinez-Ariño, J. 2019. Governing Religious Diversity in Cities: Critical Perspectives. Special Issue, *Religion, State and Society* 47(4–5): 364–73.

McCall, L. 2005. 'The Complexity of Intersectionality'. *Signs: Journal of Women in Culture and Society* 30(3): 1771–800.

Meissner, F. 2015. 'Migration in Migration-Related Diversity? The Nexus between Superdiversity and Migration Studies'. *Ethnic and Racial Studies* 38(4): 556–67.

Michell, T. 2013. 'Positive Feng Shui in Whitehorse Helps Fuel Property Market Growth, Real Estate Agents Say'. *Herald Sun*. https://www.heraldsun.com.au/leader/east/positive-feng-shui-in-whitehorse-helps-fuel-property-market-growth-real-estate-agents-say/news-story/7109f6a8acd0338422058aad5cf33df7. Accessed 13 August 2019.

Modood, T. 2018. 'Pointing to a Multicultural Future: Rethinking Race, Ethnicity, Religion and Britishness'. In Foblets M.-C., Alidadi K. (eds), *Public Commissions on Cultural and Religious Diversity, vol. 2: Internal Dialogues, Critical Compromises and Real-Life Impact*. Farnham: Ashgate.

Pascoe, B. 2018. *Dark Emu: Aboriginal Australia and the Birth of Agriculture*. Broome, WA: Magabala Books.

Phillimore, J. 2011. 'Approaches to Health Provision in the Age of Super-diversity: Accessing the NHS in Britain's Most Diverse City'. *Critical Social Policy* 31(1): 5–29.

Selby, J., Barras, A., and Beaman, L. 2018. *Beyond Accommodation: Everyday Narratives of Muslim Canadians*. Vancouver: UBC Press.

Sharifian, F., and Musgrave, S. 2013. 'Migration and Multilingualism: Focus on Melbourne'. *International Journal of Multilingualism* 10(4): 361–74.

Sigona, N. 2013. 'Imagining a New Research Agenda in an Era of Superdiversity'. *Postcards from ...* (weblog), 25 October. http://nandosigona.wordpress.com/2013/10. Accessed 12 September 2020.

Singleton, A., Halafoff, A., Rasmussen, M. L., and Bouma, G. 2020. *Freedoms, Faiths and Futures: Teenage Australians on Religion, Sexuality and Diversity*. London: Bloomsbury.

Stringer, M. 2014. 'Evidencing Superdiversity in the Census and Beyond'. *Religion* 44: 453–46.

Vertovec S. 1996. 'Multiculturalism, Culturalism and Public Incorporation'. *Ethnic and Racial Studies* 19(1): 49–69.

Vertovec, S. 2006. 'The Emergence of Super-diversity in Britain'. Centre on Migration, Policy and Society (COMPAS) Working Paper, 25, School of Anthropology, University of Oxford.

Vertovec, S. 2007. 'Super-Diversity and Its Implications'. *Ethnic and Racial Studies* 30(6): 1024–54.

Vertovec, S. 2010. 'Towards Post-Multiculturalism? Changing Communities, Conditions and Contexts of Diversity'. *International Social Science Journal* 61(199): 83–95.

Vertovec, S. 2014. 'Reading "Super-diversity"'. In Anderson B., Keith M. (eds), *Migration: A COMPAS Anthology*. Oxford: Centre on Migration, Policy and Society (COMPAS).

Vertovec, S. 2021. 'The Social Organization of Difference', *Ethnic and Racial Studies* 44(8): 1273–95, DOI: 10.1080/01419870.2021.1884733

Vertovec, S., Hiebert, D., Gamlen, A., and Spoonley, P. Forthcoming. 'Visualizing Superdiversity and "Seeing" Urban Socio-economic Complexity', under review at *Urban Geography*.

Victoria (State of Victoria). 2018a. *Victorian and Proud of It*. https://proud.vic.gov.au/wp-content/uploads/2017/02/Victorian-And-Proud-of-it-MPS-180207.pdf. Accessed 3 July 2020.

Victoria (State of Victoria). 2018b. *Population Diversity in Victoria: 2016 Census, Local Government Areas*. Melbourne: State of Victoria, Department of Premier and Cabinet. https://www.vic.gov.au/sites/default/files/2019-08/Full-Report-Population-Diversity-in-LGAs-2016-Census-Web-version-30May18.PDF. Accessed 9 April 2021.

Victoria Police. n.d. 'Victoria Police Priority Communities Reference Groups'. https://www.police.vic.gov.au/reference-groups. Accessed 16 April 2021.

Wessendorf, S. 2014. *Commonplace Diversity: Social Relations in a Super-diverse Context*. London: Palgrave Macmillan.

Williams, C. F., and Mikola, M. 2018. 'From Multiculturalism to Superdiversity? Narratives of Health and Wellbeing in an Urban Neighbourhood'. *Social Work and Policy Studies: Social Justice, Practice and Theory* 1(001): 1–12.

Wise, A., and Noble, G. 2016. 'Convivialities: An Orientation'. *Journal of Intercultural Studies* 37(5): 423–31.

Wise, A., and Noble, G. (eds). 2018. *Convivialities: Possibility and Ambivalence in Urban Multicultures*. Abingdon: Routledge.

Wooden, M., Holten, R., Hugo, G., and Sloan, J. 1990. *Australian Immigration: A Survey of the Issues*. Canberra: AGPS.

2

Attitudes towards Religious Diversity in Australia

Douglas Ezzy, Anna Halafoff, Rebecca Banham and Greg Barton

Introduction

This chapter begins with a short discussion of the history of attitudes towards religious diversity in Australia. We then report the results of national survey of Australians' attitudes towards religious diversity. The survey examines attitudes towards different faiths in Australia, education about religious diversity and the building of mosques and temples. We also examine the influence of Christian nationalist ideas on these attitudes. While Christians are often privileged, and distrustful of diverse religiosities, our data suggests that it is not commitment to Christianity, as indicated by belief or regular attendance at services, which is associated with antagonism to diverse religiosities. Rather, it is Christian nationalism, which seeks to impose Christian values and practices on all Australians, which is antagonistic to diverse religiosities.

In 2013 Anna Halafoff (2013a: 166) drew on Ulrich Beck's (2006) *Cosmopolitan Vision*, arguing that what we were witnessing was not so much a 'clash of civilisations' (Huntington 1993) but a clash *within* civilisations, between cosmopolitan pluralists and anti-cosmopolitan exclusivists. Briefly, cosmopolitanism is a social and political theory centred on respect for rights and diversity. Cosmopolitan rights and policies were institutionalised in many societies, focused on respect for cultural, gender, sexuality and multispecies diversity in the mid-late twentieth century. Multiculturalism is an example of this, as is Victoria's 1995/2010 Equal Opportunity Act. These progressive changes have, however, been strongly resisted by anti-cosmopolitans, often with a conservative religious orientation, who are threatened by these changes and wish to retain their power and privileges. This has resulted in 'culture wars' over rights and values between conservatives and progressives. Anti-cosmopolitans began to gain significant public support at the turn of the twentieth century, and particularly after the events of 11 September 2001. This has increased over the past two decades with the emergence of right-wing populism and the spread of dis/misinformation through social media (Halafoff et al. 2021).

More recently, and similar to Halafoff, Lori Beaman (2020: 24) has argued that the key tension is between 'past preserving' and 'future forming' narratives. Past preserving narratives tend to emphasise the preservation of a romanticised past, often linked to claims of retaining 'our values' and an emphasis on nationalist heritage, culture and tradition. In contrast, future-forming narratives tend to be oriented towards an emergent sense of inclusion and belonging that respects the multicultural, multifaith and super-diverse nature of society, including an emphasis on multispecies diversity and world-repairing. In this chapter we highlight the relationship between antagonism towards religious diversity, exclusivism and claims that Australia should be a Christian nation. This is examined in this chapter through the results of a national survey.

The conservative Howard federal government in Australia was a turning point in understandings of diversity. Howard was prime minister in the late 1990s and early 2000s as Australia was becoming increasingly ethnically and religiously diverse, mainly as a product of a more liberal immigration policy. Rather than embracing this diversity, the Howard government appealed to the long-held fears and insularity of Australians who were increasingly uncomfortable with the many changes they were experiencing with accelerating globalisation and cosmopolitanism. Importing policies and rhetoric from the American Christian right, the Howard government began implementing policies such as 'tightened censorship, opposition to gay and lesbian marriage and parenting, reopening the debate on abortion and capital punishment, overturning euthanasia law, a preference for faith-based over government welfare and schools, intolerance of Muslims, suspicion of outsiders, hostility to "activist" judges and a claim to exclusive, inside knowledge of "values"' (Maddox 2005: 200). The Howard government strongly equated Australian values with Christian values at this time, claiming those who did not subscribe to them were 'unAustralian' (Maddox 2005; Halafoff 2006).

Marion Maddox charts how Howard's politics of 'us and them' was designed as a political strategy, aiming to 'construct a bogey of "Them" that could galvanise a nervous "Us" to sweep Howard and his cast to power' (Maddox 2005: 109). The stigmatised others often focused on 'family values' issues such as LGBT+ people, juvenile delinquents and divorcees. The strategy also included fearful statements about Indigenous Australians, refugees, Muslims and Asians. Maddox, similar to Judith Brett (2003), argues that Howard's references to Christianity were a rhetorical political strategy, designed to articulate a vague sense of an idealised past, now lost. That is to say, the discomfort associated with the changes wrought by growing ethnic and religious diversity have been weaponised as part of a deliberate political strategy where 'Christian' and 'family' values become codes for anxieties about change. Halafoff (2014, 2022) frames this as 'anti-cosmopolitan terror', where narrow, religious nationalism, drums up fears against and hatred for others, that can result terrifying acts, such as the 2005 Cronulla riots and, more recently, the rise of Far Right violence against racial minorities and the Putin regime's horrific war on Ukraine. Halafoff first wrote on anti-cosmopolitan terror in 2014, citing terrorist Anders Breivik's references to anti-Muslim statements made by Howard, former treasurer Peter Costello and the Australian Cardinal George Pell at the height of the Australian values debate in Breivik's Manifesto.

Joseph Baker and associates (2020: 275) have also observed that in the United States, 'a variety of studies demonstrate that Christian nationalism is a powerful cultural framework that is influential beyond traditional religious boundaries'. The nationalist identification of a country as Christian is associated with the use of religious language to justify discriminatory practices towards racial, religious and other minorities. It moves 'beyond traditional religious boundaries' because it overlaps with, but is not constrained to, those who identify as and/or practice as Christians, but rather taps into a cultural imaginary of a Christian nation and values. Gary Bouma (2016: 768) argued that the relative lack of religious conflict in Australia in the mid-late 1900s was a product of an explicit multicultural policy: 'social inclusion including respect for difference and mutual respect'. The rise of Christian nationalism seeks to undermine such policies. These also relate to the White Australia Policy and multiculturalism which are discussed more extensively in Chapter 5.

Australian attitudes towards religious diversity

We included two sets of questions in a representative national panel Australian Community Survey of 1,300 Australians conducted in November 2020 by the National Christian Life Survey Research (NCLSR). The survey is a national panel survey, weighted to be representative of the general population. It presumes competency in English, and so may not adequately represent Australians from non-English-speaking backgrounds, and this should be taken into account in the interpretations of some of the findings below, particularly in relation to the attitudes of members of non-Christian religions, which have high numbers of people from non-English-speaking backgrounds. A more detailed explanation of the method is provided in an endnote to the chapter. The first set of (three) questions asked about attitudes towards diversity. We asked whether people agree or disagree that 'having people of many different faiths makes Australia a better place to live' (abbreviated below as 'Different faiths'). This provides a broad indicator of attitudes towards religious diversity. This question is quite general in nature in order to understand people's attitude towards practices that are inclusive, or antagonistic, towards religious diversity. Next we asked whether people agreed or disagreed that 'the Australian Curriculum, which sets out what students should learn in schools, ought to include a wide range of religious and nonreligious worldviews' (abbreviated below as 'Australian Curriculum'). Finally, we asked a specific question that highlighted practices of acceptance, or antagonism, towards minority religions such as Islam and Hinduism: 'Local communities should be able to prevent the construction of mosques or temples in their area if they don't want them' (abbreviated below as 'Prevent mosques and temples').

The three categories of 'Inclusive', 'Ambivalent' and 'Antagonistic' are used to describe the responses to the questions about religious diversity. We have used these three categories because the question about mosques is worded negatively, which means that people who disagree with that question have similar views to those who agree with the other two questions. 'Inclusive' refers to those who agreed or strongly agreed with the questions about Different Faiths and the Australian Curriculum or disagreed or strongly disagreed with the question about Preventing Mosques. 'Antagonistic' refers to those who disagreed or strongly disagreed with the questions about Different Faiths and the Australian Curriculum or agreed or strongly agreed with the question about Preventing Mosques.

The second set of (two) questions was designed to identify participants' attitudes towards the idea of Australia being a Christian nation. One question asked whether people agreed or disagreed that 'the Australian Federal Government should advocate Christian values' (abbreviated below as 'Government should advocate Christian values'). Respondents were also asked: 'The opening of Australian Federal Parliament includes the Christian Lord's Prayer. What do you think of this?' (abbreviated below as 'The Lord's Prayer in Parliament') and were offered possible responses:

- 'The Lord's Prayer should be used to open Parliament';
- 'Prayers from a variety of religions should open Parliament';
- 'There should be no religious prayers to open Parliament'; or
- 'Can't choose'.

These survey questions provide broad indicators of trends and patterns in attitudes of Australians towards religious diversity. We focus on the three issues of general attitudes towards the diversity of faiths in Australia, religion in the curriculum and attitudes towards building mosques and temples. These provide a general indicator of attitudes towards religious diversity, pinpointing issues that are often debated in Australia. Christian nationalism is increasingly highlighted in contemporary literature on attitudes towards diversity, and there is little literature on Australian Christian nationalism (see McLeay et al. 2023). It is important to differentiate the influence of Christian nationalist ideas from Christian membership and practice because not all Christians are nationalist in their attitudes.

Amanda Tyler (2022: 1), reflecting on the events of 6 January 2021 in the US Capitol observes that 'Christian nationalism is not Christianity, though it is not accurate to say that Christian nationalism has nothing to do with Christianity'. Many Christians are Christian nationalists, as Andrew Seidel (2022) demonstrates in his account of the role of Christians in the 6 January 2021 post-election rallies: 'They marched with crosses, images of the Virgin Mary, [and signs that said] "Jesus is my Savior, Trump is my President"' (Seidel 2022: 15). This chapter highlights that in Australia Christian nationalism similarly overlaps with Christianity, drawing on Christian imagery and language to articulate exclusivist and anti-cosmopolitan agendas, seeking to preserve a past that privileges particular groups and organisations.

Survey results

The survey results suggest that approximately one-third of Australians embrace an inclusive approach to religious diversity (Table 2.1). Forty-two per cent of Australians embrace teaching about a diversity of religious worldviews, and 37 per cent think a diversity of faiths has made Australia a better place. However, only just over one quarter (27 per cent) of Australians have an inclusive attitude towards non-Christian religions, disagreeing that a local community should be able to prevent the building of a mosque or temple. Another 30–40 per cent are ambivalent or uncertain about religious diversity.

Table 2.1 Attitudes towards religious diversity

	Inclusive	Ambivalent	Antagonistic	N
	Agree (%)	Neither (%)	Disagree (%)	
Different faiths	37	40	23	1,258
Australian curriculum	2	33	25	1,230
	Disagree (%)	Neither (%)	Agree (%)	
Prevent mosques and temples	27	35	38	1,224

Different faiths: 'Having people of many different faiths makes Australia a better place to live.'

Australian Curriculum: 'The Australian Curriculum, which sets out what students should learn in schools, ought to include a wide range of religious and nonreligious worldviews.'

Prevent mosques and temples: 'Local communities should be able to prevent the construction of mosques or temples in their area if they don't want them.'

On the other hand, approximately one quarter to one-third of survey respondents are antagonistic towards religious diversity (Table 2.1). More specifically, when asked whether a diversity of faiths makes Australia a better place to live, just under one quarter (23 per cent) disagree. Breaking the disagreeing responses to this question down further, 9 per cent strongly disagree and 14 per cent disagree. Similarly, when asked about including a wide range of religious worldviews in the Australian Curriculum, one quarter (25 per cent) disagree, with 13 per cent who strongly disagree and with 12 per cent who disagree. Finally, just over one-third (38 per cent) of Australians want local communities to be able to prevent the building of a mosque or temple if they don't want them, with 14 per cent who strongly agree and 22 per cent who agree. These attitudes are similar to that observed by Andrew Markus (2021: 63) in the Scanlon surveys where 10 per cent of Australians were 'very negative' towards Muslims and 22 per cent 'somewhat negative', noting that the Scanlon survey asks different questions. In other words, while approximately one-third of Australians are antagonistic towards religious diversity, only about 9–14 per cent of Australians are strongly antagonistic. These are still concerning statistics.

Religious identification and Christian nationalism: Attitudes towards religious diversity

The Australian Federal Government should advocate Christian values.

Table 2.2 Should the federal government advocate Christian values?

	Disagree (%)	Neither (%)	Agree (%)	N
Government advocate Christian values	30	31	38	1,221

Table 2.3 Prayers in Parliament

	Percentage
The Lord's Prayer should be used to open Parliament	26
Prayers from a variety of religions should open Parliament	10
There should not be religious prayers to open Parliament	42
Can't choose	22
N	1,306

The opening of Australian federal Parliament includes the Christian Lord's Prayer. What do you think of this?

Australians are roughly divided into thirds in response to the question about the federal government advocating Christian values (Table 2.2). Just under one-third (30 per cent) disagree, one-third (31 per cent) are undecided, and just over one-third (38 per cent) agree that the Australian federal government should advocate Christian values. There is a similar pattern with attitudes towards prayers in Parliament, although with more support for a nonreligious Parliament (Table 2.3). Slightly over one quarter (26 per cent) want Christian prayers in Parliament, 42 per cent don't want any prayers in parliament, 10 per cent want prayers from a variety of religions and 22 per cent can't choose.

The relationship between religious identification and attitudes towards religious diversity is reported in Table 2.4. Members of other religions (63 per cent) and attending Christians (47 per cent) have the most inclusive attitudes towards a diversity of faiths in Australia. Members of other religions (50 per cent) and attending Christians (61 per cent) are also strongly supportive of including education about a diversity of religious worldviews in the curriculum. Across all the groups there remains moderate levels of support for inclusive attitudes towards non-Christian religions: 45 per cent of nominal Christians, 40 per cent of attending Christians, 33 per cent of those with no religion, and 32 per cent of those who identify with other religions are antagonistic towards building mosques or temples.

Table 2.4 Religious identification and religious diversity

		No religion (%)	Nominal Christian (%)	Attending Christian (%)	Other Religion (%)
Different faiths	Antagonistic	24_a	23_a	21_a	18_a
	Ambivalent	44_a	$40_{a,b}$	33_b	19_c
	Inclusive	32_a	36_a	47_b	63_c
Australian curriculum	Antagonistic	31_a	23_b	14_c	$24_{a,b,c}$
	Ambivalent	34_a	34_a	25_b	$26_{a,b}$
	Inclusive	34_a	43_b	61_c	$50_{b,c}$
Prevent mosques and temples	Antagonistic	33_a	45_b	$40_{a,b}$	32_a
	Ambivalent	34_a	33_a	36_a	38_a
	Inclusive	32_a	22_b	24_b	$30_{a,b}$
N		512 (43%)	402 (37%)	211 (18%)	69 (6%)

Attending Christians are defined as those who identify as Christian and attend religious services at least several times a year. Nominal Christians identify as Christian and attend services yearly or less often.

Different faiths: $X^2(4, N = 1,227) = 36.138, p < .001$

Australian Curriculum: $X^2(4, N = 1,201) = 47.973, p < .001$

Prevent mosques and temples: $X^2(4, N = 1,194) = 18.952, p < .001$

Across the categories in each row, different subscript letters denote proportions within the categories of Religious identification that differ significantly from each other at the .05 level based on the SPSS z-test of proportions.

Cells with low percentages or low numbers, such as some in 'Other Religion' may not be reliable for comparison purposes.

Some have argued that the growing numbers of people with no religion is associated with increasing public antipathy towards the public expression of religion. Kim Lam (2019: 729), for example, reports that the young Australian Buddhists she interviewed had observed an 'increase in anti-religious sentiment, which had a capacity to minoritise all religious adherents on the basis of religious identification alone.' Our survey results suggest a more complex picture. On some issues, people with no religion are less positive about religious diversity than religious people, whilst on other issues nonreligious people are more inclusive than religious people. For example, in comparison to religious people, people with no religion are less likely to have inclusive attitudes towards the diversity of faiths and are more likely to be antagonistic towards the inclusion of information about a diversity of religious worldviews in the curriculum. On the other hand, people with no religion are more likely to have inclusive attitudes towards minority religions (32 per cent) than Christians (22% and 24%), as indicated by their attitudes towards building mosques or temples.

Table 2.5 Christian nationalism and religious diversity

		Christian Nationalist (%)	Undecided (%)	Secularist (%)
Different faiths	Antagonistic	33$_a$	20$_b$	24$_b$
	Ambivalent	30$_a$	43$_b$	38$_b$
	Inclusive	38$_a$	37$_a$	38$_a$
Australian curriculum	Antagonistic	19$_a$	22$_a$	39$_b$
	Ambivalent	26$_a$	40$_b$	18$_c$
	Inclusive	55$_a$	38$_b$	43$_b$
Prevent mosques and temples	Antagonistic	60$_a$	33$_b$	31$_b$
	Ambivalent	23$_a$	44$_b$	23$_a$
	Inclusive	18$_a$	23$_a$	46$_b$
N		258 (23%)	639 (54%)	279 (24%)

'Christian nationalists' are those who both agree that the federal government should advocate Christian values and that Parliament should open with the Lord's Prayer. 'Secularists' are those who disagree with the government advocating Christian values and do not want any prayers in Parliament. The 'Undecided' are any other combination of responses.

Different faiths: $X^2(4, N = 1,200) = 22.391, p < .001$

Australian Curriculum: $X^2(4, N = 1,176) = 73.444, p < .001$

Prevent mosques and temples: $X^2(4, N = 1,167) = 123.259, p < .001$

Across the categories in each row, different subscript letters denote proportions within the categories of Christian nationalism that differ significantly from each other at the .05 level based on the SPSS z-test of proportions.

The two questions about prayers in Parliament and whether Parliament should advocate Christian values can be used to examine the relationship between Christian nationalism and attitudes towards religious diversity. For the purposes of our analysis we define 'Christian nationalists' as those who both agree that the federal government should advocate Christian values and that Parliament should open with the Lord's Prayer. We define 'Secularists' as those who disagree with the federal government advocating Christian values and do not want any prayers in Parliament (Table 2.5).

Christian nationalists are roughly divided into thirds in regard to their views on the benefit of different faiths in Australia and are typically supportive of teaching about the diversity of religious worldviews in schools with 55 per cent agreeing that the curriculum should include studying a diversity of religious worldviews. However, Christian nationalists are strongly antagonistic towards non-Christian religions with 60 per cent agreeing that a local community should be able to prevent the building of a mosque or temple and only 18 per cent reporting inclusive attitudes. In contrast, secularists are more likely to have inclusive attitudes towards different faiths (38 per cent) and have inclusive attitudes towards building mosques and temples (46 per cent). Christian nationalists tend to be older, with 29 per cent of Christian nationalists being seventy or older. In contrast, only 5 per cent of secularists are seventy or older. Put the other way, 44 per cent of people seventy or older are Christian nationalists, but only 15 per cent of people are in the age group of eighteen to twenty-nine years. There are no significant differences in education levels and gender identity.

The categories of 'Christian' and 'Christian nationalist' overlap, but they are not the same. Among regularly attending Christians, 55 per cent are Christian nationalists. Among nominal Christians, 28 per cent are Christian nationalists. Or, put the other way around, only 45 per cent of Christian nationalists attend Christian services regularly, and 42 per cent are nominal Christians, with 10 per cent of Christian nationalists not identifying their religion as Christian. In other words, Christian nationalists are a distinct group that overlaps with regularly attending Christians but also extends beyond them. Christian nationalism is a set of ideas about how Australia should be, that is not necessarily linked to being Christian, as is well illustrated by the fact that 10 per cent of Christian nationalists do not identify as Christians. The presence of a group of Christian nationalists who think that Christian values and practices are good for Australia, whilst not actually identifying as Christian themselves, suggests that Christian nationalism is less about religious belief and practice, and more about conservative values and ideas.

Comparing the attitudes of Christian nationalists (Table 2.4) and practising Christians (Table 2.5) suggests that antagonism toward non-Christian religions such as Islam or Hinduism, is more strongly associated with nationalist forms of Christianity. Christian nationalists are twice as likely (60 per cent) as secularists (31 per cent) to be antagonistic towards non-Christian religions, as measured by attitudes towards building mosques or temples (Table 2.5). Among regularly attending Christians who are also Christian nationalists ($N = 113$), 57 per cent are antagonistic towards non-Christian religions. In a startling contrast, among regularly attending Christians who do not advocate Christian nationalism ($N = 89$), only 20 per cent are antagonistic towards non-Christian religions. This underlines that antagonism towards non-Christian religions such as Islam or Hinduism is more strongly associated with nationalist forms of Christianity.

Young people are significantly more accepting of religious diversity, and older people are significantly more attached to Christianity and are antagonistic

Table 2.6 Religious diversity and age

		18–29%	30–9%	40–9%	50–9%	60–9%	70–99%
Government advocate Christian values	Agree	26$_a$	28$_{a,b}$	36$_{b,c}$	36$_{b,c}$	46$_c$	65$_d$
	Neither	31$_{a,b}$	35$_b$	30$_{a,b}$	34$_b$	34$_b$	24$_a$
	Disagree	43$_a$	37$_{a,b}$	34$_b$	30$_b$	20$_c$	12$_d$
Different faiths	Antagonistic	16$_a$	24$_b$	22$_{a,b}$	27$_b$	28$_b$	26$_b$
	Ambivalent	38$_{a,b}$	35$_b$	40$_{a,b}$	44$_a$	38$_{a,b}$	43$_{a,b}$
	Inclusive	46$_a$	41$_{a,b}$	38$_{a,b,c}$	29$_c$	34$_{b,c}$	32$_{b,c}$
Australian curriculum	Antagonistic	21$_a$	24$_{a,b}$	24$_{a,b}$	30$_b$	31$_b$	21$_a$
	Ambivalent	33$_a$	34$_a$	36$_a$	32$_a$	27$_a$	33$_a$
	Inclusive	45$_a$	42$_a$	41$_a$	38$_a$	42$_a$	46$_a$
Prevent mosques and temples	Antagonistic	23$_a$	36$_{b,c}$	34$_c$	45$_{b,d}$	49$_d$	50$_d$
	Ambivalent	37$_{a,b,c}$	41$_{b,c}$	40$_c$	32$_{a,b,c}$	28$_a$	30$_{a,b}$
	Inclusive	40$_a$	23$_b$	27$_b$	23$_b$	22$_b$	20
	N	261	210	195	210	166	181

Government advocate Christian values: $X^2(10, N = 1,223) = 100.253, p < .001$

Different faiths: $X^2(10, N = 1,259) = 25.990, p < .01$

Australian Curriculum: $X^2(10, N = 1,229) = 11.837, p > .05$

Prevent mosques and temples: $X^2(10, N = 1224) = 61.748, p < .001$

Across the categories in each row, different subscript letters denote proportions within the categories of age groups that differ significantly from each other at the .05 level based on the SPSS z-test of proportions.

towards non-Christian religions (Table 2.6). Among those under thirty, only 26 per cent think the federal government should advocate Christian values, whereas nearly two-thirds (65 per cent) of those over seventy and 46 per cent of those in their sixties think the federal government should advocate Christian values. Similarly, less than one quarter (23 per cent) of those under thirty are antagonistic towards building mosques and temples, whereas approximately half of those over fifty are antagonistic towards building mosques and temples. One quarter, however, is still a significant and disturbing minority. Attitudes towards the diversity of faiths in Australia show a similar pattern, although the differences are not as strong.

People with more education tend to have more inclusive attitudes towards religious diversity, but there are some differences depending on the type of education (Table 2.7). The more education a person has, the more likely they will agree with including a wide range of religious worldviews in the Australian curriculum. Those who did not complete secondary school and those who have a diploma or trade certificate are less inclusive. Whereas those who completed

Religious Diversity in Australia

Table 2.7 Religious diversity and education

		Some Secondary or less %	Secondary completed %	Diploma or trade certificate %	Bachelor's degree or postgraduate %
Different faiths	Antagonistic	29$_a$	16$_b$	26$_a$	17$_b$
	Ambivalent	45$_a$	43$_a$	39$_a$	31$_b$
	Inclusive	26$_a$	41$_b$	35$_b$	52$_c$
Australian curriculum	Antagonistic	33$_a$	25$_b$	22$_b$	19$_b$
	Ambivalent	34$_a$	32$_a$	37$_a$	24$_b$
	Inclusive	33$_a$	43$_b$	41$_b$	57$_c$
Prevent mosques and temples	Antagonistic	44$_a$	31$_b$	39$_{a,c}$	34$_{b,c}$
	Ambivalent	37$_a$	39$_a$	36$_a$	28$_b$
	Inclusive	19$_a$	30$_{b,c}$	25$_{a,c}$	37$_b$
Government advocate Christian values	Agree	39$_{a,b}$	32$_b$	40$_a$	39$_{a,b}$
	Neither	34$_{a,b}$	38$_b$	28$_{a,c}$	26$_c$
	Disagree	27$_a$	30$_{a,b}$	32$_{a,b}$	35$_b$
N		352	227	386	258

Different faiths: $X^2(10, N = 1,256) = 53.956, p <.001$

Australian Curriculum: $X^2(10, N = 1,228) = 44.155, p <.001$

Prevent mosques and temples: $X^2(10, N = 1,223) = 31.022, p <.001$

Government advocate Christian values: $X^2(10, N = 1,222) = 13.886, p <.05$

Across the categories in each row, different subscript letters denote proportions within the categories of education that differ significantly from each other at the .05 level based on the SPSS z-test of proportions.

secondary school (but do not have a diploma or trade certificate), and those who have a university education, are more inclusive when it comes to a diversity of faiths in Australia. There is a similar, although weaker, pattern in the responses to the question about local communities being able to prevent the building of a mosque or temple.

Overall, the bivariate statistics describe two contrasting trends in response to religious diversity in Australia. Older people, less educated people and Christian nationalists tend to be more antagonistic towards religious diversity. In contrast, younger people, more educated people, people with no religion and non-nationalist Christians tend to be more embracing of diversity.

We conducted logistic regressions in order to separate out which of the various factors are more influential on attitudes towards religious diversity. In Table 2.8 we examine the sources of antagonistic attitudes towards religious diversity. Odds ratios greater than 1 indicate the variable increases the likelihood

Table 2.8 Antagonism towards religious diversity in Australia, logistic regressions

	Antagonistic to mosques and temples		Antagonistic to diversity of faiths in Australia		Antagonistic to information about religion in curriculum	
	Odds ratio	95% CI	Odds ratio	95% CI	Odds ratio	95% CI
Christian nationalist	2.81***	2.00–.96	2.25***	1.55–3.27	0.99	0.66–1.49
Secularist	0.91	0.65–1.27	1.23	0.85–1.77	1.98***	1.42–2.78
Christian	0.92	0.68–1.26	0.68*	0.47–0.96	0.86	0.62–1.20
Other religion	0.98	0.52–1.82	0.74	0.37–1.50	0.98	0.49–1.94
Attend services regularly	0.69	0.46–1.04	0.83	0.53–1.30	0.80	0.49–1.30
Pray or meditate regularly	0.94	0.64–1.36	1.25	0.83–1.88	0.89	0.58–1.38
Faith is important in life decisions	1.20	0.84–1.71	0.94	0.63–1.40	0.58**	0.38–0.88
Secondary education	0.82	0.54–1.22	0.44	0.27–0.71	0.68	0.44–1.04
Diploma or trade certificate	0.99	0.71–1.37	0.73	0.51–1.03	0.54***	0.38–0.78
Bachelor's degree or postgraduate	0.87	0.59–1.27	0.51**	0.33–0.78	0.51**	0.33–0.78
Gender (female)	0.89	0.69–1.15	0.65**	0.49–0.86	0.84	0.64–1.12
Age in years	1.016***	1.008–1.024	1.006	0.997–1.015	1.005	0.996–1.014
(Constant)	0.29***		0.40**		0.47*	
Nagelkerke R2	0.105		0.07		0.101	

*** $p < 0.001$; ** $p < 0.01$; * $p < 0.05$; $N = 1,306$.

Logistic regression. All variables are dummies, with the exception of age.

Christian nationalists: those who both agree that the federal government should advocate Christian values and that Parliament should open with the Lord's Prayer. Secularists: those who disagree with the government advocating Christian values, and do not want any prayers in parliament. The comparison for both these dummy variables are the 'Undecided' who are any other combination of responses.

Christian and Other religion are dummy variables with the comparison of no religion.

Attend services regularly: Attend several times a year or more often.

Pray or meditate regularly: Pray a few times a week, or more regularly.

Importance of faith: Religious faith or spirituality is very important, or important.

Education variables are dummy variables with the comparison: 'Some secondary education or less'.

The regression reported is with weighted data.

See the methodological appendix for further details.

of antagonism, odds ratios less than 1 indicate the variable reduces the likelihood of antagonism.

The logistic regressions in Table 2.8 suggest that *antagonism toward religious diversity in Australia is mainly associated with Christian nationalism.* Christian nationalists (odds ratio of 2.81) are nearly three times more likely to have antagonistic attitudes towards the building of mosques or temples. The only other significant influence is that of age (OR 1.016), with older people being more likely to be antagonistic towards the building of mosques or temples. This is consistent with the findings of the Scanlon survey that only 21 per cent of those aged eighteen to twenty-four had negative attitudes towards Muslims, whereas 44 per cent of those aged fifty-five to sixty-four had negative attitudes (Markus 2021: 107). None of the other indicators of religious belief or practice is significant, once the influence of Christian nationalism is controlled.

Christian nationalists (OR 2.25) are also over twice as likely to have antagonistic attitudes towards the diversity of faiths in Australia. In contrast, Christians (OR 0.68), women (OR 0.65) and people with a university education (OR 0.51) are less likely to be antagonistic to the diversity of faiths in Australia. It is notable that Christian nationalists are more likely to be antagonistic to the diversity of faiths, whereas people who identify as Christians are less likely to be antagonistic. In this case Christian nationalists and Christians have very different views.

Antagonism to including information about the diversity of faiths in the Australian curriculum seems to have different sources. Christian nationalists (OR 0.99) are not significantly more likely to be antagonistic. Rather, secularists (OR 1.98) are nearly twice as likely to be opposed to teaching about the diversity of faiths in the Australian curriculum. For the purposes of this analysis we define 'secularists' as people who indicated they do not want the government to advocate Christian values and do not want prayers to open federal Parliament (Table 2.5). Given the existing Christian privilege in the Australian curriculum, together with the relative lack of content on religion throughout it, it is not surprising that Christian nationalists are more supportive of teaching about diverse religions – including Christianity – than secularists are, particularly given secularists' long-held concerns regarding the place of religion in Australian schools (Halafoff 2013b; Byrne 2014; Maddox 2014). People who say their faith is important (OR 0.58), people with diploma and trade certificates (OR 0.54) and university education (OR 0.51) are all less likely to be opposed to including information about the diversity of faiths in the Australian curriculum. See Chapter 5 for further discussion of this issue.

Overall, the regression analyses indicate that in Australia, the strongest sources of antagonism towards religious diversity – aimed specifically at religious minorities – are Christian nationalist ideas. Indicators of the importance of one's religion or faith, regularity of attending religious services and regularity of prayer or meditation are not associated with antagonistic attitudes towards religious diversity. Rather, people who identify as Christians are more likely to agree that the diversity of faiths has made Australia a better place, once the influence of Christian nationalism is controlled.

Discussion: Experiences of diversity

Christian nationalists – defined as those Australians who both want the federal government to advocate Christian values, and the federal Parliament to open with the Christian Lord's Prayer (Table 2.5) – make up 23 per cent of the Australian population. Christian nationalism is strongly associated with antagonism towards religious diversity (Tables 2.5 and 2.8). Between one quarter and one-third of Australians are antagonistic towards the three measures of religious diversity examined here, including about 9–14 per cent of Australians who are strongly negative towards religious diversity (Table 2.1). Christian nationalists are the primary source of anti-cosmopolitan exclusivism (Halafoff 2013a) and seek to engage past preserving practices antagonistic to religious diversity (Beaman 2020).

Most contemporary Australian nonreligious workplaces do not have communal prayers as a regular part of their activities. However, the Australian federal Parliament still opens with the Christian Lord's Prayer. Only one quarter (26 per cent) of Australians support this practice (Table 2.3). It is surprising to see such public Christian prayers in a nonreligious workplace, particularly one as symbolically significant as federal Parliament. As such, it highlights the power and privilege that Christianity continues to enjoy in Australia, and the state-sanctioned resistance to inclusion and pluralism. Jay Wexler (2019) reports that many local and state governments in the United States still open their meetings with Christian prayers. When members of religious minorities challenge this practice, requesting prayers from a variety of religions, these governments in the United States often choose to have no prayers at all.

Christian nationalists are not arguing that Christians should have equal rights to other religions. Rather, Christian nationalists argue that Christians should have more rights and privileges than are provided to other religions in Australia.

Christian nationalists want to have Christian prayers in Parliament even though other religions do not have such prayers. They want local communities to be able to object to the building of an Islamic mosque or Hindu temple, even though Christians do not generally have to deal with similar objections to their churches. Christian nationalists want the federal government to advocate Christian values, because they think Christian values, ethics and practices should be the ones that guide all Australians, even those Australians who do not follow the Christian religion.

In the 1960s and 1980s 'nominal' Christians were more likely to be antagonistic towards religious and ethnic diversity, in contrast to the more inclusive attitudes of those who attended church regularly and those who said they had no religion (Mol 1966; Maddox 2005). Marion Maddox (2005: 140) reports that in Hans Mol's 1966 study of the beliefs and practices of Australians, regular churchgoing was associated with conservative moral and political attitudes on topics such as abortion and capital punishment. However, attitudes towards racial minorities did not follow this pattern: 'The more religiously active his respondents, the more likely they were to feel "friendly and at ease" with members of what he calls 'outgroups' [including …] Japanese, Italians, Catholics, Jews and alcoholics' (Maddox 2005: 140). In Mol's 1981 study, this pattern still held (Maddox 2005).

Our research shows that religious attendance is now largely unrelated to attitudes towards religious diversity. The attitudes of nominal Christians are typically similar to Christians who attend services regularly (Table 2.4). In the regression analyses, the frequency of attending religious services is not a significant predictor of any of the indicators of attitudes towards religious diversity (Table 2.8) showing that the key influence upon attitudes to diversity is now Christian nationalist ideas, rather than frequency of attending religious services. Baker and associates (2020) demonstrate that Christian nationalism in the United States is tightly interrelated with xenophobia and Islamophobia. Our data suggest a similar pattern exists in Australia, as discussed in more detail in subsequent chapters.

There is considerable additional work to be done on understanding Australian attitudes towards religious diversity (Weng et al. 2021). Markus (2014: 13) has pointed out, in relation to the Scanlon Surveys that he leads, that it is problematic to assume that one survey question can provide an accurate indicator of attitudes towards Muslims. He also argues it is useful to differentiate more extreme responses from more moderate ones. Further research into attitudes towards religious diversity could usefully adopt a similar approach using a more sophisticated set of indicators. There is also further work to be done identifying the sources of attitudes towards religious diversity. For example, Timothy Gravelle (2021: 132) found that in Australia, 'political party identification, contact with Muslims, and the local prevalence of Muslims all shape Islamophobic attitudes among majority-group Australians'.

In Australia, those who have received education about diverse religions and worldviews in secondary school have a more positive attitude to religious minorities (Singleton et al. 2021). Our data supports this observation, demonstrating that higher levels of education are associated with more inclusive attitudes towards religious diversity. Coupled together, this strongly suggests that education, and specifically improving religious literacy, will increase respect for the various religious and nonreligious identities that now make up Australia.

We argue for a more inclusive pluralist approach, oriented to future forming narratives that respect the multicultural, multifaith and super-diverse nature of Australian society, respectful of the rights of others. Approximately one-third of Australians embrace an inclusive approach to religious diversity, with a further one-third ambivalent or uncertain (Table 2.1). This demonstrates a need to increase religious literacy and interreligious understanding among Australians, to counter risks posed by Christian nationalism and the Far Right. Strategies for doing so are discussed in subsequent chapters.

Methodological appendix: Survey method details

We included a set of questions in a national survey to better understand attitudes towards religious diversity in Australia. The Australian Community Survey was an online survey conducted in November 2020 by National Christian Life Survey Research (NCLSR). The sample was drawn from a large online research panel. The survey is distributed by the Online Research Unit (ORU). ORU meets ISO 20252 and ISO 26362 standards for both market research and panel work. The Australian sample of just over 1,300 persons is representative of the adult population on age, gender and location. The dataset is weighted to reflect the demographic profile of the Australian population aged 18+ on age, gender and education, according to the 2016 Census. Nonetheless, we note that panel data may be problematic in various ways. Koivula and Sivonen (2022: 220) noted that in a comparison of a panel and probability survey the panel respondents were less likely to answer questions 'perceived as sensitive', although the panel did include better representation from groups that are often under-represented in probability surveys.

We included questions in the ORU survey that measure attitudes towards religious diversity, using the following statements with Likert scale response possibilities: 'Having people of many different faiths makes Australia a better place to live' (abbreviated in the tables as 'Different faiths'); 'The Australian Curriculum, which sets out what students should learn in schools, ought to include a wide range of religious and nonreligious worldviews' (abbreviated as 'Australian Curriculum'); 'Local communities should be able to prevent the construction of mosques or temples in their area if they don't want them' (abbreviated as 'Prevent mosques and temples'). These were all 5-point scales: strongly agree, agree, neither agree nor disagree, disagree, strongly disagree. In the analyses below the strongly agree and agree categories, and the strongly disagree and disagree categories have been combined.

Attitudes towards the separation of church and state were obtained with two questions. One asked: 'The Australian Federal Government should advocate Christian values' with a similar 5-point scale. Respondents were also asked: 'The opening of Australian Federal Parliament includes the Christian Lord's Prayer. What do you think of this?' The possible responses offered were: The Lord's Prayer should be used to open Parliament; Prayers from a variety of religions should open Parliament; There should be no religious prayers to open Parliament; Can't choose. The ORU survey included a question about religious identity: 'What is your religion?', and attendance at religious services was indicated by the question: 'Apart from such special occasions as weddings, funerals, etc., how often do you attend religious services?'

References

Baker, Joseph, Perry, Samuel, and Whitehead, Andrew. 2020. 'Keep America Christian (and White): Christian Nationalism, Fear of Ethnoracial Outsiders, and Intention to Vote for Donald Trump in the 2020 Presidential Election'. *Sociology of Religion* 81(3): 272–93.

Beaman, Lori G. 2020. *The Transition of Religion to Culture in Law and Public Discourse.* New York: Routledge.

Beck, Ulrich. 2006. *The Cosmopolitan Vision.* Cambridge: Polity Press.

Bouma, Gary. 2016. 'The Role of Demographic and Socio-cultural Factors in Australia's Successful Multicultural Society: How Australia Is Not Europe'. *Journal of Sociology* 52(4): 759–71.

Brett, Judith. 2003. 'John Howard and the Australian Legend'. *Arena Magazine* (65): 19–24.

Byrne, C. 2014. *Religion in Secular Education: What in Heaven's Name Are We Teaching Our Children?* Leiden: Brill.

Gravelle, Timothy. 2021. 'Explaining Islamophobia in Australia: Partisanship, Intergroup Contact, and Local Context'. *Australian Journal of Political Science* 56(2): 132–52.

Halafoff, A. 2006. 'UnAustralian Values'. In *Refereed Conference Proceedings, UNAUSTRALIA Conference*. Canberra: University of Canberra, 1–18.

Halafoff, A. 2013a. *The Multifaith Movement: Global Risks and Cosmopolitan Solutions*. Dordrecht: Springer.

Halafoff, A. 2013b. 'Education about Religions and Beliefs in Victoria'. *Journal for the Academic Study of Religion* 26(2): 172–97.

Halafoff, A. 2014. 'Riots, Mass Casualties, and Religious Hatred: Countering Anti-cosmopolitan Terror through Intercultural and Interreligious Understanding'. In P. Hedges (ed.), *Controversies in Contemporary Religions*. Santa Barbara, CA: Praeger, 293–312.

Halafoff, A. 2022. 'Resisting Vladimir Putin's Campaign of Anti-cosmopolitan Terror'. ABC Australia. https://www.abc.net.au/religion/putin-campaign-of-anti-cosmopoli tan-terror-anna-halafoff/13919322.

Halafoff, A., Weng, E., Marriot, E, Smith, G., Barton, G., and Bouma, G. 2021. 'Worldviews Complexity in COVID-19 Times: Australian Media Representations of Religion, Spirituality and Non-religion in 2020'. *Religions* 12(9): 682–703.

Koivula, A., and Sivonen, J. 2022. 'Different Sample Sources, Different Results? A Comparison of Online Panel and Mail Survey Respondents'. In *International Conference on Human-Computer Interaction*. Cham: Springer, 220–33.

Lam, Kim. 2019. 'Young Buddhists and the Cosmopolitan Irony of Belonging in Multicultural Australia'. *Journal of Intercultural Studies* 40(6): 720–35. DOI: 10.1080/07256868.2019.1675619Marion.

Maddox, M. 2005. *God under Howard: The Rise of the Religious Right in Australian Politics*. Sydney: Allen & Unwin.

Maddox, M. 2014. *Taking God to School: The End of Australia's Egalitarian Education?* Sydney: Allen & Unwin.

Markus, Andrew. 2014. 'Attitudes to Immigration and Cultural Diversity in Australia'. *Journal of Sociology* 50(1): 10–22.

Markus, Andrew. 2021. *Mapping Social Cohesion 2021. Scanlon Foundation Research Institute*. https://scanloninstitute.org.au/sites/default/files/2021-12/Mapping_Social _Cohesion_2021_Report_0.pdf. Accessed 1 August 2022.

McLeay, A., Poulos, E., and Richardson-Self, L. 2023. 'The Shifting Christian Right Discourse on Religious Freedom in Australia'. *Politics and Religion*, 1–22.

Seidel, Andrew. 2022. 'Events, People, and Networks Leading up to January 6'. In *Christian Nationalism and the January 6, 2021 Insurrection*. https://www.christians againstchristiannationalism.org/jan6report.

Singleton, A., Halafoff, A., Rasmussen, M., and Bouma, G. 2021. *Freedom, Faiths and Futures: Teenage Australians on Religion, Sexuality and Diversity.* New York: Bloomsbury.

Tyler, Amanda. 2022. 'Introduction'. In *Christian Nationalism and the January 6, 2021 Insurrection.* https://www.christiansagainstchristiannationalism.org/jan6report.

Weng, E., Halafoff, A., Abur, W., Campbell, D., Bouma, G., and Barton, G. 2021. 'Whiteness, Religious Diversity and Relational Belonging: Opportunities and Challenges for African Migrants in Australia'. *Journal for the Academic Study of Religions* 34(3): 289–313.

Wexler, Jay. 2019. *Our Non-Christian Nation: How Wiccans, Satanists, Atheists, and Other Non-Christians Are Demanding Their Rightful Place in American Public Life.* Stanford, CA: Redwood Press.

3

Media Representations of Worldview Diversity

Anna Halafoff, Emily Marriott, Geraldine Smith and Enqi Weng

Introduction

Previous Australian and international studies have demonstrated that media representations of religion reveal complex attitudes towards diverse worldviews – religious, spiritual and nonreligious – and their status in society (Knott, Poole and Taira. 2013; Poole and Weng 2021; Weng and Halafoff 2020, 2021). Research on media and religion after 11 September 2001 has also critiqued news media's propensity for sensationalism, depicting religion as controversial and deviant. This is especially so for media treatment of Islam and Muslims, as they continue to be frequently problematically correlated with violence, terrorism and extremism (Ewart and Rane 2011; Rane, Ewart and Abdalla 2010; Vultee, Craft and Velker 2010).

Christianity and Judaism have typically received more mixed reporting, in so-called Western societies, including the UK and Australia and have also been associated with direct violence and war and structural violence, including sexual abuse. Christianity has also often been discussed in contrast to secularism and nonreligious belief, and particularly fears of declining religious authority and morality in late modernity in previous analyses. At the same time, references to Christianity have appeared frequently across all newspaper genres, such as in place names and discussion of sport, the arts and in crosswords and quizzes (Poole 2019; Vultee, Craft and Velker 2010; Weng 2019, 2020; Weng and Halafoff 2020, 2021).

Research also reveals that media representations of religions in Western societies have tended to give more attention to the 'Abrahamic' faiths of Christianity, Islam and Judaism and thereby institutional forms of religion, which have more clearly defined beliefs and practices, and are more easily identifiable for a news audience. This has then rendered religious, spiritual or nonreligious groups that are smaller and/or more ambiguous in their organisational structure, beliefs and practices less visible in media reporting (Taira 2015; Weng and Halafoff 2020, 2021). Compared to institutional religions, more amorphous beliefs – such as spirituality, and even 'Eastern' religions like Buddhism – have tended to be presented more positively in news media compared to the Abrahamic religions, but have also been treated far less seriously, appearing most often in genres of entertainment and travel. While Christianity, Islam and Judaism have featured in news reporting and sections such as 'Prayers for the Day', far less coverage was received by spirituality, Buddhism and Hinduism, reflecting their lesser status in Western societies. References to nonreligion and the secular have also appeared less frequently than references to religion and generally have been more positive, perhaps indicating more acceptance of nonreligious views in nations such as the UK and Australia (Moore 2008; Vultee, Craft and Velker 2010; Weng 2020; Weng and Halafoff 2020, 2021).

As explained in previous chapters, the reality is that Australia has long been a culturally and religiously diverse nation, beginning with its First Nations cultures, and with subsequent waves of migration from the Asia-Pacific, European, Middle Eastern and African regions. The myth of a white, Christian Australia was fabricated by the introduction of the 1901 Immigration Restriction Act, known as the White Australia Policy. While this racist act no doubt reduced non-white migration to Australia, its far northern regions remained culturally and religiously diverse. This diversity has intensified since the act was lifted and migration increased from the 1970s onwards (Hage 1998; Halafoff et al. 2021; Weng et al. 2021a, 2021b). Consequently, previous research has demonstrated that media reporting that foregrounds, and thereby privileges, Christianity and other Abrahamic faiths in Australian newspapers does not adequately reflect the actual lived religious, spiritual and nonreligious diversity and complexity of this nation (McGuire 2008; Furseth 2017; Weng and Halafoff 2020, 2021). Two authors of this chapter, Enqi Weng and Anna Halafoff (2020: 343–5) also found that the pervasiveness of Christianity throughout Australian newspapers reflects its continued influence in Australian public and political life in both overt and more 'hidden', uncontested ways that have the ability to negatively impact the rights of others as was evident in Australia's recent marriage equality debate.

Previous research has also stressed the importance of feeling a sense of belonging for personal wellbeing and also for living well together (Yuval-Davis 2006); in particular, news media can play a significant role in creating this sense of belonging for diverse communities (Nolan, Farquharson and Marjoribanks 2018). When people feel excluded, negatively stereotyped or invisible, this can impede their sense of belonging and wellbeing (Yuval-Davis 2006). The Migration component of this Religious Diversity in Australia (RDA) study found that negative and racist discourses from political figures reported in the media have had negative impacts on Chinese, Russian and Afghan Muslim Australians (see Chapter 4). This racism intensified against Chinese diaspora and international students in Australia during the first year of the Covid-19 pandemic, when the RDA study was being conducted. The RDA project team decided to include a Media component to investigate representations of diverse worldviews – religious, spiritual and nonreligious – in Australian media, at the time of the pandemic, given Covid-19 and resulting restrictions were affecting many religious communities (Campbell 2020; Halafoff et al. 2020). The team's goal was to see how these media representations may have changed in the five years since Halafoff and Weng had conducted a similar Australian case study, as part of Lori Beaman's and Kim Knott's 'Religion on an Ordinary Day' project (Poole and Weng 2021; Weng and Halafoff 2020, 2021).

This chapter reports on the Media component of the RDA study, focused on the complexity of worldviews during the time of Covid-19. It briefly presents the project's methods and then discusses a thematic analysis of data gathered from four major newspapers read in Melbourne, Victoria, and Hobart, Tasmania – the two cities that are the main focus of the research. It concludes that many of the previous findings on media representations of religion in Australian and international studies, as discussed above, remain relevant; yet, there are also new trends emerging from this 2020 RDA Media study regarding diverse religions and worldviews, their power dynamics and state relations within Australia. In particular, this chapter reveals new insights on changing attitudes to First Nations cultures, nature and spirituality.

Methods

This study employed a thematic content quantitative and qualitative media analysis of news articles from major newspapers circulated in Melbourne and Hobart during the first year of the Covid-19 crisis in Australia from 25 January to 19 August 2020, which coincided with the data collection phase of the RDA project. The first confirmed case of Covid-19 in Australia was reported in Melbourne on 25 January 2020 (Department of Health 2020). Compared to the other states, Victoria was hit hardest by the pandemic in 2020, with an initial-month lockdown from 16 March to 12 April (Premier of Victoria 2020; ABC News 2020). A second longer lockdown began on 9 July 2020. It was meant to end on 19 August 2020, so this end date was chosen for this RDA Media study, which helped to keep the volume of data for analysis manageable. The lockdown was subsequently extended and restrictions did not start to ease for Metropolitan Melbourne until 28 October 2020. It was the longest and strictest lockdown recorded worldwide (BBC News 2020). In Tasmania, the first case of Covid-19 arrived on 2 March, and a State of Emergency was declared on 19 March requiring non-essential travellers to undergo a fourteen-day quarantine upon arriving to Tasmania. On 30 March, the Premier of Tasmania announced that they would be enforcing a four-week lockdown. However, restrictions did not begin to be eased until June 2020 (Premier of Tasmania 2020a; Storen and Corrigan 2020), and borders remained closed until 26 October when they re-opened to low-risk states and territories (Premier of Tasmania 2020b).

National and local newspapers read in Melbourne and Hobart, which reach a broad range of audience demographics, were selected for analysis: *The Australian, The Age, Herald Sun* and *The Mercury*. *The Age* is a more socially progressive newspaper owned by Nine Entertainment, while the other three are more conservative and owned by News Corporation (News Corp), also known in Australia as the Murdoch Press. *The Australian* is a national newspaper that targets business owners and elites. *The Age* is a Melbourne-based newspaper, with an educated and professional readership. *Herald Sun* is also a Melbourne-based newspaper, and *The Mercury* is Hobart-based. Both are daily right-leaning tabloids.

A mixed-method thematic quantitative and qualitative approach[1] using targeted keywords related to spirituality, religion and nonreligion identified through previous international studies on 'Media Portrayals of Religions and the Secular Sacred' led by Knott (Knott, Poole and Taira 2013) and the 'Religion on an Ordinary Day' study led by Beaman and Knott (Poole and Weng 2021; Weng and Halafoff 2020, 2021) was applied in the RDA Media study. The research team only searched for articles, thereby excluding crosswords and television guides and the like. The revised keywords searched for in the media database Factiva were: Spirituality – 'spirituality' (spiritual*), 'yoga' (yog*) and 'meditation' (meditat*); Religion – 'Religion' (religio*), 'Catholic' (Catholic*), 'Anglican' (Anglican*), 'Christianity' (Christian*), 'Islam' (*, Islam* OR Muslim*), 'Buddhism' (Buddh*), 'Hinduism' (Hindu*), 'Sikhism' (Sikh*) and 'Judaism' (Judais* OR Jew*); and Nonreligion – 'no religion' (non* religio*, no religio*, not* religio*) and 'secular' (Secular*). The researchers undertook the Factiva search for these terms coupled with the terms 'coronavirus*' and or 'COVID*', and coded the data according to themes.[2] The analysis is presented below.

Data analysis

Religion (n = 1,220) received far more mentions than Spirituality (n = 334) or Nonreligion (n = 30) (see Table 3.1) across the four newspapers. However, we discuss spirituality first in our analysis, given the much longer presence of First Nations spirituality in Australia, than Christianity and any institutionalised religion or nonreligious worldview.

Spirituality: First Nations, religious and holistic

The spirituality category, focused on the terms 'spiritual', 'meditation' and 'yoga', was mentioned 334 times across the four papers in total (see Table 3.2). Most references to spirituality were positive (n = 183), with 107 neutral, 19 mixed and only 25 negative across the papers. The *Herald Sun* and *The Age*'s reporting on spirituality was mostly positive, *The Mercury*'s mostly neutral and *The Australian* had the most negative (n = 13) mentions of spirituality of the four papers (see Table 3.3). Spirituality mentions appeared most often in Domestic News (n = 115); Features (n = 76), Entertainment/Travel/Review (n = 57), Opinion (n – 32) and Sport (n = 25) (see Table 3.4). Their presence in different genres demonstrates both a serious and more light-hearted coverage of spirituality that pervades many aspects of Australian life, as noted previously by Weng and Halafoff (2020, 2021).

For example, a positive article titled 'Top tourism spots eye local travel cash splash' in *The Australian* focused on the local travel boom during Covid-19

Table 3.1 Number of references coded in each newspaper

	The Australian	*The Age*	*Herald Sun*	*The Mercury*	Total
Spirituality	89	106	107	32	334
Religion	496	387	204	133	1,212
Secular/ Nonreligion	17	10	2	1	30
Total references					**1,584**

Table 3.2 Spirituality – references across the newspapers

	The Australian	The Age	Herald Sun	The Mercury	Total
Spiritual	46	39	18	8	111
Meditation	16	33	41	11	101
Yoga	27	34	48	13	122
Total references					**334**

Table 3.3 Spirituality – tone of references across the newspapers

	The Australian	The Age	Herald Sun	The Mercury	Total
Positive	38	61	72	12	183
Neutral	28	30	29	20	107
Negative	13	6	6	0	25
Mixed	10	9	0	0	19
Total references					**334**

Table 3.4 Spirituality – five main genres across the newspapers

	The Australian	The Age	Herald Sun	The Mercury	Total
Domestic News	29	41	33	12	115
Feature	17	17	34	8	76
Entertainment/Travel/ Review	17	18	18	4	57
Opinion	7	9	12	4	32
Sport	8	10	7	1	26

when borders were closed to international travel. Craig Bradbery, the chief operating officer of Baillie Lodges, which own the Northern Territory's Longitude 131, was reported as saying, 'he hoped Australians chose to visit the nation's "spiritual heart" in style'. He added: 'Bookings have been very strong [as] … Spring is always a great time to visit the Red Centre, with warm days and cool nights – perfect for sightseeing and stargazing' (Maddison 2020: 4). This article also reflects two major themes emerging in the spirituality category, of First Nations spirituality, and a holistic spirituality that is often associated with nature in Australia (Halafoff, Singleton and Fitzpatrick 2023). These, and religious spirituality, are discussed in more detail below.

First Nations spirituality

Many references to spirituality, across the three papers, had a First Nations focus, related in particular to sacred places and racial justice. As mentioned above, the 'Red Centre', where Uluru and Kata Tjuta are located, was said to be Australia's 'spiritual heart' (Maddison 2020: 4) in a piece in *The Australian*. Another, in the *Herald Sun*, recommended hiking trips in the Northern Territory focused on 'education about the culture and spirituality of the local Indigenous people' (Sutherland 2020: 14). Letters and articles, at the time of Black Lives Matters Protests in *The Age* also described colonisation as 'spiritual theft' (*The Age* 2020h:22), resulting in 'spiritual crisis' (Maglalogenis 2020: 23).

Religious spirituality

Many references to spirituality, particularly in *The Australian*, had a Christian focus. Controversial Hillsong founder Brian Houston was described as former prime minister Scott Morrison's 'spiritual mentor' (Savva 2020a: 12). The benefits of online worship, as a means for overcoming social and spiritual distancing (Visontay 2020), were also outlined as the centrality of 'spiritual care' for wellbeing (Lewis 2020: 4).

Articles across the three papers also mentioned spirituality in relation to other religions. *The Australian* described the Buddhist Dalai Lama as a 'Tibetan spiritual leader' (Hodge 2020c: 9) and mentioned the Noosa Satanists as claiming to help people free themselves from 'spiritual enslavement' (Workman 2020: 2). *The Age* cited Muslim AFL footballer Bachar Houli saying Ramadan was a time 'to reflect on his spiritual journey' (Ryan 2020: 38), while another article stated Ramadan was 'a spiritual boot camp' (Hope 2020: 4).

Holistic spirituality

The benefits of yoga and meditation to relieve stress and for fitness and wellbeing – in yoga studios, gyms, workplaces and schools, by everyday people, business leaders celebrities and athletes – were covered across the four papers (Chancellor and Lacy 2020; Landowski 2020; Manelis 2020; Smith 2020). Both yoga and meditation were also mentioned in relation to Buddhism and Hinduism

(Azzopardi 2020; *The Age* 2020c), Christian monasticism (Carroll 2020a) and to 'Tarawih, a form of Islamic meditation' (Topsfield and Rosa 2020: 11) in *The Age*.

Positive expressions of holistic spirituality also often occurred in relation to nature, nature-based tourism and nature-based sport. In addition to the examples stated above in First Nations spirituality on sacred places, Kelly Slater described surfing as 'a spiritual thing' in *The Australian* (Swanton 2020: 28), and *The Age* described gardening as a 'spiritual, soul-nourishing activity' (McManus 2020: 4). Spirituality also came up in discussions on art and music, including sleep apps (Allen 2020; Barns 2020; Clarke 2020; Jackson 2020).

Holistic spirituality was also critiqued in *The Age* and *The Australian* in relation to discredited spiritual gurus and their abusive practices (Hodge and Vasandani 2020; *The Age* 2020e; *The Australian* 2020a), potential Covid-19 super-spreader events and Covid-19 vaccine resistance, with particular mention of Novak Djokovic's problematic 'spiritual deep-dives' (Lutton 2020: 32).

Religion

Religion (*n* = 335) appeared most frequently, of the major religious search terms, followed by Catholicism (*n* = 311), Islam (*n* = 230), Christianity (*n* = 153); Judaism (*n* = 82), Anglicanism (*n* = 59), Buddhism (*n* = 21), Hinduism (*n* = 13) and Sikhism (*n* = 8) (see Table 3.5). This order does not match the most recent Australian census data given the smaller numbers of

Table 3.5 Religion – references across the newspapers

	The Australian	The Age	Herald Sun	The Mercury	Total
Religio*	132	108	62	33	335
Catholic*	109	108	60	34	311
Islam* OR Muslim*	122	55	30	23	230
Christian*	61	51	18	23	153
Judais* OR Jew*	34	32	14	2	82
Anglican*	21	18	10	10	59
Buddh*	6	4	5	6	21
Hindu*	7	2	3	1	13
Sikh*	3	3	1	1	8
Total References					**1,212**

Table 3.6 Religion – five main genres across the newspapers

	The Australian	The Age	Herald Sun	The Mercury	Total
Domestic News	158	150	87	78	473
Opinion	112	45	43	26	226
Feature	74	57	18	11	160
International News	87	40	13	4	144
Letters	26	59	26	9	120

Table 3.7 Islam or Muslim – tone of references coded across the newspapers

	The Australian	The Age	Herald Sun	The Mercury	Total
Positive	4	10	3	1	18
Neutral	78	34	18	21	151
Negative	38	11	9	1	59
Mixed	2	0	0	0	2
Total references					**230**

Muslim and Jewish Australians, compared to the larger Christian groups (ABS 2022). Higher numbers of references to Christianity, Islam and Judaism in this RDA Media study adds further evidence of the predominance of Abrahamic faiths in Australian public life, previously noted by Weng and Halafoff (2020, 2021). Religion also had far more ($n = 1,212$), and more serious coverage than spirituality, given that references appeared largely in Domestic News ($n = 473$), Opinion ($n = 226$), Features ($n = 160$), International News ($n = 144$) and Letters ($n = 120$).

Major religions – Islam

Islam received the most coverage of all major religions across all the newspapers, with 230 references in total. The coverage was mostly neutral ($n = 151$), then negative ($n = 59$) and with far less positive ($n = 18$) and mixed ($n = 2$) references (see Table 3.7). This was especially so in *The Australian*, *Herald Sun* and *The Mercury* News Corp papers.

Most of the negative reporting was focused on the spread of Covid-19 within Muslim communities and on Muslim pilgrimages (Baxendale and

Fergurson 2020; Bolt 2020a; Hodge 2020b; Hodge and Vasandani 2020: 13). By contrast, *The Age* highlighted more positive aspects of closing mosques, shifting Islamic practices and celebrating Ramadan online and Muslim social services helping those in need (Hodge 2020a; Topsfield and Rosa 2020; Tomazin 2020).

For example, *The Age* reported: 'Like Easter, Anzac Day and Mother's Day before, the Islamic holy festival ... Ramadan, will be kept to small family groups. Prayers will be at home and the feasts markedly less extravagant.' The article then quoted Ms Janif, who gave birth during the first week of Ramadan, and explained how online practices were a silver lining in the pandemic, making it more accessible for Muslim women: 'A beautiful thing is that during this Ramadan, it's been online ... People are providing prayers, or Koran recitations or just educational talks, which means someone like me ... is able to access. In the past you'd have to go to the mosque' (Hope 2020: 4).

Other articles that mentioned Islam and Muslims centred on issues of terrorism and extremism (Packham 2020: 4; Thomas 2020: 10) and were mainly negative and mixed. There were also a number of articles across the papers critical of China, which included empathetic concerns regarding the human rights abuse of Muslim Uyghurs and the Muslim 're-education' camps in Xinjiang (Bagshaw 2020; Bevilacqua 2020; Bolt 2020b; Panahi 2020). Additional mentions also included Islamic prayer times (*The Mercury* 2020a).

Major religions – Christianity

The Australian (*n* = 61) and *The Age* (*n* = 51) mentioned Christianity more frequently than the *Herald Sun* (*n* = 18) or *The Mercury* (*n* = 23) (see Table 3.8). Most Christian references in *The Age*, *Herald Sun* and *The Mercury* were neutral and positive. *The Age* had the most negative coverage on Christianity. *The*

Table 3.8 Christianity – tone of references coded across the newspapers

	The Australian	*The Age*	*Herald Sun*	*The Mercury*	Total
Positive	32	14	6	11	63
Neutral	24	23	11	11	69
Negative	5	11	1	0	17
Mixed	0	3	0	1	4
Total references					153

Australian, by contrast, had more positive references to Christianity, reflecting a privileging of Christianity.

Most mentions of Christianity related to Christian services and educational institutions including schools and universities being impacted by Covid-19 outbreaks and restrictions and shifting to online methods of delivery. The newspapers often depicted Anglican and Catholic Christian institutions and leaders, including the queen and the pope, as moral authorities and protectors during this crisis (Freier 2020; Johnstone 2020; Norington 2020; Reid 2020; *The Age* 2020d; Zwartz 2020). For example, The Age quoted the Catholic Archbishop of Melbourne as saying: 'This is the absolute heart of the Christian calling; how might I go out to people, in safe but creative ways, so that people don't feel isolated and alone?' (Le Grand 2020a: 6). Another feature in *The Mercury* by The Most Reverend Julian Porteous concluded that the pandemic had provided 'a new gift – the gift of time and the gift of quiet', reflecting on Christian contemplative practices (Porteous 2020: 34). By contrast, the Greek Orthodox Church in Australia and the Korean Christian Shincheonji movement were seen as deviant for flouting Covid-19 restrictions (Fowler 2020; Laurie 2020), demonstrating a persistent mistrust against the ethnic 'other', noted in other chapters within this volume.

Christianity was also the subject of critique in relation to Australian Cardinal George Pell and The Royal Commission into Institutional Responses to Child Sexual Abuse, the then prime minister Scott Morrison's Pentecostal Christian identity, particularly in *The Australian* and *The Age* (Bramston 2020; Le Grand 2020b; Savva 2020b: 10; Topsfield 2020: 2; Walker 2020: 7). A more light-hearted pervading use of Christian terms was evident in names of places and football teams across all papers.

Major religions – Judaism

Following Christianity and Islam, Judaism received the next highest number of mentions across the papers ($n = 82$), largely in relation to how Jewish communities were handling the pandemic and transitioning to digital practices. Most articles were neutral and negative (see Table 3.9) and focused on the contravening of rules such as social distancing, while positive and mixed articles praised Jewish communities for closing synagogues and praying online (Sakkal 2020: 7). Some articles and letters also stated that the suffering during the Holocaust was far worse than the pandemic (*The Age* 2020f; Penberthy 2020). For example, a letter to the editor in the *Herald Sun* stated:

Processing something of that magnitude is difficult and a new experience for those of us not old enough to remember World War II. But I mention World War II to illustrate that this still isn't the scariest moment in human history. Nazism, the Blitz in London, the scale and orchestration of the Jewish genocide … all that is worth reflecting on next time you're freaking out about the lack of toilet rolls. (Penberthy 2020: 32)

Other mentions in *The Age* and *The Australian* focused on anti-Semitism in Australia (Hutchinson and Loussikian 2020a, 2020b) and Turkey (*The Australian* 2020b).

Major religions – Buddhism, Hinduism and Sikhism

There were far less mentions of Buddhism (*n* = 21), Hinduism (*n* = 13) and Sikhism (*n* = 8) across the newspapers than the Abrahamic faiths, with most mentions being neutral or positive in tone (see Tables 3.10–3.12). Most references to Buddhism and Hinduism were related to the benefits of stillness, compassion, meditation and/or chanting to deal with stress during the pandemic (Azzopardi 2020; Davidson 2020; Joseph 2020; *Herald Sun* 2020; Wang Xin De and Zhi-Ji 2020). One article in *The Mercury* disturbingly reported that a Chinese Buddhist

Table 3.9 Judaism or Jewish – tone of references coded across the newspapers

	The Australian	The Age	Herald Sun	The Mercury	Total
Positive	0	2	2	1	5
Neutral	28	24	9	1	62
Negative	6	6	3	0	15
Mixed	0	0	0	0	0
Total references					82

Table 3.10 Buddhism – tone of references coded across the newspapers

	The Australian	The Age	Herald Sun	The Mercury	Total
Positive	1	1	3	2	7
Neutral	4	3	2	2	11
Negative	1	0	0	2	3
Mixed	0	0	0	0	0
Total references					21

Table 3.11 Hinduism – tone of references coded across the newspapers

	The Australian	The Age	Herald Sun	The Mercury	Total
Positive	1	0	1	0	2
Neutral	5	2	2	1	10
Negative	1	0	0	0	1
Mixed	0	0	0	0	0
Total references					13

Table 3.12 Sikh – tone of references coded across the newspapers

	The Australian	The Age	Herald Sun	The Mercury	Total
Positive	0	3	0	1	4
Neutral	3	0	1	0	4
Negative	0	0	0	0	0
Mixed	0	0	0	0	0
Total references					8

temple had been vandalised in 'an act of racism' against the Chinese community, who had been unfairly 'blamed for coronavirus' (Kitto 2020: 6). *The Age* and *The Mercury* also included praise for Sikh volunteering and food delivery during lockdowns, including to international students (Cowie and Precel 2020; Fitzherbert 2020; *The Mercury* 2020b). For example, *The Age* described how:

> the hard lockdown of public housing towers shone a spotlight on many individuals and organisations that quickly put concern for residents into action – such as the Sikhs who provided meals for residents, just as they did during last summer's bushfires. (Fitzherbert 2020: 19)

One negative article in *The Australian* referred to a 'Buddhist militia' in Myanmar (Hodge 2020d: 8) and another to religious persecution of Hindus in Sri Lanka (Hodge 2020e: 8).

Nonreligion

There were by far less mentions of nonreligion and the secular ($n = 30$) than of religion or spirituality across the newspapers (see Table 3.13), mostly in *The*

Table 3.13 Secular/nonreligion – references across the newspapers

	The Australian	The Age	Herald Sun	The Mercury	Total
Secular	8	7	1	1	17
Nonreligion	9	3	1	0	13
Total references					30

Table 3.14 Secular/nonreligion – tone of references across the newspapers

	The Australian	The Age	Herald Sun	The Mercury	Total
Positive	1	2	0	0	3
Neutral	11	7	0	1	19
Negative	5	1	2	0	8
Mixed	0	0	0	0	0
Total references					30

Australian (n = 17) and *The Age* (n = 10). Coverage across the papers was largely neutral (n = 18) and negative (n = 8) (see Table 3.14) appearing most often in Features (n = 11), Opinion (n = 6), Domestic News (n = 6), Letters (n = 3) and Entertainment/Travel/Reviews (n = 2) (see Table 3.15). Similarly to spirituality, this indicates that nonreligion and the secular permeate many parts of Australian life but are taken less seriously than religion.

Furthermore, and as noted above, the more conservative coverage by *The Australian* and *Herald Sun* bemoaned the rise of a 'woke', 'secular age' and decline of Christian values as a threat to morality and Western civilisation (Credlin 2020: 52; Kelly 2020: 20; Morrow 2020: 36). Both papers also raised concerns that the climate movement was the new 'quasi-religion', with nature replacing God (Carroll 2020b: 16; McCrann 2020).

Reporting on nonreligion and the secular was often linked to nature, *The Mercury*'s one neutral article reported that Charles Sturt University researcher Jennifer Watkins said that 'although funeral rituals were already becoming secular and individualistic' before the pandemic; this trend was accelerating dramatically and was likely to continue too. She stated that 'now … there's certainly a great feeling of warmth and intimacy, particularly for people having it in their own homes' and that 'more families were holding funerals in their gardens for a serene atmosphere and spiritual link to nature' (Mccann 2020: 5).

Table 3.15 Secular/nonreligion – five main news genres across the newspapers

	The Australian	*The Age*	*Herald Sun*	*The Mercury*	Total
Feature	7	4	0	0	11
Opinion	3	1	2	0	6
Domestic News	3	2	0	1	6
Letters	0	3	0	0	3
Entertainment/Travel/ Review	2	0	0	0	2

The more progressive paper, *The Age*, had more positive and wide-ranging coverage with mentions of a secular Easter bunny (Dubecki and Lam 2020: 4) and of 'religious faith and secular science' both providing meaning in ways that could be complementary (*The Age* 2020g: 22). Opinions and letters in *The Age* also critiqued people 'worshipping' neoliberal capitalism (*The Age* 2020a: 36) and former prime minister Morrison's Christianity, rejecting his 'offer of God's blessings' and asking him to 'keep it secular' (*The Age* 2020b: 21). A news article in *The Age* also noted how religion used to be 'the opiate of the masses' but that 'organised commercial sport' is the masses' current preferred drug, and that Australians are likely to suffer the impact of withdrawal from it given the Covid-19 restrictions (Wu 2020: 26).

Discussion and conclusions

Similar to findings in the other chapters of this volume, the RDA Media study revealed a privileging of Christianity in media representations of religion in Australian media, particularly in more conservative News Corp-Murdoch Press newspapers. Islam and Judaism also received more serious media attention than other minority faiths and spirituality, demonstrating the prominence of Abrahamic traditions in *The Australian* public mind, despite Australia's geographical proximity to Asia.

Not only was coverage of Christianity pervading across all media genres, it was mostly neutral and positive in contrast to reporting on Islam and Judaism, which was more negative. Ethnic forms of Christianity were also seen as deviant, and a Chinese Buddhist temple was reported as vandalised in a racist attack. While Asian traditions of Buddhism, Hinduism and Sikhism were largely seen to be more positive, they were often exoticised appearing mostly in travel and entertainment, and less visible than the Abrahamic faiths. This media reporting does not, however, accurately reflect the reality of the multicultural or multifaith composition of Australia, evident in historical records and Census data, as Weng and Halafoff (2020, 2021) observed in their previous study of Religion on an Ordinary Day (RoD) in Melbourne, Australia.

An additional concern, as this RDA Media study focused on Melbourne and Hobart, is that News Corp/Murdoch Press has a monopoly over newspapers read in capital cities across Australia, other than Sydney and Melbourne. This means that readers in Hobart are exposed to more conservative views, Christian privileging and negative reporting on Islam and other minority faiths, than those in Melbourne and Sydney. This may contribute to less religious and interreligious literacy and greater risks of Islamophobia and migrantophobia among people in smaller capital cities and towns in Australia. There are obviously other sources from which to obtain news and information; however, social media is also rife with problematic racism and religious vilification against minorities. This strengthens the case that Weng and Halafoff (2020, 2021) made previously for the need for more programmes on religious and interreligious literacy in schools, to counter misinformation and political and media biases. This is discussed in more detail in the Education chapter 5 within this volume.

This media component of the RDA study has also documented significant new insights on changing attitudes to First Nations cultures and spirituality in Australia and the sacredness of nature to Australians. There was substantively more attention given to First Nations spirituality, in reference to cultural heritage and sacred natural places, and to racial justice in the RDA study than in the previous RoD Australian study (Weng and Halafoff 2020, 2021). This demonstrates both a growing awareness of and interest in First Nations culture and social justice by mainstream Australia – and a resistance towards this recognition by a vocal minority of conservative voices, reported most often in the News Corp-Murdoch Press.

In addition, while First Nations Australians have always had a strong and enduring relational connection with Country, and nature has always played a strong and sacred role in the Australian imaginary (Tacey 2004; Bouma 2006; Halafoff et al. 2023), many references to nature and spiritual contemplative practices, particularly as a source of comfort during the pandemic, were a significant theme within this study. Spirituality also pervaded all genres and aspects of Australian life. In the RoD study this reporting was largely positive; however, this RDA Media study also revealed a critique of spirituality's relationship to capitalism, and to conspiracy theories and resulting vaccine resistance. The rise of conspiracy theories during the pandemic likely led to this spike in critical perspectives of spirituality. As Halafoff et al. (2022) have explained recently in their '(Con)spirituality in Australia' study, (con)spiritualists think of nature and their own pristine bodies as sacred, and biomedicines, including vaccines, as pollutants. Halafoff, Emily Marriott, Ruth Fitzpatrick and Weng (2022) bracketed the 'con' in 'conspirituality' (Ward and Voas 2011) to stress the internal diversity within spiritual movements, given that their pilot study showed that only a small percentage of Australians who identify as spiritual hold conspiratorial and vaccine-resistant views. Small or not, these and other risks and harms within spiritual movements, such as cultural appropriation, essentialised gender norms and sexual abuse, are serious issues of increased interest to journalists and researchers (conspirituality.com; Halafoff et al. 2022).

Finally, this RDA Media analysis also showed that even among the most secular, there was a strong connection to nature, which was in ways 'religion-like' (Knott, Poole and Taira 2013). Environmentalism was also seen as a new secular religion, further challenging extractive conservative capitalist practices, power and privilege. Yet, nothing could unsettle the sacredness of Australia's favourite religion, sport! It retained its centrality and revered status, as previously revealed in the RoD study (Weng and Halafoff 2020, 2021).

Notes

1 Halafoff decided on the search terms in consultation with Weng and Marriott. Marriott, Smith and Halafoff conducted the data analysis, and all authors contributed to the final discussion and conclusion of this chapter and an article arising from the study (Halafoff et al. 2021). Both publications were led by Halafoff.

2 Exclusion criteria were implemented to make the volume of data more accurate and manageable for this analysis. They included focusing on print articles only, and excluded articles that had no references to religion. For example, the initial searches included articles where 'Christian*' referred to a person's name, or the search term 'Jew*' also picked up references to 'jewellery'.

References

ABC News. 2020. Breakfast Show. *ABC News*, 10 April.
The Age. 2020a. 'Letters'. *The Age*, 21 March, 36.

The Age. 2020b. 'And Another Thing'. *The Age*, 25 March, 21.

The Age. 2020c. 'There'll Always Be a There'. *The Age*, 28 March, 2.

The Age. 2020d. 'Reach Out to Others in Spirit of Easter'. *The Age*, 12 April, 32.

The Age. 2020e. 'Our Pick'. *The Age*, 16 April, 8.

The Age. 2020f. 'We Have Been Looked after in This Pandemic'. *The Age*, 12 May, 20.

The Age. 2020g. 'Letters'. *The Age*, 8 June, 22.

The Age. 2020h. 'Letters'. *The Age*, 12 July, 22.

Allen, Christopher. 2020. 'Meeting Our Monsters'. *The Australian*, 25 July, 10.

The Australian. 2020a. 'Gym Still a Haven if Precautions Taken'. *The Australian*, 12 March, 14.

The Australian. 2020b. Letters to the editor. *The Australian,* March 23, 13.

Australian Bureau of Statistics. (ABS) 2022. '2021 Census Shows Changes in Australia's Religious Diversity'. Australian Bureau of Statistics, Canberra, https://www.abs.gov.au/media-centre/media-releases/2021-census-shows-changes-australias-religious-diversity. Accessed 13 July 2022.

Azzopardi, N. 2020. 'The Global Power of "Om"'. *The Age*, 10 August, 12.

Bagshaw, E. 2020. 'Australia's China Challenge in the Post-Coronavirus World'. *The Age*, 25 April, 7.

Barns, G. 2020. 'GASP Cut Highlights Great Divide'. *The Mercury*, 3 August, 14.

Baxendale, R., and Fergurson, J. 2020. 'Eid Family Feast Sparks Big Cluster'. *The Australian*, 12 June, 5.

Bevilacqua, S. 2020. 'Dropping Like Flies'. *The Mercury*, 4 April, 23.

Bolt, A. 2020a. 'Tribalism a Friend of the Virus'. *Herald Sun*, 13 July, 21.

Bolt, A. 2020b. 'Personal Insight into Regime'. *Herald Sun*, 21 May, 45.

Bouma, G. 2006. *Australian Soul: Religion and Spirituality in the Twenty-First Century*. Cambridge: Cambridge University Press.

Bramston, T. 2020. 'PM Can't Make History While He's Still a Mystery'. *The Australian*, 19 May, 10.

Campbell, H. 2020. 'The Distanced Church: Reflections on Doing Church Online'. https://hdl.handle.net/1969.1/187891. Accessed 3 June 2021.

Carroll, J. 2020a. 'Sinning against Nature Now the New Religion'. *The Australian*, 4 July, 16.

Carroll, J. 2020b. 'Key to Sailing on When Life Is Becalmed by Shutdown'. *The Age*, 1 August, 27.

Chancellor, J., and Lacy, C. 2020. 'Life's a Beach for Turnbull'. *The Australian*, 17 April, 14.

Clarke, A. 2020. 'Sound of Isolation Blues'. *The Age*, 21 May, 16.

Covid in Australia: Melbourne to Exit 112-day Lockdown (2020), [TV programme] BBC News, 3 June 2021.

Cowie, T., and Precel, N. 2020. 'Kindness, Its Catching'. *The Age*, 4 April, 12.

Credlin, P. 2020. 'We're Losing Faith'. *Herald Sun*, 14 June, 52.

Davidson, B. 2020. 'How to: Follow Your Intuition'. *The Australian*, 11 July, 3.

Department of Health. 2020. 'First Confirmed Case of Novel Coronavirus in Australia'. 25 January. https://www.health.gov.au/ministers/the-hon-greg-hunt-mp/media/first-confirmed-case-of-novel-coronavirus-in-australia. Accessed 3 June 2021.

Dubecki, L., and Lam, L. T. 2020. 'Get 'em While They're Hot'. *The Age*, 7 April, 4.

Ewart, J., and Rane, H. 2011. 'Moving on from 9/11: How Australian Television Reported the Ninth Anniversary'. *Journal of Media and Religion* 10(2): 55–72.

Fitzherbert, M. 2020. It Is Our Duty to Fix Honours System. *The Age*, 5 August, 19.

Freier, P. 2020. 'Take Heart from New Life'. *Herald Sun*, 10 April, 27.

Fowler, M. 2020. 'Secretive Cult behind Korean Outbreak Has Branches in Australia'. *The Age*, 3 March, 10.

Furseth, I. 2017. 'Introduction'. In I. Furseth (ed.), *Religious Complexity in the Public Sphere: Comparing Nordic Countries*. Cham: Springer Nature, 1–30.

Hage, G. 1998. *White Nation: Fantasies of White Supremacy in a Multicultural Society*. Annandale: Pluto Press.

Halafoff, A, Weng, E., Bouma, G., and Barton, G. 2020. 'Religious Groups Are Embracing Technology during the Lockdown, but Can It Replace Human Connection?' *The Conversation*. 1 May. https://theconversation.com/ religious-groups-are-embracing-technology-during-the-lockdown-but-can-it-replace-human-connection-135682. Accessed 11 May 2021.

Halafoff, A., Marriott, E., Smith, G., Weng, E., and Bouma, G. 2021. 'Worldviews Complexity in COVID-19 Times: Australian Media Representations of Religion, Spirituality and Non-religion in 2020'. *Religions* 12(9): 682–703.

Halafoff, A., Marriott, E., Fitzpatrick, R., and Weng, E. 2022. 'Selling (Con)spirituality and COVID- 19 in Australia: Convictions, Complexity and Countering Dis/misinformation. *Journal for the Academic Study of Religion* 35(2): 141–167.

Halafoff, A., Singleton, A., and Fitzpatrick, R. 2023. 'Spiritual Complexity in Australia: Wellbeing and Risks'. *Social Compass* 70(3): 003776862311620.

Herald Sun. 2020. 'Your Healthy Week Ahead'. *Herald Sun*, 12 April, 2.

Hodge, A. 2020a. 'Thousands Gather for Mass Prayers. *The Age*, 19 March, 7.

Hodge, A. 2020b. 'Confident Nation 'Is Heading for a Fall'. *The Australian*, 24 March, 8.

Hodge, A. 2020c. 'New Delhi Expels Pakistani Diplomats for "Espionage"'. *The Australian*, 2 June, 9.

Hodge, A. 2020d. 'West Warns of Brutal Myanmar "Genocide"'. *The Australian*, 1 July, 8.

Hodge, A. 2020e. 'Sri Lankan Election to Help Family Keep Grip on Power'. *The Australian*, 6 August, 8.

Hodge, A., and Vasandani, C. 2020. 'Balinese Lose Cool with Celebrity Flouters'. *The Australian*, 26 June, 9.

Hope, Z. 2020. 'In a Time of Pandemic, Muslims Affirm Faith in Quiet Devotion'. *The Age*, 24 May, 4.

Hutchinson, S., and Loussikian, K. 2020a. 'CBD'. *The Age*, 7 April, 2.

Hutchinson, S., and Loussikian, K. 2020b. 'CBD'. *The Age*, 8 April, 3.

Jackson, A. 2020. 'These Digital Times Call for Inventive Measures'. *The Australian*, 1 July, 12.

Johnstone, C. 2020. 'Catholics Modify Holy Sacrament'. *The Australian*, 6 March, 8.

Joseph, J. 2020. 'Faith'. *The Age*, 7 June, 23.

Kelly, P. 2020. 'Whatever It Takes' Must Be Our Motto'. *The Australian*, 21 March, 20.

Kitto, J. 2020. 'Vandals Deface Temple'. *The Mercury*, 30 May, 6.

Knott, K., Poole, E., and Taira, T. 2013. *Media Portrayals of Religion and the Secular Sacred*. Surrey: Ashgate.

Landowski, L. 2020. 'Repair the Isolation Brain Fade'. *The Mercury*, 30 May, 38.

Laurie, V. 2020. ' "Faith Will Save Us" from Communion Ills'. *The Australian*, 13 March, 3.

Le Grand, C. 2020a. 'Devilish Balance for Kind Hearts'. *The Age*, 20 March, 6.

Le Grand, C. 2020b. 'High Court Comes to Swift Judgement'. *The Age*, 3 April, 16.

Lewis, R. 2020. 'Visitor Limits Win Sector Approval'. *The Australian*, 19 March, 4.

Lutton, P. 2020. 'Djokovic Will Recover from Virus, but Leadership Won't'. *The Age*, 25 June, 32.

Maddison, M. 2020. 'Top Tourism Spots Eye Local Travel Cash Splash'. *The Australian*, 16 July, 4.

Maglalogenis, G. 2020. 'PM's Problem Hiding in Plain Sight'. *The Age*, 6 June, 23.

Manelis, M. 2020. 'Ultimate Good Guy Plays the Bad Man'. *Herald Sun*, 17 May, 4.

Mccann, A. 2020. 'Could the Pandemic Change the Way We Grieve?' *The Mercury*, 11 May, 5.

McCrann, T. 2020. 'After the Bushfires We Must Go Nuclear'. *Herald Sun*, 29 January, 49.

McGuire, M. 2008. *Lived Religion: Faith and Practice in Everyday Life*. Oxford: Oxford University Press.

McManus, B. 2020. 'Healer in the Backyard'. *The Age*, 2 August, 4.

The Mercury. 2020a. 'Services'. *The Mercury*, 26 June, 46.

The Mercury. 2020b. 'Letters to the Editor'. *The Mercury*, 18 April, 36.

Moore, R. C., 2008. 'Secular Spirituality/Mundane Media: One Newspaper's In-Depth Coverage of Buddhism'. *Journal of Media and Religion*, 7(4): 231–55.

Morrow, J. 2020. 'Uprising of Elite Wannabes'. *Herald Sun*, 20 June, 36.

Nolan, D., Farquharson, K., and Marjoribanks, T. 2018. 'Australian Media and the Politics of Belonging'. In Nolan D., Farquharson K. and Marjoribanks T. (eds), *Australian Media and the Politics of Belonging*. London: Anthem Press, 3–18.

Norington, B. 2020. 'Repent, but Be Quick about It, with Drive-by Confessions'. *The Australian*, 25 March, 3.

Packham, B. 2020. 'ASIO Power Plea to Tackle Teen Terrorists'. *The Australian*, 30 May, 4.

Panahi, R. 2020. 'Silence Falls on China's Sickening Brutality'. *Herald Sun*, 24 July, 33.

Penberthy, D. 2020. 'We Need a Little Time Out'. *Herald Sun*, 20 March, 32.

Poole, E. 2019. 'Covering Diversity'. In K. Wahl-Jorgensen and T. Hanitzsch (eds.), *The Handbook of Journalism Studies*. New York: Routledge, 469–86.

Poole, E., and Weng, E. 2021. 'Introduction: Religion on an Ordinary Day: An International Study of News Reporting'. *Journal of Religion, Media and Digital Culture* 10(2): 165–78.

Porteous, J. 2020. 'The Gift of Time and Quiet'. *The Mercury*, 10 April, 34.

Premier of Victoria. 2020. 'State of Emergency Declared in Victoria Over COVID-19'. 16 March. https://www.premier.vic.gov.au/state-emergency-declared-victo ria-over-covid-19. Accessed 3 June 2021.

Premier of Tasmania. 2020a. 'Press Conference – 30 March 2020'. 30 March. https:// www.premier.tas.gov.au/covid-19_updates/press_conference_-_30_march_2020. Accessed 7 March 2023.

Premier of Tasmania. 2020b. 'Tasmania's Air and Sea Ports Prepare for Eased Border Restrictions'. 25 October. https://www.premier.tas.gov.au/site_resources_2015/addi tional_releases/tasmanias_air_and_sea_ports_prepare_for_eased_border_restricti ons. Accessed 7 March 2023.

Rane, H., Ewart, J., and Abdalla, M. 2010. *Islam and the Australian News Media*. Carlton: Melbourne University Press.

Reid, I. 2020. 'Church Leaders Offer Words of Hope and Faith'. *The Australian*, 11 April, 7.

Ryan, P. 2020. 'Perspective and Purpose'. *The Age*, 15 May, 38.

Sakkal, P. 2020. 'Police Breakup Ultra-Orthodox Prayer Group'. *The Age*, 10 April, 7.

Savva, N. 2020a. 'Deadly Virus Offers Morrison a Lifeline to Recovery'. *The Australian*, 5 March, 12.

Savva, N. 2020b. 'Morrison Must Recharge His Batteries for the Next Phase'. *The Australian*, 16 July, 10.

Smith, L. 2020. 'Reaching Out to Embrace Change'. *The Mercury*, 14 August, 2.

Storen, R., and Corrigan, N. 2020. 'COVID-19: A Chronology of State and Territory Government Announcements (up until 30 June 2020)'. *Australian Parliament House*. https://www.aph.gov.au/About_Parliament/Parliamentary_Departments/Parliament ary_Library/pubs/rp/rp2021/Chronologies/COVID-19StateTerritoryGovernme ntAnnouncements#_Toc52275799. Accessed 7 March 2023.

Sutherland, C. 2020. Is it OK to Book for Next Year? *Herald Sun*, 9 August, 14.

Swanton, W. 2020. 'The Superstars We May Never See Again'. *The Australian*, 25 March, 28.

Tacey, D. 2004. *The Spirituality Revolution: The Emergence of Contemporary Spirituality*. East Sussex: Brunner-Routledge.

Taira, T. 2015. 'Media and the Nonreligious'. In K. Granholm, M. Moberg and S. Sjö (eds), *Religion, Media, and Social Change*. London: Routledge, 110–25.

Thomas, J. 2020. 'Local Heroes in War on Terror'. *The Australian*, 19 June, 10.

Tomazin, F. 2020. 'Ethnic Groups Try to Plug Message Gaps'. *The Age*, 26 June, 4.

Topsfield, J. 2020. 'Vandals Strike Cathedral after Pell Freed'. *The Age*, 9 April, 2.

Topsfield, J., and Rosa, A. 2020. 'The New Zoom on a Family Feast'. *The Age*, 24 April, 11.

Visontay, E. 2020. 'Faithful Find a New Way to Pray'. *The Australian*, 30 March, 5.

Vultee, F., Craft, S., and Velker, M. 2010. 'Faith and Values: Journalism and the Critique of Religion Coverage of the 1990s'. *Journal of Media and Religion* 9: 150–64.

Wang Xin De, V., and Zhi-Ji, B. 2020. 'We Are All Connected so Turn to the Light and Shun the Darkness'. *The Mercury*, 22 April, 20.

Walker, J. 2020. 'Back in Robes, Cloaked in Faith … Pell's Light Is Undimmed'. *The Australian*, 11 April, 7.

Ward, C., and Voas, D. 2011. 'The Emergence of Conspirituality'. *Journal of Contemporary Religion* 26: 103–21.

Weng, E. 2019. 'Through a National Lens Darkly: Religion as a Spectrum'. *Journal for the Academic Study of Religion* 32: 3–26.

Weng, E. 2020. *Media Perceptions of Religious Changes in Australia: Of Dominance and Diversity*. London: Routledge.

Weng, E., and Halafoff, A. 2020. 'Media Representations of Religion, Spirituality and Non Religion in Australia'. *Religions* 11: 332.

Weng, E., and Halafoff, A. 2021. 'Religion on an Ordinary News Day in Australia: Hidden Christianity and the Pervasiveness of Lived Religion, Spirituality and the Secular Sacred'. *Religion, Media and Digital Culture* 10: 225–49.

Weng, E., Halafoff, A., Smith, G., Bouma, G., and Barton, G. 2021a. 'Higher Education, Exclusion and Belonging: Religious Complexity, Coping and Connectedness among International Students During the COVID-19 Pandemic in Australia'. *Journal of International Students* 11(2): 38–57.

Weng, E, Halafoff, A., Abur, W., Campbell, D., Bouma, G., and Barton, G. 2021b. 'Whiteness, Religious Diversity and Relational Belonging: Opportunities and Challenges for African Migrants in Australia'. *Journal for the Academic Study of Religions* 34(3): 289–313.

Workman, A. 2020. 'Strewth'. *The Australian*, 19 August, 2.

Wu, A. 2020. 'What Happens to the Fans, and Society, When the Regular Fix of Sport Is Missing?' *The Age*, 22 March, 26.

Yuval-Davis, N. 2006. 'Belonging and the Politics of Belonging'. *Patterns of Prejudice* 40(3): 197–214.

Zwartz, B. 2020. 'Together in Isolation'. *The Age*, 12 April, 28.

4

Migration and Religious Diversity

Anna Halafoff, Enqi Weng, Rebecca Banham,
Greg Barton and Gary Bouma

Introduction

As discussed in previous chapters, the land now called Australia has always been culturally and religiously diverse. First Nations peoples have a diverse range of languages and cultures, living as nations across a vast continent for over 65,000 years. In more recent centuries they have had strong links with Pacific Island and Asian communities, particularly across the north of Australia, that include contact with Buddhist, Taoist, Confucian and Muslim traditions. Large numbers of men from the Asia-Pacific region travelled to Australia to work in mining, pearling and sugar cane industries in the mid- to late nineteenth century, before the introduction of the 1901 Immigration Restriction Act. The presence of substantial Chinese and Japanese communities across the north of Australia instigated anxieties among the European settler-colonisers in the south, which then led to the introduction of this racist act. Even after the so-called White Australia Policy was enacted in 1901, many parts of Australia, and especially the far north, remained diverse as children of immigrants born in Australia, those who could pass an English-language dictation test and those with exemptions to work in the pearling industry were permitted to stay. It was not until the outbreak of the Second World War that most Japanese immigrants and many Chinese immigrants left Australia. Most people are unaware of this history, and it was only after the Immigration Restriction Act was finally lifted that Australia began to be seen as a culturally and religiously diverse society from the 1970s onwards (Bouma and Halafoff 2017; Halafoff et al. 2022; Reynolds 2003).

The prevailing myth, therefore, of a White Christian Nation that still persists in Australian society does not reflect its historical and contemporary multicultural and multifaith reality. Sadly, racism, discrimination and vilification against migrants, asylum seekers and refugees remain disturbingly prevalent (Hage 1998; Halafoff et al. 2022; Weng et al. 2021a, 2021b). While a sense of belonging is widely acknowledged as a basic need, divisive discourses emanating from politicians and the media, and exclusionary immigration policies, threaten the sense of belonging of many Australians. Non-white and culturally diverse Australians have long challenged negative prejudices against them and campaigned for their rightful place in Australian society to be recognised. Diverse cultural and religious organisations and places of worship have played a significant role in assisting diaspora communities with settlement and nurturing a sense of belonging (Antonsich 2010; Baumeister and Leary 1995; Clegg 2006; Hage 1998; Weng et al. 2021a, 2021b; Yuval Davis 2006, 2016).

Global crises, such as the Second World War, the Vietnam War and the threat of terrorism after 11 September 2001 have impacted multicultural relations in Australia. In response, diaspora communities have at times partnered with state actors, such as the Department of Premier and Cabinet in Victoria and Victoria Police, to counter the negative impacts of such events on community relations, and these well-established networks have therefore been in place to deal with new crises (Bouma at al. 2007; Halafoff 2013).

This chapter presents findings of the Migration stream of the Religious Diversity in Australia study[1] conducted in 2019–20. This research project was conceived well before the outbreak of the Covid-19 pandemic, but the sudden onset of the pandemic in early 2020 provided a unique opportunity to also investigate how Covid-19 impacted diaspora communities. The research team chose to focus on Chinese and Indian diaspora, because of their long histories in Australia and because they are the largest non-white (UK or European) diaspora communities in this country (ABS 2022). In addition, the much smaller Russian and Afghan diaspora communities, which also have a long history in Australia, were studied because of what they reveal about the impact of complex and troubled relations between their countries of origin and their settlement country.

This study comprised forty-three semi-structured interviews with community, women, youth and religious leaders from Chinese, Indian, Russian and Afghan communities and stakeholders working with culturally and linguistically diverse communities in Melbourne and Hobart.[2] Melbourne is the capital city of the state of Victoria, one of the three Australian states (alongside New South Wales (NSW) and Western Australia (WA)) which attracts the majority of immigrants. Victoria has 31 per cent of its residents born overseas, NSW has 30 per cent and WA has 35 per cent. In contrast, only 13 per cent of people in Tasmania were born overseas (ABS 2022). Hobart is the capital of Tasmania and is designated a regional capital city. Consequently, Hobart attracts many migrants as the process for permanent residency (PR) is expedited in regional centres. Victorian multicultural and multifaith policies and practices are generally more advanced than Tasmania's, given that Victoria has larger and more well-established diaspora communities dating back to the nineteenth century. Nevertheless, Tasmania also has a long history of diversity, a well-established Chinese diaspora community and a fast-growing Indian diaspora community. It has small Russian and Afghan diaspora communities.

Drawing on Australian census data, the Migration stream interviews and previously published scholarship, this chapter focuses on Chinese, Indian, Russian and Afghan diaspora communities' sense of belonging in Australia, at the height of the Covid-19 pandemic. It concludes with a discussion on factors that impede or enable a sense of belonging among diasporic communities in Australia more broadly, including persistent and systemic racism and discrimination, religious settlement and social services, community and state strategies to address social inequalities and growing geopolitical tensions in the Asia-Pacific region.

Chinese diaspora in Australia

The Chinese diaspora community has a long history dating back to the mid-nineteenth-century Gold Rush. They had a significant presence, particularly across the far north of Australia, in mining and as labourers, establishing market gardens, temples known as 'Joss Houses' and 'Chinatowns' in many cities and regional areas across the continent including in Victoria and Tasmania. These temples included Taoist, Confucian and Buddhist deities and symbols, and large Chinese sections of graveyards dating back to this time can be found across the country. Many of these early Chinese communities in Australia were prosperous and powerful and were feared as a result. This led to discrimination and violence against them and their temples, and eventually to the introduction of the 1901 Immigration Restriction Act. Nevertheless, as noted above, given many Chinese families were already well established in Australia, and spoke fluent English, many stayed on to run businesses once the gold mining boom had ended. Another overlooked aspect of their history is that there were strong economic and social links between First Nations Australians and Torres Strait Islanders and Chinese peoples. Many Chinese businesses employed First Nations workers and were said to offer fairer conditions than the Europeans. There are many descendants from marriages and unions between First Nations and Chinese Australians, including prominent business families throughout Australia. With the demise of the White Australia Policy, Chinese diaspora immigration once again increased to Australia, both directly from China and from Southeast Asia. Chinese Associations, such as the Chung Wah Society, established in the nineteenth century also continue to have an active presence in Australia and have played an important role in strengthening Chinese Australian identity in the face of ongoing racism and exclusion (Choi 1975; Kok 2008; Reynolds 2003; Halafoff et al. 2022: Vivian 1986).

Little of this history is known by the average Australian, given it is not included in the Australian curriculum (see Chapter 5 on Education), and as one anonymous Chinese participant in this study noted: 'One of the biggest obviously faults we have as a country is that we don't always tell our stories well. We don't even want to admit or acknowledge our historical blemishes, we don't talk about it.' This same participant also noted that 'people tend to see the whole "Chinese community" as one homogenous group', whereas there's 'a great diversity there, that hasn't been well noted or understood' previously.

Most China-born Australians have 'No Religion' (75.6 per cent), and there are also relatively high numbers of Buddhists (10 per cent), smaller numbers of Christians not further disclosed (2.6 per cent) and Catholics (2.4 per cent). The majority of the China-born community are of high economic status and are professionals, managers and administrators, working in hospitality, hospitals and computing. Yet many people born in China living in Australia are not Australian citizens (58.3 per cent), as they are international students or temporary visa holders, so are employed far more precariously. The socio-economic status of the Chinese people living in Australia is therefore mixed (ABS 2022). Some were buffered from the economic effects of the pandemic lock-downs, as they were able to continue working from home or were eligible as citizens for government assistance, if their jobs were adversely impacted. Many were not citizens, however, and those working in hospitality and sales, or as frontline workers in hospitals, were rendered much more vulnerable to unemployment with no government support, and to the health risks of the virus.

Racism, belonging and resistance

Disturbingly but not surprisingly, many Chinese participants reported a persistent and prevailing underlying racism in Australia, which manifests subtly or overtly in everyday interactions. This racism is related to long-standing fears that there are 'too many Chinese' in Australia and negative racialised prejudices against them (Hage 2014). One Chinese community member recounted,

> I've heard stories from my parents ... that when they first arrived in Australia ... they [were] subject to some form of racism ... It has happened to me once. When I was in high school, so quite a while ago, at Kmart [department store], and we were speaking in Cantonese, and then a lady approached us and told us to go back to our own countries if we don't want to speak English ... fortunately it's been quite rare for us. [But] I guess racism does remain a concern. Especially for a lot of the Australian-born Chinese ... from talking to friends ... some do worry about their ethnicity when applying for jobs, whether they'll be disadvantaged ... you've probably heard of the bamboo ceiling?

In addition, many participants felt that negative stereotypes of their community were often circulated in political and media discourses linked to geopolitical tensions between Australia and China. One Chinese interviewee observed that there has recently been 'a big shift of attitude to the Chinese community in Australia' due to a worsening relationship between China and Australia. This resulted in slurs against Chinese community members including being called a 'communist' or 'spy'.

Even though the Chinese people have had a long history in Australia, respondents also reported that Chinese people are 'under-represented' in, and 'under-appreciated' by, mainstream society. This sentiment was echoed by several Chinese participants as a 'bamboo ceiling issue'. Some felt that this, however, is changing, with greater representation of Chinese Australians in the media, and that Chinese diaspora organisations and groups were enabling younger generations to develop confidence to play a more prominent role in Australian society. As one Chinese community member stated, 'the Asian voice is emerging'.

Other respondents also noticed a greater interest in and respect for Chinese traditions, and related traditions, such as the Lunar New Year festival, among non-Asian Australians and a greater uptake of Chinese languages in schools. For example, Brian Chung, president of the Chinese Associations of Tasmania, based in Hobart, explained how

> we ... run, one of the biggest [Lunar New Year festivals] in Tasmania ... we have 5-6000 people come to our festival and more than half are non-Asian .... We want the kids and kids from the broader community to [experience] the Dragon

Dance and the Lion Dance … The Dragon Dance has been going for a hundred years in Australia.

Impacts of Covid-19

Chinese communities received extensive media attention, when the first cases of Covid-19 were reported in China, and when the virus was first identified among returning travellers from China to Australia. Chinese Australians and Chinese students in Australia suffered as the victims of racist attacks during this period, and many Chinese businesses suffered from a lack of patronage as a result (Viala-Gaudefroy and Lindaman 2020; Woolley 2020; Zhou 2020). Most Chinese participants reported that they had either been the subject of racism or knew people who had been in the first year of the pandemic, when interviews were conducted. This occurred in childcare centres, directed at children and parents, in shopping centres and on busy streets. Interviewees reported that they were criticised for wearing masks in the first lockdown when this was not compulsory, were 'told to go back to their own country' and were physically attacked in some cases. One Chinese respondent felt that during the pandemic the way 'people treat[ed] Chinese people was not fair, was not thoughtful or rational'. Another shared a disturbing personal experiences of 'everyday racism' in Melbourne during the first wave of the virus in a supermarket, where a middle-aged man in front of them 'briefly mumbled to the cashier, about China brings virus, something like that'. The cashier remained silent. These racialised experiences were attributed to the 'pandemic [as] … a trigger' because of 'some deep -rooted bias or stereotyping against Asian people, especially Chinese people … [that] has rooted in this society for a lot of time' through the White Australia Policy (anonymous Chinese respondent).

Many Chinese community cultural associations and religious groups made statements condemning the racism and economic hardships experienced by international students during the pandemic and reached out to assist them to meet their needs. For example, the Australia China Youth Association (ACYA, 2020) immediately posted a statement of support on their website, saying that 'International students make up a large portion of ACYA's membership and are an important part of Australian universities, life and culture. International students should always be made to feel safe and welcomed in Australian society.'

Several Chinese respondents also described how Christian and Buddhist places of worship, frequented by Chinese communities in both Melbourne and

Hobart, assist Chinese international students with settlement and belonging. One Christian Chinese leader shared how their church members, many of whom were former international students, assisted Chinese students with finding jobs and housing during the pandemic, welcoming them as 'newly arrived brothers and sisters'.

While the Chinese diaspora in Australia is largely well-established and many people within it are of high socio-economic status, international students and temporary visa holders are in far more precarious positions, and those wishing to transition to permanent residency (PR) can face significant challenges in terms of finding employment and affordable housing. Chung of the Chinese Community Association of Tasmania, pointed out that the situation was even more difficult in Hobart as there are comparatively less jobs and housing opportunities in Tasmania's cities than on the mainland, given Tasmania's much smaller population. As a matter of federal government policy, those seeking PR are encouraged to move to regional areas, such as Tasmania, to expedite the PR process, yet the challenges they faced were heightened during the pandemic, given that many tourism and hospitality employees were forced to close. Again Chinese cultural and religious community organisations stepped in to assist those in need.

Chinese community members also described how Chinese youth and student groups pivoted to online activities to provide support to each other, using WeChat, Facebook, Instagram and TikTok in the first lockdown. Chinese Christian and Buddhist community members reported that they largely transitioned to online chanting, meditation, rituals and support group meetings via Zoom and WhatsApp during the lockdowns as well. Chinese participants also spoke of the difficulties for the elderly Chinese in homecare programmes transitioning to online service provision during the pandemic. Chinese communities, in partnership with the state government of Victoria, responded by providing IT equipment and training for the elderly and non-English-speaking members of the Chinese community.

Indian diaspora in Australia

Similarly to the Chinese but in far fewer numbers, the Indian diaspora first arrived in Australia in the nineteenth century as part of the labour force contributing towards Australia's economic development. They worked mainly as domestic workers in homes and in agriculture, including the sugar cane industry, with some staying on to set up their own farming businesses. The so-called early Afghan cameleers included some migrants from Afghanistan, but most were in fact Muslims and Sikhs from Baluchistan, Kashmir, Sind, Rajasthan and Punjab, in what was then British India. Their camel tracks connected mining towns and homesteads across the country, and their contribution was critical to building the telegraph line connecting the country from north to south, from Darwin to South Australia. They established the first mosques in South Australia; they also had close relations with First Nations Australians. Although Indians were seen as British subjects and had legal privilege to some degree, they remained disadvantaged in terms of employment opportunities and property rights, and were also adversely impacted by the White Australia Policy. For those who did remain in Australia, after the Second World War, the British citizenship of Indians facilitated their naturalisation process and eligibility for Australian citizenship. The lifting of the 1901 Immigration Act then led to a rise in migration of those with Indian heritage, from India and also from many parts of the Asia-Pacific region, Africa and the United Kingdom in the late twentieth century (Bilimoria 1989; Chandrasekhar 1992; Clark 1986; De Lepervanche 1984; Helweg 1992; Kabir 2004; Lahiri 1992; Roy 2006; Stephenson 2009).

There remains a high degree of religious diversity among the Indian-born population living in Australia, with the largest religious communities being Hindus (51 per cent), Sikhs (22.1 per cent) and Catholics (10.6 per cent), with significant numbers of Muslims (4.2 per cent) and the nonreligious (3.8 per cent). The socio-economic status of the Indian diaspora is similarly varied. Many Indian Australians are Australian citizens of high socio-economic status working as professionals, managers and as machine operators and community workers in computing, hospitals or aged care. However, many Indian-born people living in Australia, including international students, are not Australian citizens (48.3 per cent) and are temporary visa holders. Many of these members of Indian diaspora communities in Australia worked in hospitality or as frontline workers in hospitals, in aged care and in supermarkets and grocery stores. Unemployment (5.3 per cent) is just above the national average (4.8 per cent) (ABS 2022). This made them far more vulnerable to unemployment, without any government support, during the pandemic and also to increased health risks from the virus because of being forced to seek to make ends meet through precarious employment, in sectors such as private security, taxis, food delivery, aged care and healthcare, in environments where they were more exposed to Covid-19.

Racism, belonging and resistance

Many Indian diaspora community members reported a strong sense of belonging to Australian society, and that they were proud of their hybrid Australia-Indian identities. This is reflected in the comments of Sukhamrit Singh, representative for Gurdwara Nanakdarbar in Tasmania:

> I would say for myself and for my community ... Yes, we got our faith, as a different ethnicity, but we are Australian. We came under one flag. And really, we are very proud to be part of this country.

Hindu temples, Sikh gurdwaras and Indian community associations were all seen as very important for Indian diaspora communities in Australia, and particularly for new arrivals, as they provided a sense of home through the food they served, their cultural and religious activities and support to those in need. For example, Usha Gullapalli, treasurer of the Federation of Indian Associations of Victoria (FIAV), explained how organisations such as the FIAV were established to bring diaspora communities from diverse cultural, linguistic, religious and political backgrounds together and to engage with a wider Australian society. The FIAV acts as a peak/umbrella organisation representing diverse Indian organisations/groups in Australia and provides settlement support for new arrivals, including help with finding employment. The FIAV has more recently established the Federation of Indian Multifaith Organisation (FIMO) to represent the diverse religious needs of the Indian diaspora community. Another organisation is Hindi Niketan, which is devoted to promoting Hindi language and Indian culture. It is the oldest Indian association in Melbourne and a member of the FIAV. Ayush Kamal Bhardwaj, an international graduate student at the University of Melbourne, also shared how he joined The Indian Graduate Students Society (IGSS) 'immediately' when he arrived in Australia. He explained how participation in Indian cultural and religious festivals and events organised by the IGSS is 'important for bringing people together – away from home'.

When racial tensions were discussed by Indian participants, they were often seen as a thing of the past that had been largely resolved. To illustrate, there had been a highly disturbing spate of attacks reported against Indian international students in Melbourne in 2009 (ABC/AAP, 2009), at a time when there was a marked increase in South-Asian migration to Australia. This led the Victorian State Government to work closely with Indian and Hindu communities to counter violence and prejudices against the Indian diaspora (Halafoff 2013). One Indian community leader who preferred to be anonymous, discussed these events as being in the past and said that discrimination was no longer an issue. There was also a strong perception that sectarian conflicts between Hindus and Muslims in India were, for the most part, not carried over to the Indian community in Australia, as one interviewee observed: 'Politicians play politics in India. But here, we live together', harmoniously.

Indian community members were however willing to discuss challenges facing their communities when settling in Australia. These included difficulties in obtaining visas, including for religious leaders and teachers, and language and employment barriers for students and migrants. For example, Bhardwaj, of the IGSS, observed that as 'English is the first language of Australia', and 'whenever someone [is] hiring … [they are] going to look for … people [who] will have to know English … to communicate with the customers … so language is always a barrier'. An anonymous interviewee also mentioned these employment challenges and how the Indian diaspora community often steps in to assist students with work opportunities:

> When they apply, [employers] always ask for experience. Now as a student they don't have experience. And when they're asking for the Australian experience, they don't get it … most of the students, they end up working within [the] Indian community.

Fears were also expressed by an anonymous interviewee that these issues were 'creating a potential underclass of Indian educated, students' which could result in 'a very clear resentment by a class, that is obviously educated, but couldn't find a relevant job'. Indian community members also stated that funding provided to them by state actors, to assist with language training, employment skills and cultural activities to build understanding about Indian cultures and religions in the host community was insufficient. For example, Anu Krishnan, director of Kulturebrille, stated that state funding was often for short-term projects 'expected to provide quick fixes' and that longer-term support would be more beneficial.

Impact of Covid-19

There was considerable criticism within the Indian diaspora community of the then Australian prime minister Scott Morrison's insensitive comment to the media near the beginning of the pandemic that international students were guests in Australia and that if they could not afford to stay they should simply 'return to their home countries', when in fact it was often impossible for them to do so during a period of border closures, flight cancellations and other pandemic restrictions (Gibson and Moran 2020).

Not-for-profit organisations, such as Sikh Volunteers Australia (SVA) and The International Society for Krishna Consciousness (ISKCON), were among the first responders providing food and assistance to those in need and in quarantine, particularly during the Covid-19 outbreak that occurred in Melbourne public housing in 2020. Jaswinder Singh, of the Sikh Volunteers Australia, explained that as they had experience in delivering 300–400 meals a week to survivors during the 2019–20 summer bushfires, they already had the infrastructure and resources to assist with the sudden increase of people in need. Likewise, Bhakta Dasa, of ISKCON Australia, shared that they were able to provide 500 meals a week to international students, the homeless and people who would have usually frequented their temples, through their Meals on Wheels programme, held in partnership with Port Philip (local government) Council.

The Sikh community in particular, which represents more than one-fifth of the Indian community, received substantial positive media attention for their generous provision of these services (Grewal 2020). Bhardwaj, who volunteered for SVA and helped organise and serve these meals, reflected on the sense of immense pride that he felt being part of the Indian community in Victoria during this crisis. He felt encouraged that contributions were acknowledged by the media and the public via social media. The Sikh community's positive community work has been noted to contribute to their public image as 'good migrants'.

Gullapalli, of the FIAV, also explained how FIAV provided both direct assistance or referrals for accommodation, financial and mental-health support to those in need during the Covid-19 pandemic, especially those on temporary visas, including international students, who were ineligible for government funding support. Bhardwaj, also recounted how the Facebook group 'Indians in Melbourne' had facilitated connections between more established Indian diaspora community members and international students to help in practical ways, with housing, transport and groceries during the pandemic. As Dasa put it, the international students from India were 'really struggling'. State and federal government funding to assist with this service provision were well received by the Indian diaspora community in Melbourne. Nevertheless, many Indian diaspora community leaders called for more government funding support to help them to be able to better assist their vulnerable community members. Dasa said that as they are heavily reliant on donations, whilst demand was unprecedented, additional funding was required to 'keep our programs going' in uncertain times.

Russian diaspora in Australia

Small numbers of Russian men, seeking their fortunes in mining, pearling and whaling industries also made their way to Australia in the 1900s, and some of them stayed on to settle in Australia. Russians fleeing persecution, many of them Jews and so-called white Russians who fought against the Soviet Red Army, also migrated to Australia in the early twentieth century. Regardless of their qualifications many Russians worked as labourers, due to their lack of English-language skills, and many joined the Australian Army to fight in the First World War. A larger wave of displaced Russian persons moved to Australia via Europe and China after the Second World War, and then waves of migrants from the Soviet Union continued to arrive in Australia from the 1970s onwards (Govor 2005; Protopopov 2005; Rutland 2006; Tikhmenev 1978).

There continues to be a high degree of religious diversity among Russian Australians, with large percentages of Russian federation–born community identifying as having 'No Religion' (42.7 per cent) or being Eastern Orthodox (30.1 per cent), Christian not further defined (9.1 per cent), together with relatively high numbers (6.2 per cent) of those who identify as Jewish (compared with 0.06 per cent in Russia). The majority of Russians are Australian citizens (73.3 per cent), and full-time employed professionals, managers, administrators and community services, working in computing, higher education, hospitals and aged care. Unemployment (6.6 per cent) is just above the national average (4.8 per cent) (ABS 2022). Their socio-economic status is, accordingly, relatively high, and so many were buffered from the economic effects of the pandemic as they were able to continue working from home or were eligible for government assistance, if their jobs were adversely impacted. Nevertheless, as a high-proportion of them were frontline workers in hospitals and in aged-care, and some were international students and temporary visa holders, this still made of them as more vulnerable to the virus.

Discrimination, belonging and resistance

Members of the Russian diaspora face ongoing discrimination due to negative reporting and stereotypes in the Western, including the Australian, media. Father Alexander Abramoff, manager of the Russian Ethnic Representative Council (RERC), recalled that when he was growing up 'in the 1980s there was a lot of anti-Russian propaganda, that … Russian is Soviet, [and] all you Russians are communists'. This was an ongoing issue, as Russian Australians are still 'always fighting against the real tide of negative news and negative perceptions of the Russian community'.

Archpriest Michael Protopopov, dean of Victoria in the Russian Orthodox Church Outside Russia, shared accounts of discrimination against Russians in Melbourne, which had occurred at school, and in the workplace. He added: 'I can't say that it's a major thing but it does happen, and when it happens, specifically to you, you feel the pain of it.' The establishment of churches was important for the Russian community in exile, as sites of belonging as Protopopov explained: 'The reality of why we still are a visible Russian community is because when we came out we had nothing. The church became the personification of a lost nation.' Russian churches and synagogues were also the first community hubs where Russian migrants could express and celebrate their faiths and identities and preserve their traditions. They also continue to be the places where many new arrivals go to seek support when first settling in Australia.

Russian associations and organisations, for adults and youth, also play an important role in community belonging, service provision, sharing of culture and countering discrimination. Abramoff recounted how the Russian Ethnic Representative Council (RERC) was formed in 1983 'to bring the community together', to 'protect the Russian name' in the face of ongoing anti-Russian prejudices and to provide services to the community. Vera Kalashnikova, the founder of Club Erudite, explained how her events 'bring together people' and teach Russian kids about culture, history and language. Erudite holds events at Russia House, where the RERC is based and in Russian Church halls and other spaces. The RERC also has an active Youth Group, that has partnered with Russian student associations on events.

Nikolai Artemev, founder of the Monash Russian Club (MRC) at Monash University, explained how negative perceptions of Russians centred on Russian politics and a misperception that all Russians were Caucasian, and Orthodox Christian, with the same accent. Artemev, who was born in Siberia, explained that 'we have this diversity in Russia, [it is a] multicultural population' and that there were students in the MRC from Tatarstan and Buryat, who were Muslim or Buddhist and of Asian appearance, as well as those who were Russian Orthodox, nonreligious or Jewish, and mostly white. He also shared how before the pandemic, while 'people … have these stereotypes about Russia', there had been a high level of 'interest among students' at Monash in 'Russian culture' and 'literature'. Artemev founded the MRC to 'break' negative stereotypes and to 'introduce [Russian] culture' to other students. with a strong conviction that 'culture is the main thing which can connect Australia and Russia'. He was also a member of the Russian House Youth Group (RHYG), coordinated by Egor Sadanov, and both shared how Russian House had held annual *Maslenitsa*,[3] popular Russian cultural and religious pancake festival events, before the pandemic. Abramoff, of the RERC, remarked that *Maslenitsa* 'is really an important thing because we can highlight the colorfulness and the rich heritage of the Russian community'. The MRC and Russian House Youth Group also held Russian trivia, movie and comedy nights, such as 'Slav sport' events, made popular by YouTubers prior to the pandemic. Humour has long been utilised by migrant groups in Australia to break down barriers between migrant and host communities (Davis 2009; Weng and Halafoff 2020), and the Slav sport events had been very successful. Some Russian programmes and events were at least partially state government funded, but the Russian diaspora in Victoria had also received funding from the Russian government for their cultural activities, such as the *Maslenitsa* festival and a Russian Youth Forum that was held before the pandemic. This would be prohibited now, following the Russian government's invasion of Ukraine.

Impact of Covid-19

Most of the support provided by the Russian organisations to their communities in Melbourne during the pandemic took the form of pastoral care, and also a significant amount of service provision took place through the established aged-care home care programmes. Father Protopopov explained how his parish in Dandenong had set up online church services on YouTube and Facebook. Abramoff similarly described how the Russian church in Brunswick had transitioned to online services, and how this was 'a big *utishenya* [a comfort], to people'.

The Ruscare aged-care home care programme also had to pivot to mainly over-the-phone service consultations by its case managers or to strictly observed, socially distanced and masked home visits. Many elderly Russian people that the RERC provided aged care to at the time were living on their own and in public housing, which made them more vulnerable. RERC received funding from the state government to buy tablets for their elderly clients, and to provide them training on how to use them. This programme was very effective, and now RERC is able to provide ongoing information and telehealth consultations online.

Father Abramoff explained how people were watching the news from Russia and receiving mixed messages as to how dangerous the virus was. But for the most part, he said that the Russian community was observing the Victorian government's regulations and taking the crisis very seriously. RERC provided regular updates to the community, in-person, through mail, email and social media, regarding local restrictions. Abramoff also noted that there was a lack of direct and timely communication between state government agencies and ethnic community peak bodies, particularly when the public housing towers were suddenly locked down, and that there were also delays with translation of government material to Russian and other languages. He added that after the public housing crisis, there were more regular meetings and consultations between culturally and religiously diverse diaspora community leaders and state actors on various strategies to prevent the spread of Covid-19.

Russian international students were also adversely affected by the pandemic, as Artemev of the MRC stated, 'We face the same problems as other international students … losing jobs, and also finding jobs was difficult for us.' Some students wanted to return to Russia, when their classes were moved online, and due to the high costs of tuition fees and rent in Melbourne, but at that time they did not know when borders would safely open again. He added that the Monash Graduate Association had been 'very helpful' in assisting students who needed to intermit or defer exams, and that the university had provided free food each week to international students in need. While there was some pivoting to online activity by the student and youth groups, Sadanov of the RHYG lamented that the long lockdowns had been really challenging especially for young people and that online events did not have the same 'magic' as face-to-face events.

Afghan diaspora in Australia

As noted above, many of the so-called early Afghan cameleers in Australia included migrants from Afghanistan, who played a significant role in Australia's early development, including establishing Australia's first mosques. The next major wave of migration to Australia from Afghanistan occurred one century later, following the Soviet-Afghan war in 1979, with large numbers of asylum seekers fleeing this conflict. After the Soviet withdrawal, this included large numbers of Hazara Shi'a Muslims who are a persecuted minority in Afghanistan. Trauma from fleeing war and persecution, as well as the stress of seeking asylum and refugee status have had a negative impact on the health of the Afghanistan diaspora (Abraham and Busbridge 2014: 245; Kavian et al. 2020; Kabir 2004; Maley 2001, 2008; Stephenson 2009).

On the surface, the Afghanistan diaspora appears to the least religiously diverse of the four groups, as almost all members of the Afghan-born community are Muslims (94.3 per cent). Nevertheless, these figures hide the level of true diversity within this community, in terms not just of being Sunni or Shia Muslims (with most Hazara being Shia) but also in terms of personal belief and practice. The majority of the Afghan-born community are employed as technicians, tradespeople, labourers, machinery operators, professionals and community workers, in assorted trades, supermarkets and grocery stores, and in construction work. The level of unemployment for those born in Afghanistan is over almost triple (13.6 per cent) the national average (4.8 per cent), and the highest of the four groups (ABS 2022). Their socio-economic status is consequently significantly lower than the other three groups. Some were buffered from the economic effects of the pandemic as they were able to continue working, or were eligible for government assistance if their jobs were adversely impacted. But large numbers of them are not yet Australian citizens (44.4 per cent), rendering them vulnerable without government support. And many are employed as community and retail workers in environments where they were particularly exposed to becoming infected.

Racism, belonging and resistance

Many Afghan diaspora interviewees explained that they were concerned about 'very poor' media representations of Muslims, since the al-Qaeda terrorist attacks of 11 September 2001. They explained that as many Muslim women, and most Afghan women, wear a hijab or veil to cover their hair, they are visibly Muslim. Many Afghan women have experienced vilification and discrimination, in person and online. As one anonymous interviewee described: 'If the women are on the street with their hijab and alone, then they face more general abuse.' Gula Bezhan, of the Afghan Women Association Victoria (AWAV), also stated that 'there are a lot of such challenges' for women wearing headscarves and that they are 'not treated good' and 'not given jobs they are applying for'. Bezhan, who worked as a medical doctor in Afghanistan, started working in community development to mentor other women in her community. She explained how most Afghans arrived in Australia through humanitarian programmes and struggled in their initial years of settlement. Many of them, like Bezhan, come from professional backgrounds, such as doctors, specialists and diplomats, but have had to make career changes when their qualifications have not been recognised. She described how she initially struggled to settle in Australia and had to retrain when she arrived. As a result, Bezhan still experiences ambivalence regarding her sense of belonging in Australia, despite being meaningfully employed, and being a key figure in the Afghan diaspora community. She shared how:

> I think it's all the same, nothing has changed … For first step you don't know any English, and you're coming, and in five or ten years time, we find ourself. And we are more a strong and we fight, and still I saw so many Afghan people are suffering a lot … And for this reason, every day I'm more working with community to empower them to give them a strong understanding to stand up. And I told them, 'You belong to Australia and this is our country.' But unfortunately, it often still feels like we don't really belong.

Marzia Wardak, who works for an Afghan women's support organisation in Melbourne, alluded to the fact that, like so many in the community, she had not left Afghanistan by choice and spoke of the grief she felt about her displacement and leaving her beloved homeland: 'If our country was peaceful and we didn't have war or anything, nobody would like to come to this country or any other country.' Bezhan also shared the difficulties faced in acclimatising to a culture with very different norms: 'For us it's not easy to come to Australia …. Not everyone enjoys 100%, because we got something but we lose most of our stuff … in Australia, everyone is individual, me, me, and we don't know the neighbour.'

Afghanistan diaspora community organisations, such as the AWAV and Bakhtar Cultural Association (BCA), have well-established relationships of rapport and trust with their communities in Melbourne and also with government agencies providing support to them. Miriam explained how, 'when I finished [school], I joined Bakhtar Cultural Association, which is an Afghan Association and there I met lots of Afghan people and also lots of Muslims, which made me to feel more at home'. She also added that funding from the government 'truly helps [the] Afghan community'.

Interviewees also mentioned the positive role that the Afghan community has with both Victoria Police and Tasmania Police, and how events such as mosque open days have assisted in generating better understanding and building positive relations with the broader public. An anonymous interviewee recounted how:

> Every year we have Hobart Mosque Open Day. We sometimes have some public community event[s]. So we find people coming to our mosque, visiting our mosque, asking questions and just making good with the other Muslim communities.

The outpouring of support from the police and Hobart community after the Christchurch massacre was also mentioned as a significant peacebuilding event.

> For the Muslim communities, it really helped. For example, after the massacre when the community was in a bit of shock. After the visit by the Tasmanian police, then the wider community came to the mosque with the flowers and placards, saying sorry for what happened in Christchurch and showed their sympathy and empathy for the Muslim's, the community. That sort of things converted the fear into love.

Bezhan of the AWAV, also spoke positively about Victoria Police yet was more critical of the government and its migration policies and practices: 'The government doesn't know what is going on for migrant people … most of the time is according Australian culture, not according the migrant. Government doesn't care about migrant. Unfortunately, so much migrant of the community is left behind.'

Impacts of Covid-19

AWAV and BCA were ideally placed to provide assistance to Afghan women and their families during the Covid-19 health crisis. Bezhan described how the AWAV secured some funding from the Victorian government to purchase and distribute required medical supplies such as gloves, masks and hand sanitisers to families in her community. She also spoke to between ten and twenty families each day, she said, not only to check in on their current condition but also to relay relevant health instructions regarding the pandemic from the authorities to the community. Mariam Siar, a youth leader and board member at BCA, similarly spoke to many Afghan diaspora community members in Dari or Pashto to translate relevant information and to assist them with their needs.

An initial attempt to reach out to the Afghan community – by the Victorian Chief Health Officer (CHO) Brett Sutton at a time contract tracing revealed a rapid spread though large Afghan family clusters – unfortunately backfired rather badly. Afghan diaspora community leaders turned to the media to say that they had felt unfairly singled out by public statements of concern for their community made by the CHO, given that the virus had been spreading throughout many communities in Victoria and not just the Afghanistan diaspora community. Sutton, who had previously worked in Afghanistan, moved quickly to apologise for his comments in a public statement of contrition delivered in Dari (Mitchie 2020).

Discussion and conclusion

Belonging is a basic need, and a source of wellbeing. The place of belonging can be, and often is plural, as people can have more than one place or community where they feel at home in (Anthias 2013; Yuval Davis 2006, 2016). A sense of belonging can also be eroded or even prevented from taking root if people are subject to forms of exclusion, such as racism, vilification and discrimination, and also protracted citizenship processes. This 'politics of belonging', framed by discourses around national values, can also be exclusionary, particularly if they are framed in a narrow way, linked in Australia's case to Judeo-Christian values, and Western democracy, rather than universal values and principles (Antonsich 2010; Halafoff 2006, 2015; Healy 2019; Yuval Davis 2006). As Henderson (2007) notes, there are 'hierarchies of belonging', and no matter how long a migrant has lived in Australia, their place of birth, skin colour and religion prevent them from feeling like they have an equal place in the white, Christian, Australian imaginary (Antonsich 2010). As discussed earlier in this volume, this myth of a white, Christian, Australia, created by the socially engineered White Australia Policy, does not reflect the multicultural and multifaith reality of Australia, both pre-, during and post-colonisation. This white, Christian, fantasy seeks to erase the sovereignty of First Nations peoples, and also the rich and complex histories of migrant communities in Australia (Hage 1998; Halafoff et al. 2021; Weng et al. 2021a, 2021b), including all of the communities included here in the Religion and Diversity in Australia (RDA) Migration Study.

Australian governments and education departments do not adequately teach about the historical cultural and religious diversity of this nation, the contributions of Chinese, Indian, Russian and Afghan communities and their relationships with First Nations and European communities (see Education chapter 5). Instead Australian multiculturalism is falsely seen to be a relatively recent phenomenon that only emerged in the late twentieth century. The fact that all of these communities have had a strong presence in Australia, and contributed significantly to its development, since at least the mid-nineteenth-century, and some before then, is a major finding of this study. This type of truth-telling is powerful, not only in challenging and dismantling the myth of a white, Christian, Australia but also in providing an alternate narrative of the culturally and religiously diverse reality of Australia. This will assist those of us from migrant backgrounds with a feeling that we truly belong here, respectful of the fact that this was, is and always will be Aboriginal land that was never ceded.

Concurrently, the RDA Migration Study research demonstrates that the legacy of the White Australia Policy continues to shape Australian attitudes and policies to migration and ethnic diaspora communities. There is a prevalent and prevailing racism in this nation, that is both numerological and existential, that is often triggered by crisis events. Non-white, Chinese, Indian and Afghan communities have all experienced racism in Australia, at many different times, dating back to early waves of migration in the 1900s. Despite the formal lifting of the racist White Australia Policy, and the institutionalisation of policies of multiculturalism, the Chinese diaspora was targeted by white nationalists, such as Pauline Hanson, in the 1990s. Post 9/11, racism, religious discrimination and anti-asylum-seeking 'boat people' discourses were levelled particularly at the Muslim community, including the Afghan diaspora, and especially against women who were more visible. These discriminatory discourses also had negative impacts on Sikh men, with many religiously observant Sikhs wearing turbans being mistaken for Muslims (which is sadly ironic, and speaks to links between ignorance and hate, given the fact that very few Muslim men in Australia wear turbans). In the late 2000s, the Indian diaspora community also bore the brunt of racially motivated attacks, as much larger numbers of migrants and international students from India were living and settling in Australia. During the Covid-19 pandemic the negative effects of racism have been particularly and painfully felt by Chinese diaspora.

There is another form of racism and discrimination that has been highlighted in this article, and that is shaped by geopolitical tensions exacerbated by political discourses and media reporting. Chinese and Russian diaspora communities in Melbourne both continue to suffer as a result of this. This all also provides further evidence of how 'othering shifts' (Bouma et al. 2007) from community to community, depending on global crisis events and their repercussions in Australia.

Discrimination against Russian diaspora communities has substantially intensified after Russia's horrific invasion of Ukraine. These anti-Russian stereotypes and prejudices continue to be prevalent in popular culture (Brown 2020), and in ways that aren't tolerated by progressives when expressed against other cultural and religious minorities (Halafoff 2022). This has also translated into less Australian state support for Russian community's cultural and peacebuilding activities. It is thus vital that we better distinguish between the Russian regime – including President Putin and Patriarch Kirill – and the Russian people and culture more broadly, and recognise that many Russians, in Russia and in Russian diaspora communities, leaving Russia strongly oppose

Putin's war in Ukraine (RAWC 2022) and should not be tarred with the same brush as Putin's sympathisers.

In addition many Australians do not seem to understand that asylum seekers, refugees and diaspora communities are often composed of people who are exiled from their places of origin, and who are often very much victims of the oppressive regimes that are governing them. The governments in all four countries of origin that this study focused on have become more conservative and authoritarian in the years since this project commenced. Ultra-nationalist discourses about Chinese values, Hinduism, Russian Orthodoxy and Sunni Islamic purity figure prominently in narrow populist re-imaginings of identity. As in Britain and Australia, this rise of nationalism, while positively instilling a sense of diasporic pride, has also been problematic for cultural and religious minorities excluded from these imaginings. At the same time this religious nationalism fuels debates on religious freedom, and creates tensions regarding competing rights and claims between, for example religious and sexuality rights. Virtually all Afghan Australians fled the violence and oppressive presence of the Taliban and reject the Taliban's extremist interpretations of Islam and of Afghan culture. Many Chinese Australians have recently settled in Australia from Hong Kong, or from the Chinese mainland, to escape the increasing authoritarianism of the Chinese Communist Party regime. Many members of the Indian diaspora community in Australia strongly oppose Hindu nationalist persecution of Muslims and other minorities under Prime Minister Modi, and almost half of all Indians in Australia are not Hindus. And many Russians in Australia are opposed to the authoritarian regime of President Putin in Russia, with many leaving Russia because of authoritarianism.

A key finding of this study is the level of cultural and religious diversity *within* diaspora communities. It follows that there are also a wide diversity of political orientations within these communities, including between progressives and conservatives. This is something that many Australians, including some leaders, have yet to grasp, given that they are often uncritically inclined to prejudicial stereotypes of Russians, Chinese and Muslims as enemies, and Indians as being equated with 'peace' and the British Commonwealth. Once again the best way for state actors to understand this complexity is to work with diverse representatives of diaspora communities to stem direct and structural violence (such as against women and LGBTI+ people), in all communities, including the host community, cognisant of the need to abide by overriding human rights frameworks instituted in both Victoria and Tasmania.[4]

While racism, religious vilification and ethnic discrimination – and state policies and practices shaped by narrow nationalism such as citizenship tests based on Australian values – persist in Australia, non-white and non-Christian Australians will continue to have their sense of belonging eroded and feel excluded, no matter what they do. If there is no genuine mutual respect and recognition, and if citizenship is increasingly conditional and impossible to conform to and achieve, it is unrealistic to expect people to feel a deep sense of connectedness and loyalty to this society (Noble and Poynting 2010; Yuval David 2006, 2016). How can we belong together to something we are not really seen as part of, or that we chose not to be part of given its injustice, if the everyday racism and discrimination demonstrate that we are not one of the 'us' but one of 'them'? And on top of all of this, the dominant culture has also long been uncomfortable with economic success, both on the part of individuals and entire communities, in part because it unsettles power relations. Migrants, it would appear, are welcome, only as long as they stay in their place. So either way, we are damned when we do succeed and damned when we don't.

This also illustrates, as Hage (1998) argued, that migrants are still so often perceived as 'a problem', for example at the height of the pandemic the RDA data demonstrates how the Chinese, Indian and Afghan Muslim communities were at various stages blamed for the spread of the virus, with little awareness or understanding of how a lack of citizenship rights and lower socio-economic status actually made many of them more vulnerable to the virus, giving they were often in higher-density living situations and employed in higher-risk service occupations. Another major finding of this study, in that the contribution of migrant and religious communities to caring professions, such as in the health, aged-care and childcare sectors remains undervalued by broader Australian society. As Yuval-Davis (2016: 374) notes, a 'care gap' exists in neoliberal societies, that is largely filled by 'migrant and immigrant workers'. Chinese, Indian, Russian and Afghan community members were often the frontline workers during the pandemic, and religious organisations provided significant social supports to the most vulnerable, yet rather than being praised for this, they were instead ignored, or worse, vilified.

Nevertheless, this study has also revealed the 'multicultural Real' (Hage 1998) and multifaith Real. Cultural and religious diaspora communities, and religious, women's and youth associations and/or groups within them, continue to grow and flourish in Australia; they are organised, and highly engaged in assisting their members with settlement, and in resisting racism and exclusion. In times of crisis they have ensured access to services, fought for parity of participation and have maintained and strengthened a deep sense of belonging to this society, while also maintaining and strengthening a sense of belonging to their transnational diaspora. These communities do so despite, but also to cope with and combat, the ongoing racism and exclusion that exists in Australian society, often in partnership with state government actors in Victoria and Tasmania, including the police forces, who have a strong commitment to respect for cultural and religious diversity and provide numerous services and extensive funding support to these communities.

During times of crisis, state government actors are not impervious to errors, which can have devastating impacts, such as those that occurred during the public housing at the time of Covid-19 outbreaks in Melbourne in 2020. Yet there is a pattern previously observed by researchers (Bouma et al. 2007; Halafoff 2013), and seen again during the pandemic, of diaspora community and religious leaders holding these state leaders accountable, and working with them to address pressing issues, until they are resolved. This provides yet more evidence of the power, resilience and resistance of diaspora communities.

Another key finding is that the responsibility for addressing racism and discrimination, and building bridges between migrant and host communities, seems largely to be the responsibility of migrant and religious communities and organisations. Even when some receive significant funding and support to do so from state governments, particularly in Victoria, it is most often a short-term programme or event funding, and there is no corresponding push for the host community to take responsibility for such activities. As Anu Krishnan observed, belonging is problematically seen as the 'responsibility of the migrant … the outsider' and that there is 'both overt and covert expectation that the person migrating will make all the effort [but] there has to be welcome on both sides'.

This chapter concludes by echoing Hage's (1998: 26) call for 'the dominant White culture' to actually open 'up to the decentralising effect migration and globalisation have had on the status of Whiteness' in Australia, and for publics and state actors to instead deepen their awareness of and commitment to a more caring, compassionate and 'far-reaching multiculturalism', rather than resisting the multicultural and multifaith Real. It is here particularly, that mainstream Australian society has much to learn from feminist (Nussbaum 2001; Yuval Davis 2016) and diaspora communities about more relational models of care, at times founded on religious principles of assisting those in need, which present cogent challenges to neoliberal norms that preference individualism and economic success above community support and wellbeing (Weng et al. 2021b).

Notes

1 The Migration stream was led by Anna Halafoff and Greg Barton (Deakin University). Enqi Weng and Rebecca Banham worked as research fellows and Siew Mee Barton, Geraldine Smith worked as research assistants on this project stream. Human Research Ethics approval was provided by University of Tasmania and Deakin University, and an amendment approved to include questions pertaining to the coronavirus. The authors of this chapter come from a mix of European-descent and non-white backgrounds, and all have extensive experience conducting research in partnership with culturally and religiously diverse (CALD) communities. Halafoff was born in Australia into a white, Russian orthodox family and converted to Buddhism in her early thirties. Weng is of Chinese-Singaporean heritage and a first-generation Australian migrant. Bouma was of white, Dutch heritage but was born in the United States. He was also an Anglican priest. Barton was born in Australia and is of white, Anglo heritage. Banham is Australian-born of white Anglo heritage, and identifies as nonreligious.

2 Research participants' names and affiliations are provided in this chapter if they consented to being identified. Where research participants were not comfortable being identified, no name or identifying context has been included, only their ethnic diaspora group and a broad description of their position, that is community leader. The inconsistent levels of comfort to exposure further demonstrates the significant variety of the lived experiences and restrictions on freedom of speech in countries of origin of these members of diaspora communities. Notably, most Chinese community members decided to be anonymised.

3 *Masla* means butter, which is traditionally melted and poured over pancakes eaten with pickled herring and caviar before Lent begins.

4 The Victorian government has, for example, funded a wide range of projects and events in recent years to foster respect for LGBTI+ communities and prevent violence against women, in partnership with many LGBTI+, women's, ethnic and religious community organisations. See https://www.agmc.org.au/about-agmc/ and https://www.vic.gov.au/dffh/prevent-family-violence-2021-grant-program.

References

Abraham, I., and Busbridge, R. 2014. 'Afghan-Australians: Diasporic Tensions, Homeland Transformations and the "2014 Syndrome". *Journal of Muslim Minority Affairs* 34(3): 243–58.

Anthias, F. 2013. 'Moving beyond the Janus Face of Integration and Diversity Discourses: Towards an Intersectional Framing'. *Sociological Review* 61: 323–43.

Antonsich, M. 2010. 'Searching for Belonging – An Analytical Framework'. *Geography Compass* 4(6): 644–59.

Australian Bureau of Statistics (ABS). 2022. 2021 Search Census Data (QuickStats Country of Birth). https://www.abs.gov.au/census/find-census-data/search-by-area. Accessed 28 March 2023.

Australia China Youth Association. 2020. 'ACYA's statement of support for international students', 1 April. http://www.acya.org.au/2020/04/acyas-statement-of-support-for-international-students/. Accessed 4 February 2021.

Baumeister, R. F., and Leary, M. R. 1995. 'The Need to Belong: Desire for Interpersonal Attachments as a Fundamental Human Emotion'. *Psychological Bulletin* 117(3): 497–529.

Bouma, G., and Halafoff, A. 2017. 'Australia's Changing Religious Profile – Rising Nones and Pentecostals, Declining British Protestants in Superdiversity: Views from the 2016 Census'. *Journal for the Academic Study of Religion* 30(2): 129–43.

Bouma, G. D., Pickering, S., Dellal, H., and Halafoff, A. 2007. *Managing the Impact of Global Crisis Events on Community Relations in Multicultural Australia.* City East, Qld: Multicultural Affairs Queensland and the Victorian Office of Multicultural Affairs.

Brown, C. 2020. 'The Perfect Amorality of Killing Eve'. *The Article*, 21 June. https://www.thearticle.com/the-perfect-amorality-of-killing-eve. Accessed 14 October 2020.

Bilimoria, P. 1989. *Hinduism in Australia: Mandala for the Gods: A Story of the Coming of Hindus and Hinduism to Australia.* Melbourne: Spectrum.

Bilimoria, P., Bapat, J. B., and Hughes, P. (eds). 2015. *The Indian Diaspora: Hindus and Sikhs in Australia.* New Delhi: Printworld.

Chandrasekhar, S. 1992. 'A Short History of Australian Immigration Policy with Special Reference to India's Nationals'. In S. Chandrasekhar (ed.), *From India to Australia: A Brief History of Immigration, the Dismantling of the 'White Australia' Policy, Problems and Prospects of Assimilation.* La Jolla, CA: Population Review Publications, 11–35.

Choi. 1975. *Chinese Migration and Settlement in Australia.* Sydney: Sydney University Press.

Clark, M. 1986. *A Short History of Australia.* Victoria, Australia: Penguin.

Clegg, J. W. 2006. 'A Phenomenological Investigation of the Experience of Not Belonging'. *Journal of Phenomenological Psychology* 37(1): 53–83.

Davis, J.M., 2009. '"Ethnic Comedy" in Contemporary Australia'. *Australian Author* 41(3): 20–2.

De Lepervanche, M. M. 1984. *Indians in a White Australia: An Account of Race, Class, and Indian Immigration to Eastern Australia.* Sydney: George Allen & Unwin.

Gibson, J., and Moran, A. 2020. 'As Coronavirus Spreads, "It's Time to Go Home" Scott Morrison Tells Visitors and International Students'. *ABC News*, 4 April. https://www.abc.net.au/news/2020-04-03/coronavirus-pm-tells-international-students-time-to-go-to-home/12119568. Accessed 14 October 2020.

Govor, E. 2005. *Russian Anzacs in Australian History.* Sydney: UNSW Press.

Grewal, P. 2020. ' "Duty to Serve": Sikh Volunteers Serve Free Food after Public Housing Towers Face Lockdown in Melbourne'. *SBS Punjabi*. 1 October. https://www.sbs.com.au/language/english/audio/duty-to-serve-sikh-volunte ers-serve-free-food-after-public-housing-towers-face-lockdown-in-melbourne. Accessed 14 October 2020.

Hage, G. 1998. *White Nation: Fantasies of White Supremacy in a Multicultural Society*. Annandale: Pluto Press.

Hage, G. 2014. 'Continuity and Change in Australian Racism'. *Journal of Intercultural Studies* 35(3): 232–7.

Halafoff, A. 2006. 'UnAustralian Values'. In *UNAustralia*, refereed conference proceedings from the Cultural Studies Association of Australasia Annual Conference 6–8 December, University of Canberra.

Halafoff, A. 2013. *The Multifaith Movement, Global Risks and Cosmopolitan Solutions*. Dordrecht: Springer.

Halafoff, A. 2015. 'Special Religious Instruction and Worldviews Education in Victoria's Schools: Social Inclusion, Citizenship and Countering Extremism'. *Journal of Intercultural Studies* 36(3): 362–79.

Halafoff, A. 2022. 'Resisting Vladimir Putin's Campaign of Anti-cosmopolitan Terror'. *ABC Religion and Ethics*, 7 June. https://www.abc.net.au/religion/putin-campaign-of-anti-cosmopolitan-terror-anna-halafoff/13919322. Accessed 1 December 2022.

Halafoff, A., Lam, K., Weng, E., and Smith, S. 2022. 'Buddhism in the Far North of Australia Pre-WWII: (In)visibility, Post-Colonialism and Materiality'. *Journal of Global Buddhism* 23(2):105–28.

Healy, M. 2019. Belonging, Social Cohesion and Fundamental British Values'. *British Journal of Educational Studies* 67(4): 423–38.

Helweg, A. 1992. 'Indians of the Professions in Australia: Some Theoretical and Methodological Considerations'. In S. Chandrasekhar (ed.), *From India to Australia: A Brief History of Immigration, the Dismantling of the 'White Australia' Policy, Problems and Prospects of Assimilation*. La Jolla, CA: Population Review Publications, 76–90.

Henderson, A. 2007. *Hierarchies of Belonging (2007): National Identity and Political Culture in Scotland and Quebec*. Montreal: McGill-Queen's University Press.

Kabir, N. A. 2004. *Muslims in Australia: Immigration, Race Relations and Cultural History*. London: Routledge.

Kavian, F., Mehta, K., Willis, E., Mwanri, L., Ward, P., and Booth, S. 2020. 'Migration, Stress and the Challenges of Accessing Food: An Exploratory Study of the Experience of Recent Afghan Women Refugees in Adelaide, Australia'. *International Journal of Environmental Research and Public Health* 17: 1379.

Kok. 2008. *Chinese Temples in Australia: Hall of the Ranking Sages, Darwin, Northern Territory*. Bendigo: Golden Bridge Museum.

Lahiri, A. K. 1992. 'Diaspora Hindus and Hinduism in Australia: A Sketch'. In N. C. Habel (ed.), *Religion and Multiculturalism in Australia; Essays in Honour of Victor Hayes*. Adelaide: Christian Research Association, 199–213.

Maley, W. 2001. 'Security, People-Smuggling, and Australia's New Afghan Refugees'. *Australian Journal of International Affairs* 55(3): 351–70.

Maley, W. 2008. *Looking Back at the Bonn Process. Afghanistan: Transition under Threat*. Waterloo: Wilfrid Laurier University Press.

Mitchie, F. 2020. 'Casey Coronavirus Outbreak in Melbourne's South-East "under Control", Sutton Apologises to Afghan Community'. *ABC News*. 19 September. https://www.abc.net.au/news/2020-09-19/victoria-coronavirus-casey-cluster-under-control-brett-sutton/12680222. Accessed 14 October 2020.

Noble, G., and Poynting, S. 2010. 'White Lines: The Intercultural Politics of Everyday Movement in Social Spaces'. *Journal of Intercultural Studies* 31(5): 489–505.

Nussbaum, M. 2001. *Upheavels of Thought: The Intelligence of Emotions*. Cambridge: Cambridge University Press.

Protopopov, M. A. 2005. *The Russian Orthodox Presence in Australia: The History of a Church Told from Recently Opened Archives and Previously Unpublished Sources*. Victoria, Australia: Australian Catholic University.

RAWC. 2022. Russian Anti-War Committee. https://antiwarcommittee.info/en/committee/. Accessed 1 March 2023.

Reynolds, H. 2003. *North of Capricorn: The Untold Story of Australia's North*. Crows Nest, New South Wales: Allen & Unwin.

Roy, A. 2006. *The Companion to Tasmanian History: Indian Community*. https://www.utas.edu.au/library/companion_to_tasmanian_history/I/Indian%20community.htm. Accessed 10 September 2019.

Rutland, S. D. 2006. *The Jews in Australia*. New York: Cambridge University Press.

Stephenson, P. 2009. 'Keeping It in the Family: Partnerships between Indigenous and Muslim Communities in Australia'. *Aboriginal History* 33: 97–116.

Tikhmenev, P. A. 1978. *A History of the Russia-American Company*. Edited by Richard A. Pierce and Alton S. Donnelly. Seattle: University of Washington Press, 185.

Viala-Gaudefroy, J., and Lindaman, D. 2020. 'Donald Trump's "Chinese virus": The Politics of Naming'. *The Conversation*. https://theconversation.com/donald-trumps-chinese-virus-the-politics-ofnaming-136796. Accessed 14 October 2020.

Vivian, H. 1986. *Tasmania's Chinese Heritage: An Historical Record of Chinese Sites in North East Tasmania*. Hobart: University of Tasmania.

Weng, E., and Halafoff, A. 2020. 'Media Representations of Religion, Spirituality and Non-religion in Australia'. *Religions* 11(7): 1–15.

Weng, E., Smith, G., Bouma, G., and Barton, G. 2021a. 'Higher Education, Exclusion and Belonging: Religious Complexity, Coping and Connectedness among International Students during the COVID-19 Pandemic in Australia'. *Journal of International Students* 11(2): 38–57.

Weng, E., Halafoff, A., Abur, W., Campbell, D., Bouma, G., and Barton, G. 2021b. 'Whiteness, Religious Diversity and Relational Belonging: Opportunities and Challenges for African Migrants in Australia'. *Journal for the Academic Study of Religions* 34(3): 289–313.

Woolley, S. 2020. 'Coronavirus: University of Melbourne International Students Assaulted in Unprovoked Racist Attack'. *7 News*, 17 April. https://7news.com.au/lifestyle/health-wellbeing/coronavirus-university-ofmelbourne-international-students-assaulted-in-unprovoked-racist-attack-c-983675. Accessed 14 October 2020.

Yuval-Davis, N. 2006. 'Belonging and the Politics of Belonging'. *Patterns of Prejudice* 40(3); 197–214.

Yuval-Davis, N. 2016. 'Power, Intersectionality and the Politics of Belonging'. In W. Harcourt (ed.), *The Palgrave Handbook of Gender and Development*. Basingstoke: Palgrave Macmillan, 367–81.

Zhou, N. 2020. 'Asian Australians Threatened and Spat on in Racist Incidents Amid Coronavirus'. *The Guardian*. Australia. https://www.theguardian.com/australia-news/2020/jul/24/asian-australiansthreatened-and-spat-on-in-racist-incidents-amid-coronavirus. Accessed 14 October 2020.

5

Worldview Diversity and Education in Australia

Anna Halafoff and Ruth Fitzpatrick

Introduction

Education has long been associated with nation-building. National and state curricula shape our knowledge of history, which informs our understanding of the present. Education in Australia has, until recently, been the responsibility of the various states. The vision of a national curriculum gathered significant momentum during the conservative prime minister John Howard's era, after the events of 11 September 2001 (9/11) and the 7 July 2005 (7/7) London bombing and increased state interest in preventing 'homegrown terrorism'. Young people, and particularly young Muslims, were problematically viewed as potential risks to society, and also as being at risk of radicalisation. As a result, education, including civics and citizenship and interreligious programmes, became part of preventing/countering violent extremism (P/CVE) strategies in many parts of the world, notably in the UK, EU, Canada, New Zealand, Asia and Australia (Halafoff 2013; Jackson 2014).

Interreligious education programmes, and substantive research on them in the UK and Nordic countries, well predated what has been labelled as the post-9/11 and post-7/7 'securitisation' of religion, and securitisation of religious education (Gearon 2012; Jackson 2015). There is however no doubt that government, UN and academic interest in civics, citizenship, interreligious and later worldview education – to include emphasis on religious and nonreligious worldviews – increased from the mid-2000s onwards. These events have also had a significant impact on how content on religion and diverse worldviews has been included in the Australian and its various state curricula during this period. The place of religion in Australian government schools, in particular, has been the subject of intense debate since these schools' inception in the late twentieth century. This chapter will present a brief history of this debate in Australia before presenting a critical discourse analysis of the treatment of diverse worldviews in both the Australian and Victorian curricula,[1] exploring power dynamics, issues of equality and inequality, inclusion and exclusion, freedom and harms within them. It presents data arising from these two curricula, given the foci of the Religion and Diversity in Australia (RDA) study is on Victoria and Tasmania, and as Tasmania, as a state with a much smaller population, does not have its own version but rather teaches the national Australian Curriculum. This also provides an opportunity to compare the treatment of diverse worldviews at the national and Victorian state levels.

As discussed in previous chapters, Victoria's practices and policies on religious diversity are generally more advanced than Tasmania's or Australia's, given significantly larger numbers of culturally and religiously diverse communities in Victoria, and the Victorian state leadership has been more progressive and proactive in affirming cultural and religious diversity. This is certainly revealed in this analysis of education curricula, which reveals a privileging of Christianity and securitisation of religion particularly in the Australian Curriculum, and a more considered and equitable treatment of diverse worldviews, religious and nonreligious, in the Victorian Curriculum. Both curricula, however, do not adequately reflect the historical facts or the contemporary, complex and lived worldview diversity and reality of young Australians, and are marred by outdated 'world religion' frameworks, and a privileging of 'Abrahamic' faiths. This will be explained in more detail below.

Worldview diversity in Australian schools

As discussed in previous chapters, the land now called Australia has always been a culturally and religiously diverse country, evident in First Nations knowledge systems, languages and beliefs, and subsequent flows of trade and migration to and from Asia, Europe and the rest of the world. First Nations peoples in the Far North of Australia have long and deep ties with neighbouring Muslims, of what is now called Indonesia. From the mid-end of the nineteenth century large communities of Chinese and Japanese workers and migrants, who practised Taoism, Confucianism and/or Buddhism, engaged in mining, pearling and sugar cane industries, outnumbered Europeans across the Far North. Fears regarding their numbers and economic strength led to the introduction of the

1901 Immigration Restriction Act, known as the White Australia Policy. A myth of a White Christian Australia was thereby socially constructed at federation, through the introduction of this racist act, and perpetuated throughout much of the twentieth century, until the institutionalisation of policies of multiculturalism in the 1980s. Forty years on, in the 2020s, Australia is still caught in contestation around these two competing versions of its national identity, the White Christian 'fantasy' versus the multicultural and multifaith 'real' Australia (Bouma and Halafoff 2017; Hage 1998: 18, 232; Halafoff et al. 2021, 2022; Weng et al. 2021a, 2021b). This battle has also long been played out in relation to the place of religion in schools.

Prior to 2008, when a national curriculum began to be developed in Australia, each Australian state was responsible for developing its own curriculum. Victoria, New South Wales and Western Australia still adapt the Australian Curriculum to their own context, while the other states and territories, with smaller populations, teach the Australian Curriculum as is. Australia's earliest government schools established in the mid-1800s included some teaching of Christianity, yet by the turn of the twentieth century, in most states they moved to 'free, compulsory and secular' education, despite vehement protest from Christian organisations. As a result Australian government schools have never had dedicated Religious Education (RE) subjects or substantive content on religion in their prescribed curricula.[2] By contrast, many state education systems in the UK, central EU and Nordic countries, which initially had Christian Religious Education in their schools, shifted to a 'world religions' model of education – teaching about the major religions of Hinduism, Buddhism, Judaism, Christianity and Islam – in the late twentieth century, as a result of changes in religious demographics and advocacy by major interfaith organisations.[3] Many faith-based schools in Australia, including Catholic, Anglican, Uniting and Jewish schools, have also taught a world religions General Religious Education (GRE) since that time (Bouma and Halafoff 2009; Byrne 2014; Erebus International 2006; Halafoff 2013; Maddox 2014). These programmes have increasingly included content on ethics and/or nonreligious worldviews and are often described now in Australia and internationally as Worldviews Education (WE) programmes (Jackson 2014).

The Australian Curriculum was conceived during the conservative Liberal prime minister John Howard's years, as part of his nation-building agenda, including an emphasis on 'Australian Values'. Following the events of 9/11, and particularly 7/7, and the 2002 and 2005 Bali bombings, and as part of Australia's emerging 'culture wars', conservative actors, such as Howard, promoted 'Judeo-Christian values' and a narrow nationalism harking back to the myth of a White Christian Australia. This shift away from multiculturalism at the national level at the turn of the twenty-first century was highly problematic, as it was accompanied by Islamophobic and migrantophobic discourses, which exacerbated an underlying racism in Australia, fuelled the Far Right and undermined the very social harmony that Howard's 'Values Education' was designed to engineer. Australian scholars argued that these problematic discourses about adhering to Judeo-Christian values excluded and potentially alienated non-white, non-Christian and particularly Muslim young Australians. Consequently, this increased the risk of racism and religious discrimination against them, and also potentially rendered these young people more vulnerable to radicalisation as a result of social exclusion (Bouma and Halafoff 2009; Bouma at al. 2007; Halafoff 2006, 2013; Maddox 2005).

The more socially progressive Labor prime minister Keven Rudd was elected in 2007, and The Melbourne Declaration on Educational Goals for Young Australians was published in 2008 and shaped the drafting of the Australian Curriculum by the Australian Curriculum Assessment and Reporting Authority (ACARA). It included a much more inclusive approach to intercultural and interreligious understanding and social cohesion, than the Howard government's Australian values rhetoric (Halafoff 2006, 2015; MCEETYA 2008).

The Melbourne Declaration highlighted the need for schools to 'play a vital role in promoting the intellectual, physical, social, emotional, moral, spiritual and aesthetic development and well-being of young Australians, and in ensuring the nation's ongoing economic prosperity and social cohesion'. It also stated that processes of globalisation have created 'new and exciting opportunities for Australians' thus 'heighten[ing] the need to nurture an appreciation of and respect for social, cultural and religious diversity, and a sense of global citizenship' (MCEETYA 2008: 4). It also explained how the commitment to 'promoting equity and excellence in Australian schooling' required school sectors to provide education 'that is free from discrimination based on gender, language, sexual orientation, pregnancy, culture, ethnicity, religion, health or disability, socio-economic background or geographic location' and to 'ensure that schooling contributes to a socially cohesive society that respects and appreciates cultural, social and religious diversity' (MCEETYA 2008: 7).

Yet, the subsequent draft of the first national Australian Curriculum did not include GRE or WE as one of its key Learning Areas of the Arts, Civics and Citizenship, Design and Technology, Economics and Business, English, Geography, Health and Physical education, History, Information and Communication Technology (ICT), Languages, Mathematics, Science, or as one of its General Capabilities of Critical and Creative Thinking, Ethical Understanding, ICT Capability, Intercultural Understanding, Literacy, Numeracy, and Personal and Social Capability. Instead, ACARA decided to problematically position the main content on contemporary religion in Australia in the Civics and Citizenship Learning Area, which reflected the prevalent and problematic securitisation of religion in policy and scholarship in a post-9/11 and 7/7 world (Gearon 2012). Australian scholars and diverse religious and nonreligious organisations made recommendations to ACARA's first draft of the Australian Curriculum to address this, as part of an open consultation submission process in 2011 and 2012. While these scholar's submissions did not have any impact on changing already set Learning Areas and General Capabilities, it did at least result in the acknowledgement of Australia being described as 'a secular and multifaith society' in content on religion in Civics and Citizenship. Other content on the major religions appeared across the Australian Curriculum in a limited and haphazard capacity, and mainly in History and Languages (Halafoff 2015).

The religion in schools debate became the focus of substantive scholarship in Australia during this period, examining in particular what Cathy Byrne (2014: 1) declared as its 'Christian privilege' and also issues of state accountability. Australian scholars have documented the history of this debate in Victoria, NSW and Queensland (Bouma and Halafoff 2009; Byrne 2007, 2014; Halafoff 2013, 2015; Maddox 2014), and have also drawn on research from the UK, Europe and Canada, regarding similar debates and best practices (CoE 2008; Jackson 2014; ODIRH 2007). Such studies have been a 'hot topic' globally in analysing how well, and in many cases how badly, states have been adjusting to the changing worldview composition of their societies.

Broadly speaking, in contrast to narrow nationalism and espousing of national or regional (i.e. Australian, British, EU or Asian) values, experts on religious diversity note that education about diverse worldviews – including spiritual, religious and nonreligious worldviews – can increase interreligious understanding and thereby social inclusion, belonging and harmony in diverse societies. They argue that this education must be critical and equitable, and not place particular worldviews above others or only speak of their virtues. Curricula must also address religious and/or spiritual harms and violence, direct and structural. Diverse worldviews' ambivalent contributions to both violence and peace-building need to be examined, and multiple perspectives considered in such a critical education, which would in no way contravene secular principles (Halafoff 2015; Jackson 2014).[4]

A review of the Australian Curriculum was undertaken in 2014, following the election of conservative, Catholic prime minister Tony Abbott. It was conducted by Professor Kenneth Wiltshire AO and Dr Kevin Donnelly. Their capacity to do so was widely questioned (Beder 2014), particularly given that the Education Standards Institute (ESI), which Donnelly founded and directed at the time, favoured 'an education system based on ... a commitment to Christian beliefs and values', as stated on the ESI's home page (Halafoff 2015).[5]

Briefly, Donnelly and Wiltshire chose to overlook the statements on respect for religious diversity in the Melbourne Declaration and only highlighted its emphasis on 'spiritual and moral values' (Donnelly and Wiltshire 2014: 97). They also heeded recommendations made in 413 submissions, including by the conservative Institute for Public Affairs and The Australian Christian Lobby, that the Review's authors themselves described as 'part of a campaign arguing that the Australian Curriculum needed to be revised to ensure a more balanced and objective treatment of Christianity and the debt owed to Western civilisation' (Donnelly and Wiltshire 2014: 158). The 2014 review concluded with a list of recommendations, including Recommendation 15, which made no mention of religious diversity, and instead stressed the need 'to better recognise the contribution of Western civilisation, our Judeo-Christian heritage ... and the democratic underpinning of the British system of government to Australia's development (Donnelly and Wiltshire 2014: 246). This resulted in privileging of Christianity in Civics and Citizenship in the subsequent version of the Australian Curriculum.

By contrast, Victoria chose not to highlight Christian heritage in its revised curriculum, and instead, following international best practices and research recommendations (Jackson 2014), included new dedicated sections on Learning about Worldviews and Religions in the Humanities and in Ethical Capability. While this dedicated content is certainly more inclusive, as discussed in detail below, it is still largely focused on major religions and Humanism and Rationalism, reflecting an outdated 'world religions' approach, which largely excludes First Nations spirituality, and spirituality more broadly. This does not adequately reflect the current and complex worldview diversity – spiritual, religious and nonreligious – of young Australians, as documented by the Australian Generation Z (AGZ) study. The findings of the AGZ project and a critical discourse analysis of the treatment of diverse religions in the Australian and Victorian Curricula are presented below.

This brief history of the religion in schools debate in Australia also demonstrates how vexed and political the issue of worldviews education is, and how the competing narratives – the myth of a white, Christian Australia versus the reality of a culturally and religiously diverse Australia (Hage 1998; Halafoff et al. 2021, 2022; Weng et al. 2021a, 2021b) – are still very much at play in the drafting and delivery of curricula in Australia. It also disturbingly reveals how controversy regarding the place of religion in state schools continues to impede the development of religious literacy and interreligious understanding among young Australians (Halafoff 2015).

The worldviews of Australia's Generation Z

Two major international studies of religion in Western societies, including Australia were being conducted in the 2000s, which both included a focus on education: The Religion and Society Programme (RSP) in the UK, led by Linda Woodhead, and the Religion and Diversity Project, led by Lori Beaman. The RSP included a study on young people's perceptions of diverse religions, led by Prof. Robert Jackson, a leading authority in this field (Jackson 2014; Arweck and Jackson 2014). This study, in particular, informed the Worldviews of Australia's Generation Z (AGZ) study, conducted in 2016–19. The AGZ study comprised three stages: (1) eleven focus groups with a total of ninety-four students in Years 9 and 10 (ages fifteen to sixteen), (2) a nationally representative telephone survey of 1,200 people aged between thirteen and eighteen and (3) thirty in-depth, follow-up interviews with survey participants (Singleton et al. 2021).

The AGZ study found that 52 per cent of Australian teens identified as non-religious, 39 per cent as Christian, 3 per cent as Muslim, 2 per cent as Buddhist and 1 per cent as Hindu. Two per cent did not respond to the religious affiliation question. The AGZ study also used latent class analysis to identify six statistically distinct Worldview Types of AGZ teens, which revealed a worldview complexity among young Australians: 23 per cent 'this-worldly'/strongly nonreligious, 15 per cent indifferent, 18 per cent 'spiritual but not religious', 8 per cent 'seekers'/ religious and spiritual, 20 per cent nominally religious and 17 per cent religiously committed (Halafoff et al. 2019; Singleton et al. 2021: 60–3). Indeed, the strong identification with spirituality among Gen Z Australians was a significant finding of this study.

The AGZ project also revealed that there was a moderate level of religious literacy among AGZ focus-group participants, and while it was broad it was relatively shallow. This was not surprising given that 41 per cent of AGZ teens had had no lessons or information on religion at all at school, and that they were sourcing information on religion mainly from family, social media and peers. While most AGZ teens (93 per cent) thought having people of many different faiths makes Australia a better place to live, disturbingly 20 per cent of them had neutral or negative views about religious minorities. Of particular importance is that the AGZ study also revealed that students who have received GRE, which often included nonreligious worldviews as well, largely in Catholic and other faith-based schools, had the most positive views of religious minorities in Australia. By contrast, students who have had *no* GRE are somewhat more likely than those who have had GRE to hold negative or neutral views towards Australia's religious minorities, even when controlling for factors such as age, gender, school type, socio-economic status and religious identity. In addition, 93 per cent of AGZ students who had had GRE agreed or strongly agreed that it was helpful in developing an understanding of other people's religions, and 82 per cent agreed or strongly agreed that GRE was something important to study (Singleton et al. 2021: 149). Many AGZ participants were also engaged in debates about religious freedom and did not want religious views imposed upon them or society, particularly those beliefs which caused harm or impeded the freedom of others (Halafoff et al. 2019; Singleton et al. 2021: 182–3).

Religious diversity in Australia: Education stream

Building on findings of previous studies on religious diversity and education in Australia, including the AGZ project, the RDA Education stream set out to investigate how diverse worldviews were included and represented in the Australian Curriculum (AC) and the Victorian Curriculum (VC). A mixed-method thematic quantitative and qualitative approach,[6] using targeted keywords related to spirituality, religion and nonreligion identified through previous international studies – 'Media Portrayals of Religions and the Secular Sacred' led by Kim Knott (Knott et al. 2013) and the 'Religion on an Ordinary Day' study, led by Beaman and Knott, which was part of the Religion and Diversity Project (Poole and Weng 2021; Weng and Halafoff 2020, 2021) – was applied in the RDA Media study and the RDA Education studies. The keywords searched for in the AC and VC were: Spirituality – 'spirituality' (spiritual*); Religion – 'Religion' (religio*), 'Christianity' (Christian*), 'Islam' (*, Islam* OR Muslim*), 'Buddhism' (Buddh*), 'Hinduism' (Hindu*), 'Sikhism' (Sikh*) and 'Judaism' (Judais* OR Jew*); and Secular/Nonreligion – 'secular' (Secular*) and 'no religion' (non* religio*, no religio*, not* religio*).

The curricula were coded using the data analysis tool AntConc.[7] This analysis found that most content on diverse worldviews – spiritual, religious and non-religious – in the AC and VC, and particularly on worldviews in the Australian context, was situated in The Humanities Learning Areas of History, Geography, Civics and Citizenship (C&C) and Economics and Business (E&B). While considerable content on diverse religions and spirituality was also located in Languages, it was largely focused on contexts beyond Australia. There were also far more limited mentions of spirituality in the Arts, Dance and English. This chapter thereby presents quantitative and qualitative critical discourse analyses, investigating the positioning and representation of diverse worldviews across Foundation to Year/Level[8] 10 (F-10) Humanities in the AC and VC. Coding and analysis reveal that diverse worldviews receive unequal attention across both of these curricula, in different ways, discussed in detail below.

Diverse worldviews in the Australian and Victorian curricula: Quantitative and qualitative analysis

Spirituality

AC and VC Years/Levels 3&4 History explore the relationship between language, Country, place and spirituality of First Nations peoples. AC Year 5 Economics and Business (E&B) mentions First Nations Australians' 'spiritual connections to the land, sea, sky and waterways'. Students also study the spiritual value of water, landscapes and landforms, including providing spiritual wellbeing for First Nations Australians AC and VC Years/Levels 7&8 Geography. And AC Year 7 Civics and Citizenship (C&C) discusses the diversity of spiritualities among First Nations peoples.

Table 5.1 Spirituality – AC and VC Humanities

	Aus Curriculum (AC) F-10	Vic Curriculum (VC) F-10
Spiritual or Spirituality (spiritual*)	14 3 History 8 Geography 2 C&C 1 E&B	12 7 History 5 Geography

Number of times these keywords appeared in the respective curricula

AC and VC Years/Level F-2 History explore the contemporary significance of a local historical site of 'spiritual importance'. AC and VC Years/Level 3&4 Geography ask students to explain how 'people's connections with their environment' can have a spiritual dimension. AC Year 5 History investigates the role of spiritual leaders in 'shaping of a colony'. AC Years/Level 5&6 Geography examines the similarities and differences in 'spiritual traditions' in Australian, Asia and 'other' parts of the world. The spiritual significance of water to Asian cultures and how spiritual connections to places may have links with 'environmental sustainability' are also studied in AC and VC Year/Levels 7&8 Geography.

It is evident from this analysis, that spirituality is largely associated with the First Nations people and cultures in Australia, in Geography and History. First Nations spirituality is associated here with Country/place and wellbeing. Spirituality is also discussed more generally in relation to places, the environment and Asian cultures. This reflects Australian's sacred connection to nature, also noted in the RDA Media and the AGZ studies (Halafoff et al. 2023), and also an awareness of Australia's geographical proximity to Asia, and of Asian spiritualities on Australian life, albeit that there is only one reference to Asian spirituality in each curricula. There are similar numbers of references to spirituality in the AC (14) and VC (12), and far less mentions of spirituality than religion in both the AC (49) and VC (49). Religion received far more serious attention than spirituality across the Humanities in both curricula.

Religion

The Humanities section of the AC includes a general preamble (Humanities and Social Sciences (HASS) General) with seven mentions of religion/religions/ religious that cover the content across the Learning Areas analysed below. By contrast, the 2016 VC includes a dedicated section on Learning about

Table 5.2 Religion – AC and VC Humanities

	2015 Aus Curriculum (AC) F-10	Victorian Curriculum (VC) F-10
Religion, Religions or Religious (religio*)	49	49
	7 HASS General	14 LWR
	24 History	20 History
	5 Geography	8 Geography
	13 C&C	7 C&C

Worldviews and Religions (LWR) in its Humanities landing page, which links to a pdf and focuses on the 'key premises of major religions' and secular/non-religious worldviews. The LWR section includes fourteen mentions of religion/religions/religious. The AC does not have a similar dedicated section on diverse worldviews, instead it has a brief entry on Australia's diverse religions, in Year 8 C&C. This content on specific religions and nonreligious worldviews is discussed in more detail in the next two sections of this chapter.

A large amount of content on contemporary religious diversity in Australia in both the AC and VC is found in the curricula's early years. AC and VC Years/Levels F-4 History, Geography and Civics and Citizenship, explore religious places, activities, buildings, figures. affiliation, belonging and festivals in student's local communities.

The religious festivals in both AC Foundation and VC Levels F-2 History are listed in the following order: 'Easter, Ramadan, Buddha's Birthday (AC)/ Buddha day (VC), Feast of Passover'. Primacy is given here to Christianity and Islam, above Buddhism, and Hinduism and Sikhism are not included here at all. Religious celebrations in AC and VC Year 3 History include 'Christmas Day, Diwali, Easter, Hanukkah, the Moon Festival and Ramadan'. Again Christianity is allocated primacy here. Followed by Hinduism, Judaism, Buddhism and then Islam, with no mention of Sikhism. The order of the religions in both the AC and the VC versions in these early years of History do not align either with their historical presence in Australia, or the percentages of their current religious affiliation.

AC and VC Years/Levels 5&6 History investigate the role of religious leaders and groups in 'shaping of a colony', yet there is no other mention in either curriculum of the long history of religious diversity in Australia. AC Years 5&6 HASS also ask students to identify religious stereotypes in the media.

AC and VC Years/Levels 5–8 Civics and Citizenship (C&C) both include the most content on contemporary religious diversity in Australia, exploring religious freedom, religious identity and belonging. However, the treatment of religion here varies the most significantly across the two curricula. AC Year 5 C&C discusses the importance of 'freedom of religious belief' as a 'key value' of Australian society, and both AC and VC Years/Levels 7&8 C&C discuss 'freedom of religion' as one of the 'freedoms that enable active participation in Australia's democracy within the bounds of law'.

As mentioned above, a significant difference in the description of Australia's worldview composition occurred after the Donnelly and Wiltshire (2014) review of the Australian Curriculum, where Australia began to be

Table 5.3 AC and VC Year 7&8 Civics and Citizenship

AC – Year 7 C&C	VC – Levels 7&8 C&C
How Australia is a secular nation and a multifaith society with a Christian heritage	Describe how Australia is a secular nation and a multifaith society

described as not only being a 'secular nation' and 'multi-faith society', but also as having 'a Christian heritage' in AC Year 7 C&C. By contrast, the revised VC C&C chose to retain the focus on a secular and multifaith society and did not add the emphasis on Christian heritage. A notable omission here, when describing Australia's worldview composition, in both of the AC and VC is the lack of mention of First Nations worldviews, despite recommendations from scholars made to the Donnelly and Wiltshire (2014) Review to include them before all other worldviews that have subsequently been introduced into Australia. As stated above, these recommendations were ignored by the review's authors, who chose instead to privilege Christianity above all other worldviews. The AC Year 7 C&C section only has a brief sub-section that mentions Indigenous Australians and Torres Strait Islanders' spirituality, including their spiritual traditions and their adoption of religions of Christian and Islam.

Both AC and VC Year/Levels 7&8 C&C also ask students to explain how religious and cultural groups express their identities, and how this influences their perceptions of others and others' perception of them. And, as mentioned above, AC Year 8 C&C has specific content about the diverse 'values and beliefs of religions practised in contemporary Australia, including Christianity', once again preferencing Christianity. This content is analysed in more detail below, when discussing the diverse religions individually.

AC and VC Years/Levels 9&10 C&C examine religious group's contribution to civic life and discuss this in relation to religious group's participation in fostering 'interfaith understanding or social justice'. They also explore continuity and change in religious beliefs in Australia. In AC and VC Years/Levels 9&10 History students also study religious group's reactions to Charles Darwin's *Origin of Species*

The dominant place of Christianity when studying religion is evident in both curricula, but especially in the AC. The writers of the AC also chose to primarily position content on religion in C&C, rather than in History, or in a dedicated section on worldviews, which reveals a securitisation of religion, given that most serious content and discussion of the role of religion in contemporary Australian society in the AC is related to being a good, law-abiding citizen. The lack of content on Australia's early history of worldview diversity, before the 1901 Immigration Restriction Act, also demonstrates that the AC plays a role in perpetuating the myth of a white, Christian Australia, rather than reflecting Australia's historical and contemporary worldview diversity, of First Nations, spiritual, religious and nonreligious worldviews.

Furthermore, the most considered content on diverse religions occurs in History and Geography, focusing on religion/s 'in other places' and often in 'ancient' times. AC and 2016 Years/Levels 5&6 Geography discuss similarities and differences between religions and spiritualities in 'a number of countries', and specifically between Australia and Asia. And AC and VC Year Levels 7&8 History cover the religions 'of the ancient world' including Egypt, Greece and Rome and the religions of India, China, the Pacific region and the Central America. There is also a particular focus on 'Viking religion' and the global spread of Christianity and Islam. Once again Christianity receives more attention here than the 'other religions' as further demonstrated in the analysis of specific religions below.

Diverse religions

Most content on specific diverse religions can be found in History in both the AC and the VC, in the AC in Civics and Citizenship and in the VC in the Humanities dedicated section on Learning about Worldviews and Religions. It is of great interest to note the positioning of the different religions here in relation to subject areas, as well as their amount of mentions, and the content of the mentions. Again, this analysis reveals a securitisation of religion in the AC, with substantive content in C&C and History, and thereby at the national level. By contrast, the placement of most content on diverse religions in the VC in LWR and History is more considered and inclusive, reflecting the state of Victoria's genuine commitment to respecting religious diversity.

As stated above, the VC's dedicated section on LWR is located on its Humanities landing page. It includes a link to a pdf with dedicated sections on the main tenets of Buddhism, Christianity, Hinduism, Islam, Judaism and Secular humanism and rationalism. Its content is focused on key figures, texts, tenets and practices, and examines the worldviews in alphabetical order, ascribing equal significance to all. Of note is that nonreligious worldviews precede religions in the LWR's title, yet content on the diverse religions precedes that of secular worldviews in the pdf.

Table 5.4 Diverse religions – AC and VC Humanities

	Aus Curriculum (AC) F-10	2026 Vic Curriculum (AC) F-10
Christianity or Christian (Christian*)	16 10 History 6 C&C	16 11 History 5 LWR
Islam or Muslim (Islam* or Muslim*)	10 8 History 2 C&C	12 6 History 6 LWR
Judaism, Jew or Jewish (Judai* or Jew*)	3 2 History 1 C&C	11 2 History 9 LWR
Buddhism or Buddhist (Buddh*)	5 4 History 1 C&C	10 4 History 6 LWR
Hinduism or Hindu (Hindu*)	3 2 History 1 C&C	5 2 History 3 LWR

These entries are described in more detail below on each religion, and also in the next section on Secular and Nonreligious Worldviews.

By contrast, the AC does not have a dedicated section on religion and instead the AC's brief Year 8 C&C mention is focused on the diverse 'values and beliefs of religions practised in contemporary Australia, including Christianity'. Here students are asked to identify 'Christian traditions that have influenced the development of Australian society, democracy and law' and the 'values and beliefs of religions practiced in contemporary Australia (for example, Christianity, Judaism, Buddhism, Islam, Hinduism)'. This section again privileges Christianity, and then Judaism above 'other' religions in Australia, signalling the problematic perceived alignment of Australian values with Judeo-Christian values discussed above. Once again Buddhists, Muslims and Hindus are 'other' minorities/groups, positioned after Christians and Jews. Sikhs are not mentioned here either.

Moreover, there are far more references to Christianity and Islam in the AC's Humanities content than other religions. The VC's Humanities content has more mentions of Christianity, Judaism and Islam. This emphasis on Abrahamic faiths again does not reflect Australian Census or AGZ study data, historical facts or Australia's geographical proximity to Asia. Treatment of Christianity and Islam in the AC and VC is also far more considered than that of other so-called minority worldviews, except for in the VC dedicated section on LWR.

Christianity

The VC LWR entry on Christianity discusses God, Christ and the Holy Spirit, love, justice, an afterlife and the Bible's Old and New Testament. In addition to the religion content in LWR, the list of festivals in the early years of History in both the AC and VC and the mentions of Christianity in AC Years 7&8 C&C discussed above, Christianity mostly features in secondary History in both curricula. AC and VC Years/Levels 7–10 History examine that BC stands for Before Christ, Christianity in the Roman, Viking and Ottoman periods, Christianity's global spread, Gregorian chants, conversion to Christianity in Asia and Central America, and Christian missions and missionaries in India and China. There are more mentions of Christianity across both the AC (16) and the VC (16) Humanities, and the content is detailed and considered.

Islam

The VC LWR section on Islam mentions Allah/God, Muhammad, prophets, worship of God, doing good, an afterlife, interfaith relations, justice, the Quran, rituals, Ramadan and Hajj pilgrimage. Ramadan is also mentioned in the list of community festivals in the early years of History in the AC and VC. AC and VC Years/Levels 7–10 History include a focus on the Western and Islamic World, and specifically the global spread of Christianity and Islam. This section and another on the Ottoman Empire focus on the Crusades, the global spread of Islam, including Islamic art and design, Islamic law and Islamic inventions adopted by the West. While the content on the Ottoman Empire is quite thorough, and Islam receives more mentions than any other minority faith in Australia in both the AC (10) and VC (12), it is still often described very much in the shadow of the West and Christianity.

Judaism

The VC LWR Judaism entry is focused on God, God's laws, the promised land of Israel, an afterlife, social justice, the Written and Oral Torah/Talmud and the Sabbath. The feast of Passover and Hanukkah are also mentioned in the list of community festivals in the early years of History in the AC and VC. Judaism receives the most mentions after Christianity and Islam, in the VC (11), largely in LWR. By contrast, AC and VC Years/Levels 7&8 History mentions of Judaism are scant and far less considered than Christianity and Islam, referring only to the tolerance of the Ottomans towards the Jews and the persecution of Jewish people during the fourteenth century Black Death plague.

Buddhism, Hinduism and Sikhism

The VC LWR section on Buddhism includes content on Buddha, key teachings on impermanence, karma, suffering, cessation of suffering and meditation, and the VC LWR Hinduism content focuses on Brahma, Gods, karma, liberation from rebirth, the Vedas, the Upanishads, the Mahabharata and the Ramayana, and rituals. There is no entry for Sikhism.

Only the Buddha's birthday, the Buddhist Moon Festival and the Hindu festival of Diwali are all included in the discussion of community celebrations in the early years of History in the AC and VC. AC and VC 7&8 History examines 'Hinduism, Buddhism and Jainism' as belief systems of India with 'harmonious relations with the natural world', the spread of Hinduism and Buddhism across and beyond India during the Mauryan Empire and the rise of Theravada Buddhism during the Khmer Empire. These mentions of Buddhism and Hinduism are quite random, compared to the content on Christianity and Islam discussed above.

This data on the amount and positioning of mentions of diverse religions in years F-10 of the AC and VC once again shows a strong preference of Christianity among religions, and also of Islam and to a lesser extent Judaism. Despite the geographical proximity to Asia and the long history of Buddhism, Hinduism and Sikhism in Australia, the religions of Asia receive far less attention than the Abrahamic faiths. The fact that all content on the so-called minority faiths, except for Islam, is quite scant and haphazard in the AC in particular, in terms of what is included and excluded, is also troubling. The VC at least attempts to grant all diverse worldviews and religions equal status.

Secular and nonreligious worldviews

The VC's dedicated section on LWR mentions 'non-religious worldviews' once in its preamble. While worldviews are mentioned before religions in the title, the section on 'Secular humanism and rationalism' appears last, following all of the religion content, and is focused on the 'natural universe', people having one life and no afterlife, purpose, meaning, ethics, reason, science, common humanity, wellbeing, rights, ancient Greek and Roman philosophy and the modern Age of Enlightenment.

Table 5.5 Secular and nonreligion – AC and VC Humanities

	Aus Curriculum (AC) F-10	Vic Curriculum (VC) F-10
Secular (secular*)	4 4 C&C	9 5 C&C 4 LWR
Nonreligious, no religion, or not religious (non* religio*/no religio*/ not* religio*)	0	1 1 LWR

Most of the mentions of secular occur in AC and VC Years/Levels 7–8 C&C, including of Australia's 'secular system of government', and Australia being a 'secular nation'. In Year 7/Level 7&8 C&C Australia is described first as a secular nation and then a multifaith society in both the AC and VC, and with a Christian heritage in the AC, as discussed above. The secular and nonreligion receive far less mentions and attention than do religion and spirituality in both the AC and VC, and this content is mostly in C&C in the AC and in LWR and C&C in the VC.

Conclusion

Similar to the RDA Media study's findings (see Chapter 3 and Halafoff et al. 2021) the RDA Education study reveals a privileging of Christianity and Abrahamic faiths in both the AC and VC. This is particularly the case in the AC, and is also accompanied by a troubling securitisation of religion, with most content on diverse worldviews of Australia being positioned in C&C. By contrast the VC includes a dedicated section on LWR that treats diverse religious and non-religious worldviews equally and does not accord primacy to Christianity. AC C&C describes Australia as a secular, multifaith society 'with a Christian Heritage'. VC C&C only refers to Australia as secular and multifaith. This reveals a very different treatment of diverse worldviews at the Australian national level to the Victorian state level, with the AC upholding the myth of a Christian nation and Victoria reflecting its multifaith reality.

However, both the AC and VC are still hampered by being constrained to an outmoded world religions model that does not adequately acknowledge First Nations worldviews, the significance of spirituality more broadly or nonreligion in Australian society. While the AC and BC briefly mention the need for religious freedom to be limited by the 'bounds of the law', they also do not engage in any depth with religious or spiritual harms, or the ways in which religion and spirituality have contributed to direct and structural violence, such as against sexuality and/ or gender-diverse peoples. It this way both the AC and VC do not reflect the worldview diversity and complexity of, or issues of concern to, Australia's young people. Instead the AGZ study shows that young people are learning about diverse worldviews largely from family, social media and peers, rather than in schools. This renders young Australians particularly vulnerable to misinformation when it comes to religion and spirituality, and to negative stereotypes of minority religions.

This RDA Education study thereby provides further evidence that education about diverse worldviews in Australia, and even in Victoria, is currently inadequate, and that a more critical, considered and inclusive approach to learning about diverse worldviews is as yet to be developed and delivered in Australia. As the AGZ study has indicated, this type of education can actually increase religious and worldview literacy and parity in Australia, and thereby contribute to reducing negative perceptions of religious minorities, and religious harms against other minorities, in broader society.

Notes

1 A new version of the Australian Curriculum was released in 2022, and the Victorian Curriculum is currently under review in 2022–3 at the time of writing this chapter. This chapter presents an analysis therefore of the previous Australian and the current Victorian Curricula, that were both being taught at the time that the Religion and Diversity in Australia study was being conducted in 2018–21. An analysis of the treatment of diverse worldviews in the 2022 Australian Curriculum by Anna Halafoff, of the RDP team, was presented in her Presidential Lecture on 'Christian Privilege and the Australian Curriculum' at the Australian Association for the Study of Religion's 2022 Annual Conference (available at: https://www.youtube.com/watch?v=nzEDPTAH4vc).

2 By the 1950s, at the height of the White Australia Policy and amid rising fears of communism, while religion could not be taught in state schools by teachers, clergy and religious volunteers were permitted to provide Christian and Jewish religious instruction/education (RI/RE) to students, despite strong opposition from secular education advocates (Byrne 2014; Halafoff 2015; Maddox 2014).

3 The debate regarding RI/RE in Australian state schools intensified in the 1970s, when reviews of RI/RE practices were conducted in most states. These reviews all made similar recommendations for RI/RE programmes to be replaced by World Religion/GRE, taught by qualified teachers as part of the curriculum. These recommendations were based on international best-practices in the UK and EU.

Due to the lack of an already embedded Christian RE programme in the curricula, and also as Australia did not yet have a large-enough interfaith movement at that time to lobby for similar changes, only South Australia discontinued its RI/RE programme. NSW and WA kept RI/RE and also taught limited GRE content, and Victoria and Tasmania simply kept RI/RE due to considerable pressure from Christian and Jewish RI/RE providers and their supporters. By the 1990s many minority faith communities in Australia began providing RI/RE programmes, but the vast majority of RI/RE programmes in state schools are still Christian (Byrne 2014; Halafoff 2013, 2015; Maddox 2014).

4 Secular communities and Australian scholars of religion also continue to argue that GRE and WE should replace RI/RE programmes taught by religious volunteers in state schools, to cease the privileging of Christianity, and its associated issues outlined above, and to provide a more critical and equitable WE by teachers within the curriculum (Bouma and Halafoff 2009; Byrne 2007, 2014; Halafoff 2013, 2015; Halafoff et al. 2019; Maddox 2014). Victoria finally permitted the teaching of GRE in secular state schools in 2006, and eventually replaced RI/RE with WE in 2015. By contrast, debates about RI/RE remain heated and are ongoing in NSW and Queensland where RI/RE is still delivered by religious volunteers (Halafoff and Bouma 2019; Halafoff 2022). A more detailed discussion of RI/RE is beyond the scope of this chapter, which is focused on WE in the Australian and the Victorian Curricula.

5 Donnelly's current website introduces him as 'one of Australia's leading conservative public intellectuals and cultural warriors' and author of *The Dictionary of Woke: How Orwellian Language Control and Group Think Are Destroying Western Societies.*

6 Halafoff decided on the search terms in consultation with Enqi Weng and Emily Marriott, for the RDA Media study, and adapted these slightly to the RDA Education study. Ruth Fitzpatrick and Halafoff conducted the data analysis of the RDA Education study, and Halafoff and Fitzpatrick contributed to the analysis presented in this book chapter.

7 AntConc was recommended to the RDA Education research team by Elenie Poulos, who used it in her analysis of religious freedom debates in the Australian media.

8 The AC refers to individual Years, i.e. Year 3, whereas the VC refers to Levels that include two Year groups, i.e. Levels 3&4. Throughout this chapter we refer to AC and VC Years/Levels X&X when the content is the same in both curricula. When it is different we refer to the relevant AC Year or VC Levels.

References

Arweck, E., and Jackson, R. (eds). 2014. *Religion, Education and Society: Young People, Religious Identity, Socialisation and Diversity.* London: Routledge.

Beder, S. 2014. 'The Wrong Men behind Curriculum Review'. *The Age*, 14 January. http:// www.theage.com.au/comment/the-wrong-men-behind-curriculum-review-20140113-30qmc.html. Accessed 15 November 2014.

Bouma, G., and Halafoff, A. 2009. 'Multifaith education and social inclusion in Australia'. *Journal of Religious Education* 57(3): 17–25.

Bouma, G., and Halafoff, A. 2017. 'Australia's changing Religious Profile – Rising Nones and Pentecostals, Declining British Protestants in Superdiversity: Views from the 2016 Census'. *Journal for the Academic Study of Religion* 30(2): 129–43.

Bouma, G. D., Pickering, S., Dellal, H., and Halafoff, A. 2007. *Managing the Impact of Global Crisis Events on Community Relations in Multicultural Australia*. City East, Qld: Multicultural Affairs Queensland and the Victorian Office of Multicultural Affairs.

Byrne, C. 2007. 'Spirit in the "Expanding Circle": Why Learn about Religion in Australia in the Twenty-First Century? Can comparative Religion Knowledge Enable Cultural Diversity Capacity?' Master's Thesis. University of Queensland.

Byrne, C. 2014. *Religion in Secular Education: What in Heaven's Name Are We Teaching Our Children?* Leiden: Brill.

Council of Europe. 2008. 'Recommendation CM/Rec(2008)12 of the Committee of Ministers to Member States on the Dimension of Religions and Non-Religious Convictions within Intercultural Education'. *Council of Europe*. https://wcd.coe.int/ViewDoc.jsp?id=1386911andSite=CM. Accessed 15 November 2014.

Donnelly, K., and Wiltshire, K. 2014. *Review of the Australian Curriculum – Final Report*. Canberra: Australian Government Department of Education.

Erebus International. 2006. *Encouraging Tolerance and Social Cohesion through School Education*. Canberra: Department of Education, Science and Training.

Gearon, L. 2012. 'The Securitization of Religion in Education'. In van der Zee T. and Lovat T. (eds), *New Perspectives in Religious and Spiritual Education*. Münster: Waxmann, 215–33.

Hage, G. 1998. *White Nation: Fantasies of White Supremacy in a Multicultural Society*. Annandale: Pluto Press.

Halafoff, A. 2006. 'UnAustralian Values'. In *UNAustralia*, refereed conference proceedings from the Cultural Studies Association of Australasia Annual Conference 6–8 December, University of Canberra.

Halafoff, A. 2013. *The Multifaith Movement, Global Risks and Cosmopolitan Solutions*. Dordrecht: Springer.

Halafoff, A. 2015. 'Special Religious Instruction and Worldviews Education in Victoria's Schools: Social Inclusion, Citizenship and Countering Extremism'. *Journal of Intercultural Studies* 36(3): 362–79.

Halafoff, A. 2022. *Christian Privilege and the Australian Curriculum*. Australian Association of Religion 2022 Conference, Presidential Lecture, University of Melbourne, 30 November.

Halafoff, A., Lam, K., Weng, E., and Smith, S. 2022. 'Buddhism in the Far North of Australia Pre-WWII: (In)visibility, Post-Colonialism and Materiality'. *Journal of Global Buddhism* 23(2): 1–23.

Halafoff, A., Marriott, E, Smith, G., Weng, E., and Bouma, G. 2021. 'Worldviews Complexity in COVID-19 Times: Australian Media Representations of Religion, Spirituality and Non-religion in 2020'. *Religions* 12(9): 682–703.

Halafoff, A., Singleton, A., Bouma, G. D., et al. 2019. 'Want a Safer World for Your Children? Teach Them about Diverse Religions and Worldviews.' *The Conversation.* 21 March. https://theconversation.com/want-a-safer-world-for-your-child ren-teach-them-about-diverse-religions-and-worldviews-113025?fbclid=IwAR2mj yEwsDpj0BrNRDOWHzTUuPK5y9A2N3NS1Re8JvUr0C4wLlUofAI4jS0. Accessed 25 March 2019.

Halafoff, A., Singleton, A., and Fitzpatrick, R. 2023. 'Spiritual Complexity in Australia: Wellbeing and Risks'. *Social Compass* 70(3): 003776862311620.

Jackson, R. 2014. *'Signposts': Policy and Practice for Teaching about Religions and Non-religious Worldviews in Intercultural Education*. Strasbourg: Council of Europe Publishing.

Jackson, R. 2015. 'The Politicisation and Securitisation of Religious Education? A Rejoinder'. *British Journal of Educational Studies*, Special Issue on Education, Security and Intelligence Studies 63(3): 345–66.

Knott, K., Poole, E., and Taira, T. 2013. *Media Portrayals of Religion and the Secular Sacred*. Surrey: Ashgate.

Maddox, M. 2005. *God under Howard: The Rise of the Religious Right in Australian Politics*. Sydney: Allen & Unwin.

Maddox, M. 2014. *Taking God to School: The End of Australia's Egalitarian Education?* Sydney: Allen & Unwin.

Ministerial Council on Education, Employment, Training and Youth Affairs (MCEETYA). 2008. *Melbourne Declaration on Educational Goals for Young Australians*. Melbourne: Ministerial Council on Education, Employment, Training and Youth Affairs.

Office for Democratic Institutions and Human Rights Advisory Council of Experts on Freedom of Religion or Belief (ODIHR). 2007. *Toledo Guiding Principles on Teaching about Religions and Beliefs in Public Schools*. Warsaw: OSCE Office for Democratic Institutions and Human Rights. http://www.osce.org/odihr/29154?download=true. Accessed 15 November 2014.

Poole, Elizabeth, and Weng, Enqi. 2021. 'Introduction: Religion on an Ordinary Day: An International Study of News Reporting'. *Journal of Religion, Media and Digital Culture* 10(2): 165–78.

Singleton, A., Halafoff, A., Rasmussen, M., and Bouma, G. 2021. *Freedom, Faiths and Futures: Teenage Australians on Religion, Sexuality and Diversity*. London: Bloomsbury Academic.

Weng, E., and Halafoff, A. 2020. 'Media Representations of Religion, Spirituality and Non-religion in Australia'. *Religions* 11: 332.

Weng, E., Smith, G., Bouma, G., and Barton, G. 2021a. 'Higher Education, Exclusion and Belonging: Religious Complexity, Coping and Connectedness among International Students during the COVID-19 Pandemic in Australia'. *Journal of International Students* 11(2): 38–57.

Weng, E., Halafoff, A., Abur, W., Campbell, D., Bouma, G., and Barton, G. 2021b. 'Whiteness, Religious Diversity and Relational Belonging: Opportunities and Challenges for African Migrants in Australia'. *Journal for the Academic Study of Religions* 34(3): 289–313.

6

The Multifaith Movement in Australia: Representational and Relational Bodies

Geraldine Smith and Anna Halafoff

Introduction

This chapter is about how different types of organisations in the multifaith movement facilitate respectful relationships between religiously diverse people in Australia. To paint a picture of what the multifaith movement looks like in the world, you could imagine a small event in the local library on a Sunday afternoon where ordinary people are invited to discuss their diverse understandings of the nature of God; a school programme where a rabbi, imam and priest stand at the front of a classroom and teach the students about religious differences; a meeting room where representatives from diverse faith traditions sit around a large table for hours discussing how they will fund their initiatives; a group of activists inspired by religious and spiritual principles staging a protest together at the site of a controversial coal mine; or friends from different traditions sharing a meal together on a religious holiday. All of these types of initiatives take place in the multifaith milieu in Australia.

Rather than examining multifaith as an abstract theological discussion between religious traditions – what Moyaert (2019: 5) calls the 'dialogue-centred model of interfaith engagement' – the purpose of this chapter is to describe the multifaith movement as it is lived out in day-to-day life. Drawing on leading scholars in the field of material religion, such as Birgit Meyer (2012), Meredith McGuire (2008) and Marianne Moyaert (2019), this chapter takes a performative, embodied and material lens which focuses on what people are doing – the organisational practices of the multifaith movement. In this chapter, we discuss real-world examples of how different types of multifaith organisations, groups and networks operate in Australia.

This Interfaith component of the Religious Diversity in Australia study focuses on an analysis of interviews, conducted between 2019 and 2020, with people who worked in multifaith organisations and attendees to multifaith events, as well as autoethnographic fieldwork at multifaith events.[1] Anna Halafoff (2013:110) previously observed that the multifaith movement operates on multiple levels with differing strategies and approaches. This vast social movement manifests into many different types of organisations who work at local and global scales. Often, local issues and global events have mutual influence upon one another, and actors work in these spheres simultaneously. As Patrice Brodeur noted, and as was reiterated by Halafoff, the multifaith movement is 'glocal in nature' (Brodeur 2005: 43, quoted in Halafoff 2013: 110). Halafoff's research involved many multifaith actors who performed diverse roles, such as small discussion groups, groups attached to local government councils, non-governmental organisations delivering educational programmes, faith-based climate activist groups, youth-based initiatives and representative bodies. Halafoff (2013: 51) identifies four main goals of the multifaith movement: (1) 'developing understanding of diverse faiths and of the nature of reality', (2) 'challenging exclusivity and normalising pluralism', (3) 'addressing global risks and injustices' and (4) 'creating multi-actor peacebuilding networks for common security'. However, each multifaith body has a unique set of capabilities and limitations, they have different emphases and different ways of *performing* these goals in practice. There are possibilities present in some types of groups that are not available in others. In this chapter, we compare top-down and grassroots approaches and unpack why collaboration between these spheres is needed more than ever to energise the multifaith movement in today's world of religious diversity.

Halafoff (2013) argued that what underpins these diverse groups, organisations and bodies under the multifaith movement is a cosmopolitan vision. A cosmopolitan vision, as articulated by Ulrich Beck (2006), is firstly a description of the current situation of modernity. It describes the interdependent nature of global challenges, such as nuclear war, climate change, terrorism and social inequality, which threaten the common security of all – regardless of nation-state boundaries. It is secondly a prescriptive vision that argues that these challenges must be addressed through glocally collaborative and equally distributed solutions (Beck 2006; Halafoff 2013). Halafoff (2013: 20) explained that cosmopolitanism entails transnational alliances across multiple levels of religious, state and nonstate actors, an emphasis on respect for equal rights, respect for religious, cultural and multispecies diversity and a recognition of the interdependence of human and non-human life. Importantly, these networks are 'concentrated at local and global, as opposed to national, levels' (Halafoff 2013: 20). What makes the movement capable to address these challenges, Halafoff (2013: 52, italics in original) concluded, is that it is '*responsive, preventive, creative, collaborative, radically reflexive* and *deliberative*'. She argued that, in the face of contemporary challenges the multifaith movement is always searching for solutions and shifts according to the challenges presented before it: 'multifaith actors ... respond to their context, and particularly to local and global crisis events. They seek to prevent further crises, and to create new conditions within which future risks can be avoided' (Halafoff 2013: 52). Multifaith actors have a unique role to play in addressing these global challenges as religious organisations transcend national boundaries, therefore the multifaith movement operates through global and local networks (Halafoff 2013).

As we explore in the examples below, this vision differs according to the sphere of influence, access to resources and scale of different groups. The two main approaches this chapter explores are *representational bodies* and *relational bodies*. These two approaches are often interrelated but refer to a distinct set of practices that affect how the cosmopolitan goals of the multifaith movement are lived out. In using the term 'bodies', we seek to allude to not only organisations, institutions and structures, but also the flesh-and-blood bodies of the people living out these structures in performative and material ways. This attention to bodies operating in a material world is sometimes referred to as a 'lived religion' approach which describes how people live out their religious and spiritual worldviews through their everyday practices, rather than through belief, doctrine or texts (Orsi 2003; McGuire 2008). McGuire (2008) was critical of examining religion solely from the perspective of religious leaders who dictate the orthodoxy of a religious tradition through a focus on belief, texts and dogma. McGuire (2008: 13) argued that, through religious practises, 'the individual is able to experience, rather than simply think or believe in, the reality of her or his religious world'. In this way, 'the sacred is made vividly real and present through the experiencing body' (McGuire 2008: 13). Applying this to the multifaith movement, it is not only thought about and discussed in dialogue, but is something that people practise and make real through their bodies. These ideas are further explored in the first section below on material religion and a critique of dialogue-centred models of multifaith.

The second section explores the Faith Communities Council of Victoria (FCCV), which is what in Australia is often termed an umbrella body (an umbrella of peak bodies), which is a board of delegates who represent the interests of their respective peak body communities and seek to work together on a common goal. The FCCV has a vast sphere of influence and co-ordinates multifaith activities across the Australian state of Victoria. They are exemplary of the representational approach to multifaith. It involves people in positions of leadership in religious organisations operating as representatives with the goal of encouraging multifaith collaboration among diverse groups and using their influence and resources to enact broad change from the top-down. The third section contrasts this group to a small local discussion group called Sacred Conversations, which operates in Hobart, Tasmania. This is a group that focuses upon the relationships between religious individuals, rather than entire traditions, thus we describe it as relational. It is about building up trust, respect and safety within interpersonal relationships between different people. It lacks the same broad influence of representational bodies, but it is a site of creativity and critique. It also holds the potential of being more inclusive to those who possess hybrid religious, spiritual and nonreligious worldviews, First Nations voices, minority religions and New Religious Movements (NRMs), as well as other social groups that find themselves excluded from positions of leadership, such as young people. Each of these sections begin with a story based in interview and fieldwork data which paint a picture of what these practices look like on the ground.

The goal of the multifaith movement is to find common values and actions in a religiously diverse world. It inspires religious, state and nonstate actors to collaborate, and is underpinned by a shared moral imperative to address the world's suffering (Knitter 1995; Halafoff 2013). It is worth understanding these two approaches because there are several current trends in religious, spiritual and nonreligious worldviews that present a significant challenge to the continuation of the multifaith movement. Religious diversity is growing in what Inger Furseth (2018: 16) describes as 'religious complexity', which refers to the contradictory trends of both growth and decline of different types of religion. Gary Bouma, Anna Halafoff and Greg Barton (2022: 196–7) similarly observe the emergence of 'diversity of diversities' whereby religious identity becomes intersected with other identities, related to sexuality, gender, ethnicity, class and so on, it starts to 'become even further diversified by its intersection with other diversities'. Bouma et al. (2022: 197) describe this as 'worldview complexity', to address the lived reality that spiritual and nonreligious worldviews are also part of this complexity. Other significant trends are the rise of nonreligion, which is now the fastest growing 'religious' group in much of the modern Western world (Thiessen and Wilkins-Laflamme 2017). In Australia, those identifying as having 'no religion' on the census increased from 30 per cent in 2016 (Australian Bureau of Statistics 2017) to 38.9 per cent in 2021 (Australian Bureau of Statistics 2022). Significant numbers of nonreligious young people also identify as spiritual (Singleton et al. 2021).

Furthermore, the emerging generations of Gen Z and millennials are presenting a challenge to the succession of the multifaith movement as they are at the forefront of worldview complexity (Halafoff 2020; Smith 2022). Millennials and Gen Z have particularly spiritual, nonreligious or hydridic worldviews. They have adopted eclectic worldviews crafted from a range of religious, spiritual and nonreligious influences; are highly critical of religious institutions, particularly their treatment of LGBTI+ people; and as a result, are moving further to the margins of religious traditions (Halafoff et al. 2020; Halafoff 2020; Halafoff and Gobey 2018; Shipley et al. 2016; Shipley 2018; Singleton et al. 2021). These generational shifts are causing a crisis of succession in multifaith organisations as fewer millennials and Gen Z are taking up leadership positions (Smith 2022). However, there has been some success in youth-based multifaith organisations who move away from representational approaches and emphasise personal relationships, storytelling and social action such as the Interfaith Youth Core (now known as Interfaith America) (Brodeur 2005; Brodeur and Patel 2006; Patel and Meyer 2010; Patel, Kunze and Silverman 2008; Patel 2016); InterAction, which focused on building relationships through social activism (Halafoff and Gobey 2018; Halafoff 2020); and Youth PoWR, which used grassroots forums to construct their multifaith charter, the Sydney Statement (Smith 2022). In this context of worldview complexity, nonreligion and generational change, there are serious questions regarding what the future holds for the multifaith movement in Australia, and countries that have similar trends of worldview complexity.

Material multifaith

Birgit Meyer (2012: 11) argued that a focus on texts, doctrine and belief in the study of religion is the result of a 'Protestant legacy' present in the early development of religious studies, which presented Protestant Christianity as the 'normative and theoretical template' (Meyer 2012: 9) of all religions. This developed into the World Religions Paradigm (WRP), whereby early scholars used this normative template based on Protestant Christianity to identify five major world traditions – Buddhism, Christianity, Hinduism, Islam and

Judaism – and present them as homogenous, unchanging and isolated traditions (Cotter and Robertson 2016). Marianne Moyaert (2019: 2) explained that a Protestant bias similarly dominates the study of the multifaith movement. The dialogue-centred model posits multifaith actors as representatives of entire religious traditions, who, endowed with the legitimacy of their religious institutions, share the spiritual wisdom and religious truth with other delegates of religious traditions (Moyaert 2019: 5). The goal of this exchange, according to the dialogue-centred model of multifaith, is the greater understanding of reality for everyone (Cornille 2008; Swidler 1983). This theological ideal affects how multifaith bodies (both in the institutional and embodied sense) are organised on the ground.

A dialogue-centred model can fail to recognise the ways that the multifaith movement has developed as a social movement within diverse political, historical and social contexts and power dynamics (Fahy and Bock 2020: 2). It can imply that religious traditions are homogenous entities that lack internal diversity (Hedges 2010: 80–1); therefore they can fail to recognise the religious complexity developing within each tradition. John Fahy and Jan-Jonathan Bock (2018: 69) state that too much emphases on dialogue can be problematic as it 'uncritically accepts religious leaders and scholars as representatives of complex and heterogenous traditions'. By framing the multifaith movement as a dialogue between traditions, it also limits who can be a representative as they must be part of the educated elite; have a highly proficient grasp on textual, theological and philosophical tradition; and be considered internally legitimate representatives (Scheffler 2007: 175). Scholars writing from a feminist and/or postcolonial perspective have also pointed out how a focus on dialogue can ignore the efforts of people outside of official leadership such as women (Kwok 2005), 'lay' people within religious communities (Swamy 2016) and ignore issues related to sociopolitical power relations.

A focus on texts and belief can also sideline engagement with the 'messy' aspects of how religion is played out as an embodied experience – sometimes in paradoxical and unexpected ways (Fahy and Bock 2018: 68). Moyaert (2019) argued that the dialogue-centred model presents religious identities as clear and fixed, rather than as multilayered, fluid and complex. It overlooks the exchange of ideas and practices between traditions, movements and organisations; the constructed nature of religious categories; other intersecting identities; and the complex ways in which people identify with a diverse range of religious, spiritual and nonreligious worldviews. In the same vein as the lived religion approach, Moyaert (2019: 3–4) described interreligious/interfaith studies as a multidisciplinary field that explores the encounters between religiously diverse people. She explained that it seeks to move beyond too much scholarly emphasis on theological and philosophical exchanges between representatives of religious traditions (Moyaert 2019: 4). She further argued, 'theological exchange is important, but it is only one form of interreligious interaction' and interreligious studies seeks to broaden the discussion to encounters 'that may revolve around art, song, ritual, or socio-political activism (or a combination of these)' (4). Moyaert (2019) especially focused on the role of ritual in the interreligious exchanges. Not all organisations in the multifaith movement follow the dialogue-centred model but is a dominant paradigm that affects what is possible in practice. There is a diversity of organisations where multifaith actors explore and nurture new possibilities for the future of the multifaith movement, and focus more on embodied action (Halafoff 2013). In the next section, we explore two organisations in Australia who represent the possibilities of representational and relational multifaith.

Representational bodies

In the 1980s, the religious communities of Dandenong and Springvale in Victoria, Australia, co-authored a multifaith declaration that would continue to hold precedence for the next forty years. The authors of the statement wanted to affirm a mutual commitment of respect for the immense religious and cultural diversity in their local area and promote peace and co-operation in the community. They called it the Common Statement. The coalition of religious representatives then presented the Common Statement to the members of the Dandenong Council and the Mayor, who promised to serve in a way that reflected its principles. This action formed an important connection between representatives of religious communities and the official spheres of local government. The coalition of religious communities eventually formed into the Interfaith Network of the City of Greater Dandenong (INGD), and each year they perform the Common Statement ceremony in more or less the same fashion. Rituals, such as these, are central activities within the multifaith movement because they help to embody the abstract cosmopolitan ideals of multifaith into material actions and relationships that can be seen, felt and heard (Moyaert 2019; Griera 2019). Smith attended the ceremony in 2019, which took place within the Victorian Interfaith Networks Festival (VINF). Each year the FCCV partners with a multifaith/interfaith network operating in a Local Government Area (LGA) to host the VINF. Fortunately, in 2019, it was the

INGD's turn to run the event in partnership with the FCCV, therefore the Common Statement ritual came to be included as part of the VINF proceedings and Smith was able to witness this significant occasion.

The Springvale Town Hall served as the venue for the VINF as it was able to accommodate the hundreds of multifaith actors, religious leaders and community members invited from religious communities from all parts of Victoria. The day began with attendees sharing a meal and getting to know one another on large round tables. The president of the INGD, Agnes Kean, stood before a long table at the entrance to the hall with the book of signatures for the Common Statement before her and invited religious representatives and leaders to sign it as they arrived. The proceedings of the event commenced with a First Nations' Elder performing a Welcome to Country. The host then asked representatives from each religious community who sat upon the stage to stand side by side and they passed the microphone along one by one to announce which community they represented. Then the representatives and the audience, who were also asked to stand, read out the Common Statement together, and the signed Common Statement was presented to the Dandenong Mayor, who went to podium to say a few words. The proceedings ended with the whole hall singing a song written by the INGD network, at the same time the representatives on stage each rang a coloured bell along with the music.

The story above is a vivid image of representational approaches to multifaith. It also demonstrates the complex relationships between grassroots and top-down multifaith organisations who often work in tandem with one another. The Faith Communities Council of Victoria FCCV consists of a board of representatives from religious peak bodies within Victoria, such as the Bahaí Council of Victoria, Brahma Kumaris Australia, Buddhist Council of Victoria, Hindu Council of Australia (Vic), Islamic Council of Victoria, Jain Council of Victoria, Jewish Community Council of Victoria, Sikh Interfaith Council of Victoria and the Victorian Council of Churches. The FCCV plays a co-ordinating role for all other multifaith activity in Victoria. It balances between broad national and transatlantic multifaith networks, global events and the domains of officialdom, and the concerns of local communities and grassroots initiatives. In Halafoff's 2013 research on the multifaith movement in Australia and internationally, she found that multifaith actors strongly valued being able to work across both local and global spheres (Halafoff 2013: 110). Global events affect what happens in local communities, thus representational bodies are indispensable in organising common responses across vast global networks of religious, state and multifaith actors – they are a good example of the glocal nature of the multifaith movement. Yet, 'representational structures' (Halafoff 2013: 110) can reinforce dominant power hierarchies as those who operate in this sphere must possess institutional authority. Also, too much focus on a global perspective can overlook issues particular to each local area and the important work carried out by people on the ground (Halafoff 2013). Therefore, finding a balance between these spheres is part of the remit of representational multifaith bodies.

To understand how the FCCV balances these responsibilities, Smith interviewed its multifaith officer, Sandy Kouroupidis. He explained several roles that the FCCV plays on a glocal level. The FCCV promote multifaith activity across Victoria on their website, social media platforms and a monthly e-newsletter; maintain a Multifaith Calendar that provides information to schools, universities, government institution and private organisations about religious Holy Days; run the annual VINF in partnership with a local multifaith network; release statements on local or global issues; and run long-term social initiatives that usually span two to three years. Some of their initiatives include developing Religious Education Resources to assist teachers in teaching religious literacy in schools and providing training programs to faith leaders and their communities for the prevention of family violence. They encourage smaller multifaith groups and liaise with the government and other peak bodies for religious organisations, and act as intermediaries between grassroots groups, religious communities and state actors.

Sandy explained that on an everyday level, this means that when there is a multifaith event in Victoria, Sandy will usually get an email informing him about it, then he promotes it on the FCCV's social media, website and/or e-newsletter: 'I'll post it on the website, I'll send it out in a newsletter, put it up on Facebook so everyone that pretty much follows those things knows exactly where the next event's going to go.' He said that the FCCV supported other local multifaith councils and groups and co-ordinated glocal responses to crisis events. For example, in response to the Christchurch Attack in 2019, the FCCV released a statement condemning the attacks and to 'invite our interfaith friends and people, both locally and internationally, to join us in this endeavour and to commit to love, peace, and understanding in place of violence and hatred' (Faith Communities Council of Victoria 2019).

The FCCV formed in the follow-up of the 2009 Parliament of the World's Religions in Melbourne. In the early days of the FCCV, the Victorian state government provided them with significant support and funding as a counterterrorism response to events such as 11 September 2001, the 2002 Bali Bombings and the 2005 London Bombings. In the 2000s, the multifaith movement was seen as a conduit for counterterrorism strategies by increasing broad interreligious understanding, preventing violent extremism and promoting social cohesion (Halafoff 2013: 80). However, throughout the 2010s the multifaith movement was increasingly critiqued for being a 'soft' and ineffective strategy to counter violent extremism (Halafoff 2013: 167). The global focus also shifted away from religious involvement in violence and terrorism. As a result, multifaith organisations noticed that their state funding was dwindling and finding appropriate financial support for multifaith initiatives became increasingly difficult (Halafoff 2013: 83–4).

Sandy explained that from 2017 the Victorian state government no longer directly funds multifaith initiatives and consequently, many multifaith organisations had become less effective. He said the changes in funding greatly affected multifaith activity in Victoria: 'Multifaith organisations have either ceased to exist, reduced their activity, or have survived by focusing on issues that the state sees as high priority and willing to fund, such as women's issues, youth issues, family violence prevention, gender diversity etc.' To apply for state funding, the FCCV also had to change tact and set up programmes that conform to the interests of the Victorian state government. He emphasised that working on these social issues were important, but that these issues are harder to find consensus on and difficult for a representative body to navigate. He added that, ideally, they ought to have funding to run social initiatives and have enough resources to also do their 'core work' of promoting respectful relationships between diverse religious, spiritual and nonreligious individuals, and communities – as both were equally valuable.

In other words, this new funding model does not allow much room for more relational aspects of multifaith – which we explore below. Many interview participants in this study noted that funding was one of the biggest challenges they currently faced. The FCCV are continually seeking new ways to fund their multifaith and social justice initiatives and successfully conducted the Prevention of Family Violence project where they provided family violence prevention training to religious leaders and their faith communities: 'How we survived was by getting funding for ... training faith and community leaders in what to do in instances of family violence – that's how we're actually surviving.' Sandy continued, 'We were unable to receive funding for our core work which is bringing people of various faiths together ... So how are we surviving? By being creative.' The FCCV's adaptability is an important hallmark of the multifaith movement that has allowed it to shift through changing social and historical contexts. The FCCV joined a Multifaith Advisory Group (MAG) to participate in the 'Faith Communities Supporting Healthy Family Relationships' project, led by the University of Melbourne and funded by Multicultural Affairs, which aimed to implement the recommendations 163 and 165 of the Victorian Royal Commission into Family Violence. The outcome of this research were programmes and resources that could be used by multifaith bodies to educate religious leaders on issues of family violence, which has since been carried out by the FCCV and other multifaith groups in Victoria (Multicultural Centre for Women's Health, 2019).

The Prevention of Family Violence project is an example of the glocal dynamics of the movement. Religious representatives, state actors, academics and social justice advocates came together to address issues of patriarchal traditions, gender inequality and violence against women by working on changing attitudes and educating religious leaders within local communities and through local multifaith networks. Whilst this project was aligned with the interests of the FCCV, it reveals a precedent that to receive funding multifaith organisations must conform to state interests. Whilst religious and state actors alike may find a common cause in countering social issues such as gambling, homelessness or domestic violence prevention, funding for multifaith initiatives *for its own sake* – that is improving interreligious understanding, addressing religious-based violence and teaching people to be respectful to the religious other – is left unaddressed. This governmental funding model limits what social justice causes multifaith actors choose to address, it becomes a tool to fulfil state agendas, and suppresses the multifaith movements' capacity to be critical of the state (Halafoff 2016). Furthermore, there are some issues, such as gender and sexuality, religious freedom and climate change, which are contentious, and difficult for religiously and politically diverse networks to find consensus on.

Representational bodies coordinate vast networks of many religious, state and nonstate actors to achieve broad social change, the representational model of multifaith itself is also limited in its capacity for social critique. On the one hand, a co-authored statement on a particular issue released by a multifaith representative body can be, as Sandy noted, 'a very powerful voice'. On the other, some issues 'are hard to reach an agreement on from a peak body perspective'. The members of the representative body can only represent official positions of their institutions, are occupied by small circle of legitimate participants, and can exclude minority religions, nonreligious worldviews and other forms of spirituality that live outside of traditional definitions of 'religion.' Sandy explained that on the representational level, the role of the FCCV is to present the official perspectives of organisation's or faith tradition's, 'so they [the representatives] can't speak on an individual point of view, they can only say what their peak body says so it's an official statement.' This affords them a high degree of legitimacy in presenting the official positions of their tradition, but limits what is possible.

The FCCV, however, does not always operate on a representative capacity and instead support smaller multifaith organisations, such as the INGD in the story at the beginning of this section. He described grassroots multifaith groups as comparatively 'wild and free,' because it is made up of volunteers who may not necessarily represent the official positions of their institution. He said that volunteers generally have 'very open-minded ideas and the predominant interfaith activity is at the grassroots level'. He said on certain issues, such as gender, 'grassroots people are more supportive ... whereas if you go up the peak body point of view and you ask the same questions, you'll get the official line'. He said that both forms of multifaith were necessary and make mutually beneficial contributions. He said that much of the 'person-to-person' work where people are meeting each other happens at the grassroots, whereas peak bodies 'are a point of reference for government and media, and work on official statements and projects in line with theological perspectives' In grassroots, he also noted there were more minority groups involved 'in the higher level those minority faiths are cut off, as only recognised players are allowed to control that space'. Representational bodies, by its very nature, can be exclusive not only to individuals who hold leadership but to what are considered 'mainstream' religious groups.

A further complexity is that the FCCV provides support to grassroots multifaith groups, by sending representatives to participate in grassroots multifaith events. At these events, a panel discussion may be made up of official peak body representatives and grassroots volunteers. The mixture of 'official' representatives and volunteers means sometimes there can be confusion regarding what perspective participants are speaking from. Whilst a volunteer may come from particular religious tradition, they are likely to express personal opinions that may not be the official position of the tradition. However, as Sandy noted, this can be helpful as it allows for people to learn about different perspectives of the same tradition, and it can be valuable for people from the grassroots level to challenge official perspectives. Again, this evokes the glocal nature of multifaith work. Rather than operating in separate domains, top-down and grassroots multifaith actors are interconnected and thus the concerns of official representatives and community members interact with one another which often involves the blurring between grassroots and top-down spheres of the movement. Representative bodies still involve a great deal of relational and creative work, as they are organisations where people must work together. Relational spheres, by the same token, can be sites where theological dialogue takes places and requires representational actors to participate. Relational spheres may also involve representative roles, and some organisations blend the two in their initiatives. We highlight this to note to the reader that representative and relational approaches are rarely dichotomous and can overlap with one another.

Relational bodies

Sacred Conversations is a local multifaith group that formed in Hobart, Tasmania, in 2018 by Julian McGarry. In Smith's interview with Julian, he explained that his interest in multifaith was inspired partly in his experiences being part of an exclusivist Christian denomination and undergoing a significant paradigm shift that made him more open to the value of other religions. He then came across an esoteric/philosophical text called The Urantia Book. The Urantia Book discusses the nature of God, reality and humankind and contains similar multifaith themes such as the unity of humanity under shared spiritual goals and experiences. He explained that the ideas in this book inspired him participate in the multifaith movement. Tasmania's main multifaith activity is initiated by Religions for Peace Tasmania, who diligently performs a representational role; however, Julian felt the need to initiate more personal relationships between religious communities, so he began Sacred Conversations. Julian hoped that this group would initiate a network that would eventually take on their own life and sees his role as its facilitator. The goal of the group, he explained, was to bring people together to facilitate 'exposure to other belief systems in an environment that was well controlled and respectful and safe'. Each month, Julian sends out a newsletter invitation and his attendees meet in the University of Tasmania's Multifaith Centre to have conversations on topics such as morality, philosophy, God and worship.

The Multifaith Centre is a tiny room that sits at the basement of the student association building, even its placement alludes to its subaltern status in comparison to the realms of officialdom occupied by organisations such as the FCCV. When Smith performed fieldwork at these meetings, Julian placed the chairs in concentric circles, so everyone is facing into the circle. A coffee table lay at its centre. Items on the coffee table included singing bowls, a tissue box, flowers, books and Julian's laptop. During the event, he runs the meeting in a way that evokes his background as a therapist and gently facilitates the discussion. The discussions are based around a wide range of spiritual topics from who is God, to social issues such as peacebuilding, and sometimes he has someone present on their own religious community. His approach to these meetings signals a high regard for people's emotional, inner and personal experiences of encountering people who are different from one another. The event revolves around people talking to each other, sometimes the discussion is slightly argumentative, other times there is an atmosphere of curiosity and learning. After a discussion, the participants are invited to informally have an 'afternoon tea' of tea, coffee and biscuits and the participants stand around chatting to one another.[2]

In contrast to representational bodies like the FCCV, we now narrow the frame to the local and grassroots to a group who operates on the fringes of the movement. Smaller and grassroots-led multifaith groups may lack the same access to resources and recognition, yet they are creative and critical spheres where the multifaith movement may expand into new directions, experiences and goals. Sacred Conversations receives no state funding or support, and it is by the generosity of the University of Tasmania that they are allowed to use the Multifaith Centre.[3] As we noted in the previous section, the dialogue-centred model posits that the multifaith movement's goal is to generate dialogue between traditions, not individuals. In the early 2000s, multifaith activity was dominated by Jewish, Christian and Muslim relations, while Hindu, Buddhist and Indigenous voices were sidelined, but great efforts have been made since to include minority religions (Halafoff 2013: 104). Yet, there is still work to be done. Halafoff argued that 'multifaith engagement should ideally strive to be inclusive of all diverse faiths and spiritualities, including Indigenous, Pagan, Hindu, Buddhist, Sikh, Jewish, Christian, Muslim, and New Religious Movements (NRMs)' (Halafoff 2013: 105). This inclusion should also extend to nonreligious worldviews (Halafoff 2013: 105). However, as Terry Shoemaker and James Edmonds (2016: 204) noted, the focus on representational religious identities at multifaith events, which they call the 'interfaith identity paradigm', is problematic when it comes to the inclusion of nonreligious people. It calls people to give themselves bounded and fixed identities based on the differentiation to the 'other', thus limiting the possibilities of movement by reinforcing normative ways of identifying with religious and spiritual worldviews (Shoemaker and Edmonds 2016: 205–6).

This section suggests that relational groups are zones where there is less pressure to perform the interfaith identity paradigm. Julian's purpose for Sacred Conversations is less about finding common causes of social action, dispersing official statements or identifying funding streams. Their emphasis is on fostering respectful ways of engaging with the religious other and facilitating personal transformations in how participants understand and relate to a religiously diverse world. Julian explained:

> It's a place where we come and have conversations about sacred subjects where we know we're going to come into contact with difference, but we'll learn to manage our feelings about that and hopefully we will learn new things that we didn't know before which may in some way shape us differently, might lead to some changes within ourselves. Hopefully a coming together of people in a more united sense.

Julian had a strong focus on the emotional work that goes into multifaith relationships. He wanted to foster emotions of safety, comfort and trust because these are key tools that facilitate the harrowing processes of encountering religious difference. He said, 'There's a lot at stake for a lot of people and nobody wants to be attacked.' He was also emphatic about the practices of multifaith relationships, rather than theological or philosophical ideas. For example, he spoke about the need to teach people how to listen to one another and create an atmosphere where they too will be listened to. Julian's approach echoed other multifaith actors who were interviewed, who commonly used words such as 'safety', 'trust' and 'respect' to describe the kinds of relationships they were fostering.

In interviews with attendees to the Sacred Conversations meetings several people admitted that they had marginal, complex or hybrid religious identities and did not see themselves as representative of any tradition. The goal of attending Sacred Conversations, for some interview participants attending, was not to represent their worldview but to learn about other religions and spiritualities as part of their own exploration of worldviews. One person suggested that their interview would not be useful because they had a unique interpretation of their tradition and could not give an official representation. Several participants found Sacred Conversations to be a space where they could comfortably occupy an ambiguous identity. However, Sacred Conversations does draw on representative models when speakers are invited to present on their religious tradition, to educate attendees on the main beliefs and practices. Furthermore, on an autoethnographic note, Smith attended these events identifying as nonreligious and did not always find attending these events compatible when faced with questions about how one understands God or what spiritual values motivated them. Shoemaker and Edmonds (2016) make a similar finding, whereby upfront religious identification is not always necessary but becomes implicit in the activities at the event. Thus, relational groups may be places where more ambiguous identities are included, but exclusions can still arrive. Attempts at inclusion can be uncomfortable and even fail.

Like most multifaith organisations, limited resources make running Sacred Conversations a continuous struggle for Julian. In the interview, Smith asked Julian what kind of resources he thought Sacred Conversations needed to continue to run and grow. He said it needed more 'exposure' and for more people to be made aware of it. He had trouble convincing religious groups to provide ongoing representatives, found that motivating volunteers was difficult and struggled to attract new members. He recognised that multifaith work involved building up trust over time and persisting in encouraging people to join. Julian demonstrated a great deal of hope and perseverance, which Smith also found reflected in other multifaith volunteers she met whilst attending multifaith events.

> I've determined interfaith is definitely a long-term thing, you have to have a long-term view of things. It's not something that's going to happen rapidly and you could easily get discouraged and think 'oh well maybe I don't get huge turnups at the meeting and don't get a lot of keen interest from the faith organisations' but I said 'Julian, you've just got to be patient and you've just got to plug away and you keep sending invitation out,' they don't respond to it, you do it again.

Julian's persevering attitude reflects a ruggedness of grassroots multifaith work that appeared in other interviews with volunteering multifaith actors. Terry Sussmilch, who is the branch convenor for Religions for Peace Tasmania, and a long-serving volunteer, emphasised that most of the multifaith movement was ran by volunteers who 'pack a punch'. Grassroots groups have greater freedom to choose what they do according to their goals, concerns and experiences without the pressures that come with state funding. Also, there is greater breadth for participants who do not fit into a single religious tradition to join the meetings, without being bound to representing the official positions of their traditions. Albeit sometimes finding representational voices is also important for groups like Sacred Conversations who require support from more influential representative bodies to continue their work. Their approach, however, reflects a more interpersonal and embodied perspective of multifaith as it focuses upon the work of building respectful relationships between religiously diverse individuals and communities.

Discussion/conclusion

The goal of this chapter is to emphasise that these organisations are embodied, lived and material. They come into being through the actions taken by the people who work on the ground. Representational bodies play a balancing act between the realms of officialdom, global events and transatlantic networks, and the local concerns of their communities. Grassroots bodies may lack the same access to resources and recognition, yet they are creative and critical spheres where the multifaith movement may expand into new directions, experiences and goals. Many Millennials and Gen Z do not hold positions of leadership in their religious organisations, they do not belong to any particular religious institution, or they are not given the legitimate authority to act as representatives in multifaith organisations (Smith 2022). Therefore, a representational approach to multifaith has limited appeal for younger generations. However, in organisations that have a relational approach, where representational status is unnecessary, young people may find more inclusion. Yet, Sacred Conversations also had few young people. The data suggests that young people tend to stay within multifaith organisations who have a youth-focus because they are allowed to lead in a way that better reflects their goals, concerns and experiences (Halafoff and Gobey 2018; Halafoff 2020; Smith 2022). Hence, relational bodies too may have work to do in terms of creating spaces where young people can lead.

Religious leaders have a great deal of influence and power to enact broad social change, but they are also constrained in what kinds of activities they can be involved in. Climate change, for example is considered a divisive topic in Australia; therefore involvement in common social action for climate change is seen as problematic by some. Again, this cause has been taken up by grassroots relational multifaith bodies, the most notable example being the Australian Religious Response to Climate Change (ARRCC) (see Smith and Halafoff 2020). Nevertheless, this is not to say that the reluctance to be involved in social issues due to fears of divisiveness can escape critique. Most of the multifaith movement are made up volunteers, and many are currently not represented in the leadership of multifaith organisations. The dialogue-centred model, which places emphasis on multifaith as a dialogue between religious traditions delegated through the educated elite of traditions, excludes other forms of religion and spirituality – such as holistic spirituality, NRMs, Indigenous, naturalistic or nonreligious voices. The focus on religious leadership also means that people who are less likely to hold leadership positions in religious traditions, such as women and young people, are excluded from these spheres of power and influence. By the same token, grassroots groups may also be spheres of exclusion when one considers other intersectional dynamics at play. For example, nonreligious and NRM participants can experience implicit exclusions.

The generational changes occurring in the multifaith movement, and the subsequent crisis of succession, may indicate that the balance of power within the multifaith movement is subject to change. In the context of decline in state support for multifaith initiatives, rising nonreligion, worldview complexity and the emerging generations, the multifaith movement may need to call upon its capacity to be '*responsive, preventive, creative, collaborative, radically reflexive* and *deliberative*' (Halafoff 2013: 52, italics in original) and develop a new vision for the changing times. In fact, there are several organisations, such as Youth PoWR, who are already re-articulating the cosmopolitan vision of the multifaith movement. Representational and relational bodies must work collaboratively with each other – they often do. Representational bodies have a large sphere of influence and can enact broad social change. Relational groups are potentially more inclusive, they are more willing to accept people who occupy marginal positions as participants and can be hotbeds of creativity and critical thought. However, they operate on smaller scales, can struggle to find recognition and support and, therefore, their sphere of influence is limited. Reconciliation between these approaches requires constant negotiation between the local and global, relational and representative, and the grassroots and top-down. Yet, the fluidity of the multifaith movement allows multifaith organisations to shift according to the changing times.

Notes

1 This research was part of doctoral thesis conducted by Geraldine Smith, under the supervision of Anna Halafoff and Douglas Ezzy.
2 This research, and the subsequent interviews, had ethics approval as part of Smith's research. See Smith (2022) for more details.
3 'Sacred Conversations' meetings now take place in the Baha'i Centre for Learning for Tasmania.

References

Australian Bureau of Statistics. 2022. '2021 Census Shows Changes in Australia's Religious Diversity'. *Australian Bureau of Statistics*, Canberra, https://www.abs.gov.

au/media-centre/media-releases/2021-census-shows-changes-australias-religious-diversity. Accessed 13 July 2022.

Australian Bureau of Statistics. 2017. '2016 Census Data Reveals "No Religion" Is Rising Fast'. *Australian Bureau of Statistics*. https://www.abs.gov.au/AUSSTATS/abs@.nsf/mediareleasesbyReleaseDate/7E65A144540551D7CA258148000E2B85. Accessed 13 July 2022.

Beck, U. 2006. *The Cosmopolitan Vision*. Cambridge: Polity Press.

Bouma, G., Halafoff, A. and Barton, G. 2022. 'Worldview Complexity: The Challenges of Intersecting Diversities for Conceptualising Diversity'. *Social Compass* 69(2): 186–204.

Brodeur, P. 2005. 'From the Margins to the Centres of Power: The Increasing Relevance of the Global Interfaith Movement'. *Crosscurrents* 55(1): 42–53.

Brodeur, P., and Patel, E. (eds). 2006. *Building the Interfaith Youth Movement: Beyond Dialogue to Action*. Lanham: Rowman & Littlefield.

Cornille, C. 2008. *The Im-possibility of Interreligious Dialogue*. New York: Crossroad Publishing.

Cotter, C. R., and Robertson, D. G. (eds). 2016. *After World Religions: Reconstructing Religious Studies*. New York: Routledge-Taylor & Francis.

Fahy, J., and Bock, J.-J. 2018, *Beyond Dialogue? Interfaith Engagement in Delhi, Doha and London, Woolf Institute*. https://www.researchgate.net/publication/326682225_Beyond_Dialogue_Interfaith_Engagement_in_Delhi_Doha_and_London. Accessed 1 May 2019.

Fahy, J., and Bock, J.-J. (eds). 2020 *The Interfaith Movement: Mobilising Religious Diversity in the 21st Century*. New York: Routledge.

Faith Communities Council of Victoria. 2019. Statement on Acts of Violence on Two Mosques in Christchurch, New Zealand. https://www.faithvictoria.org.au/news-a-articles/780-statement-on-acts-of-violence-on-two-mosques-in-christchurch-new-zealand. Accessed 1 May 2020.

Furseth, I. 2018. *Religious Complexity in the Public Sphere: Comparing Nordic Countries*. Cham: Springer International Publishing.

Griera, M. 2019. 'Interreligious Events in the Public Space: Performing Togetherness in Times of Religious Pluralism'. In M. Moyaert (ed.), *Interreligious Relations and the Negotiation of Ritual Boundaries*. Cham: Springer International Publishing, 35–55.

Halafoff, A. 2013. *The Multifaith Movement: Global Risks and Cosmopolitan Solutions*. Dordrecht: Springer Netherlands.

Halafoff, A. 2016. 'Governance and Religious Diversity in Australian Multifaith Relations and Religious Instruction in the State of Victoria'. In A. Dawson (ed.), *The Politics and Practice of Religious Diversity: National Contexts, Global Issues*. New York: Routledge, 101–17.

Halafoff, A. 2020. 'InterAction Australia: Countering the Politics of Fear with Netpeace'. In J. Fahy, and J.-J. Bock (eds), *The Interfaith Movement: Mobilising Religious Diversity in the 21st Century*. New York: Routledge, 68–86.

Halafoff, A., and Gobey, L. 2018. '"Whatever"? Religion, Youth, and Identity in 21st Century Australia'. In P. L. Gareau, S. Culham Bullivant and P. Beyer (eds), *Youth, Religion, and Identity in a Globalizing Context*. Leiden: Brill, 255–77.

Halafoff, A., Shipley, H., Young, P. D., Singleton, A., Rasmussen, M. L., and Bouma, G. 2020. 'Complex, Critical and Caring: Young People's Diverse Religious, Spiritual and Non-Religious Worldviews in Australia and Canada'. *Religions* 11(4): 1–12.

Hedges, P. 2010. *Controversies in Interreligious Dialogue and the Theology of Religions*. London: SCM Press.

Knitter, P. F. 1995. *One Earth, Many Religions: Multifaith Dialogue and Global Responsibility*. New York, Maryknoll: Orbis Books.

Kwok, P.-L. 2005, *Postcolonial Imagination and Feminist Theology*. London: SCM Press.

McGuire, M. B. 2008. *Lived Religion*. Oxford: Oxford University Press.

Meyer, B. 2012. *Mediation and the Genesis of Presence: Towards a Material Approach to Religion*. Utrecht: Faculteit Geesteswetenschappen, Universiteit Utrecht.

Moyaert, M. 2019. *Interreligious Relations and the Negotiation of Ritual Boundaries: Explorations in Interrituality*. Cham: Springer International Publishing.

Multicultural Centre for Women's Health (MCWH). 2019. 'About the Project'. https://www.mcwh.com.au/project/faith-communities-supporting-healthy-family-relationships/. Accessed 7 February 2023.

Orsi, R. A. 2003. 'Is the Study of Lived Religion Irrelevant to the World We Live In? Special Presidential Plenary Address, Society for the Scientific Study of Religion, Salt Lake City, November 2, 2002'. *Journal for the Scientific Study of Religion* 42(2): 169–74.

Patel, E. 2016. *Interfaith Leadership: A Primer*. Boston: Beacon Press.

Patel, E., and Meyer, C. 2010. 'Religious Education for Interfaith Leadership'. *Religious Education* 105(1): 16–19.

Patel, E., Kunze, A., and Silverman, N. 2008. 'Storytelling Is a Key Methodology for Interfaith Youth Work'. *Journal of Ecumenical Studies* 43(2): 35–46.

Scheffler, T. 2007. 'Interreligious Dialogue and Peacebuilding'. *Die Friedens-Warte* 82(2/3): 73–87.

Singleton, A., Halafoff, A., Rasmussen, M. L., and Bouma, G. 2021. *Freedoms, Faiths and Futures: Teenage Australians on Religion, Sexuality and Diversity*. London: Bloomsbury.

Shipley, H. 2018. 'Apathy or Misunderstanding? Youth's Reflections on Their Religious Identity in Canada'. In P. L. Gareau, S. C. Bullivant and P. Beyer (eds), *Youth, Religion, and Identity in a Globalizing Context*. Leiden: Brill, 191–211.

Shipley, H., Young, P., and Cuthbertson, I. A. 2016. 'Religion, Gender, and Sexuality among Youth in Canada: Some Preliminary Findings'. *Bulletin for the Study of Religion* 45(1): 17–26.

Shoemaker, T., and Edmonds, J. 2016. 'The Limits of Interfaith? Interfaith Identities, Emerging Potentialities, and Exclusivity'. *Culture and Religion* 17(2): 200–12.

Smith, G., and Halafoff, A. 2020. 'Multifaith Third Spaces: Digital Activism, Netpeace, and the Australian Religious Response to Climate Change'. *Religions* 11(105): 1–16.

Smith, G. 2022, 'From Dialogue to Activism: How to Get Generation Z and Millennials to Participate in the Multifaith Movement in Australia'. *Social Compass* 69(1): 648–65.

Swamy, M. 2016. *The Problem with Interreligious Dialogue: Plurality, Conflict and Elitism in Hindu–Christian–Muslim Relations.* London: Bloomsbury Academic.

Swidler, L. 1983. 'The Dialogue Decalogue: Ground Rules for Interreligious Dialogue'. *Horizons*, 10(2): 348–51.

Thiessen, J., and Wilkins-Laflamme, S. 2017. 'Becoming a Religious None: Irreligious Socialization and Disaffiliation'. *Journal for the Scientific Study of Religion* 56(1): 64–82.

7

Legislation and Religious Diversity

Douglas Ezzy, Rebecca Banham, Lori G. Beaman and Geraldine Smith

Introduction

In this chapter we examine the impact of the law on the negotiation of religious diversity in Australia. Effective religious anti-discrimination and anti-vilification legislation protects members of minority religions, including Muslims, Hindus, Buddhists, Sikhs, Jews, Pagans and others from some of the harmful discrimination and vilification they too commonly experience. However, effective laws are not legislated federally, and state legislation varies significantly in its coverage and nature (Rees, Rice and Allen 2018).

Legislation to protect religious freedom has often not served to protect members of religious minorities. Saba Mahmood (2015: 145) argues: 'Through much of its modern history, the right to religious liberty has served as a means to either promote campaigns of religious proselytization to win Christian converts or to consolidate the majoritarian ethos of the emergent modern state.' There are elements of this in the proposed, but now withdrawn, federal Religious Discrimination Bill, which is discussed below. It would have legalised forms of discrimination that benefit privileged conservative Christian organisations and harm minority religions, including Islam, Hinduism, Buddhism and Sikhism.

The chapter begins with a discussion of the vilification and discrimination that religious minorities experience. This is documented in their submissions to the first exposure draft of the federal Religious Discrimination Bill. Next, we demonstrate that the Victorian religious anti-discrimination and equal opportunity legislation reduces these harms. We focus on two main aspects: (1) the facilitation of reflective self-understanding by privileged Christian groups and (2) the process of legal agonism that constrains the public expression of harmful attitudes and behaviours. We then move back to a national perspective through an analysis of submissions by privileged Christian conservatives to the first exposure draft of the federal Religious Discrimination Bill. Not all Christians are conservative, and many are not privileged. However, there is a group of conservative Christian organisations who wield considerable institutional and financial power who are actively seeking to shape Australian responses to religious diversity in ways that maintain their power and privilege.

Christian privilege is a key theme in the following analysis. By privilege, we mean that some Christian social actors and institutions have considerable financial resources and institutional influence in Australian society. This privilege is associated with power. For example, the Australian Catholic Bishops Conference notes:

> The Catholic Church provides Australia's largest non-government grouping of hospitals, aged and community care services, providing approximately 10 per cent of health care services in Australia. It provides social services and support to more than 450,000 people across Australia each year. There are more than 1,750 Catholic schools with more than 94,000 staff providing education to more than 765,000 Australian students. (Australian Catholic Bishops Conference 2019: 1)

The policies and practices of Catholic education, healthcare and social welfare have broad impacts on the general Australian population. This influence is not simply a product of the number of Catholics in Australia. The influence is also a product of very substantial government funding they receive to provide education, healthcare and welfare provision. That is to say, state support is both tacit and explicit. When Christian conservatives, including some Catholics, argue for their right to engage in discriminatory practices in these sorts of organisations, they are arguing to be allowed to engage in practices that have a broad impact on the Australian population well beyond the impact on practising Catholics.

While somewhat smaller in scale, Christian groups such as the Salvation Army, Anglicare, the Baptist Union and the Uniting Church are also privileged and powerful as a product of their size and involvement in government-funded service provision to the Australian public. Christians also dominate in the provision of classes on Special Religious Instruction in the state of Victoria (Halafoff 2016). Other religious groups, such as Muslims, Hindus, Buddhists, Sikhs and Pagans, do not have anything similar to these forms of institutional and financial power.

The discussion in this chapter is not about what religious people might do in their churches, synagogues, temples or mosques. We do not discuss, for example, the movement for gender equality in various Christian groups. Rather the focus of the chapter is on acceptable behaviour in the public sphere. For example, is it acceptable for Muslims, Buddhists, Hindus and Sikhs to be discriminated against in the context of religiously affiliated government-funded schools, hospitals, social welfare and aged care, which provide services to the general public?

We agree with Lori Beaman (2017) that it is a mistake to overemphasise the conflictual and problematic nature of the negotiation of religious difference. There is an ethic of equality and respect that is deeply embedded in everyday social practices where religious difference is negotiated in unproblematic and constructive ways. Similarly, Anna Halafoff's (2013) description of cosmopolitanism in the Interfaith movement begins with a recognition of the interdependence of all life and combines a respect for diversity with an emphasis on equal rights and radical reflexivity. Both deep equality and cosmopolitanism are central to diverse religious communities living well together, as is clearly described in other chapters in this volume (for example, see Chapter 6 on Interfaith). Alongside these, in this chapter we argue that the law plays a role in the negotiation of heated conflicts which are sometimes associated with religious difference, power and privilege.

We argue that effective religious anti-discrimination and anti-vilification laws provide 'a moral etiquette for relating to' otherness by imposing limits on powerful and privileged groups and individuals that protect people's right to live free from vilification and discrimination (Ezzy 2018: 279; Ezzy, Banham and Beaman 2022). This means that religiously motivated attitudes might sometimes still be hateful, discriminatory or profoundly offensive. What we describe as 'legal agonism' (Ezzy, Banham and Beaman. 2022) *constrains* such attitudes, restricting their public expression. Courts and administrative tribunals provide venues for negotiating religious difference that can contribute to such legal agonism. The legal forums require participants to respect the participants' right to present their positions, even if their views are passionately different.

Religious discrimination legislation in Australia

Australia does not currently have federal religious anti-discrimination or anti-vilification legislation. However, in 2019 the Australian attorney general released the first exposure draft of the Religious Discrimination Bill 2019 and associated legislation (Australian Government 2019). Submissions were invited from the Australian public. We conducted a thematic analysis of some of the submissions, focusing on submissions from key religious groups. There are over 6,000 submissions, and we only examined a selection of them. The proposed Australian federal legislation has now been withdrawn and, as a result of a change of government, is unlikely to be reintroduced.

All three versions of the federal Religious Discrimination Bill have two key, and quite different, aspects: a 'shield' and a 'sword' (Elphick, Maguire and Hilkemeijer 2019; Beck 2021). First, the legislation would protect religious and nonreligious people from being discriminated against on the basis of their faith or lack of faith (a 'shield'). This aim is widely supported, particularly by members of minority religions. For example, when the third version of this legislation was introduced into federal parliament, one of the few Muslims in parliament, Labor MP Anne Aly, 'spoke from her experience as Muslim woman about the need for religious discrimination protections to pass' (Karp 2022: 1).

Second, the legislation allows religious people and religious organisations to discriminate against other people where the conduct is backed by genuinely held religious beliefs (a 'sword'). This second aspect is highly controversial because it makes some harmful behaviours legal if they are religiously motivated. It is this 'sword' aspect of the legislation that would result in the consolidation of Christian privilege and influence and facilitate their proselytization activities, noted by Mahmood (2015) above. This aspect of the legislation was present in the first exposure draft, although it was more developed in later drafts (Elphick, Maguire and Hilkemeijer 2019). The third draft of the bill makes it explicit that religiously affiliated schools, hospitals and aged care facilities would be able to discriminate in their employment of staff to maintain their 'religious ethos' (Beck 2021: 1). 'For example, a Catholic hospital would be able to have a Catholics-only hiring policy' (Beck 2021: 1).

Much of the public and parliamentary debate focused on the treatment of LGBTQ+ students. It is unclear to what extent the legislation would also be used by Christian organisations to discriminate against Muslims, Hindus, Buddhists, Sikhs, members of other religious minorities and nonreligious people. Discrimination and vilification towards religious minorities are certainly enabled by the legislation. Commenting on the 'sword' aspect of the second exposure draft, Simon Rice (2020: 1) observed: 'A person of one religious belief will be free to disparage, demean and humiliate a person of another religious belief, even within the same faith: Hindus against Christians, Buddhists against Muslims, Orthodox Jews against progressive Jews, Catholics against Anglicans, or Shia against Sunni Muslims.'

The chapter also discusses religious anti-discrimination and equal opportunity legislation in the state of Victoria, Australia. Victoria has developed one of Australia's most sophisticated legislative responses to religious diversity. Victoria is unique in Australia for having both the Equal Opportunity Act 1995/2010 and the Racial and Religious Tolerance Act 2001 (RRTA). The Victorian legislation exemplifies the 'shield' aspect of such legislation. Cases drawing on this legislation are typically heard first in the Victorian Civil and Administrative Tribunal (VCAT). We interviewed twelve people who had appeared before VCAT in relation to either the RRTA or the Equal Opportunity Act, and/or had been subjected to legal and/or police action, and/or were well networked in their community with extensive relevant knowledge (see Ezzy, Banham and Beaman 2021 for details). We also reviewed all publicly available cases heard at VCAT from 2001 until June 2018 that deal substantially with religion (see Ezzy, Banham and Beaman 2022 for details). The data relating to Victoria reported below is from these two studies.

We use the term 'Concerned Minorities' to refer to religious groups including Jews, Muslims, Hindus, Buddhists, Sikhs, Pagans and other religious minorities. We use the term 'Privileged Conservatives' to refer to large Christian organisations, typically conservative in orientation, and some smaller groups who share their goals. We also note that our analysis often focuses on statements made by the leadership of groups. It is probable that the views of the laity of these groups may be different, at least to some extent, to these statements by the leadership, as McIvor (2020) suggests is the case for conservative Christians in the UK.

The Concerned Minorities

Submissions made by the Concerned Minorities to the first exposure draft of the federal Religious Discrimination Bill emphasise the desire of individuals to practise their religion in all spheres of life without being subject to discrimination and vilification. Submissions in this category include *Australian Jewish Association, Australian Sikh Association and United Sikhs, Christian Science, Forum of Australia's Islamic Relations (FAIR), Joint Submission by the Australian Muslim Community, Rabbinical Council of Australia and New Zealand* and *the Australian Federation of Islamic Councils.*

The main concern of submissions made by Islamic bodies is for strong laws that clearly penalise discrimination and vilification. The Forum on Australia's

Islamic Relations Inc. (FAIR) (2019) describe the behaviours that will not be protected by the bill, such as verbal abuse or threats, physical assault, non-verbal harassment, written harassment, and damage or graffiti. They provide a long list of disturbing concrete reports of 'what Australian-Muslims have been facing for the larger part of the past two decades' such as women being attacked on trains, verbal abuse on the street, being followed, being reported to the police and online threats (FAIR 2019: 4). Similarly, the Joint Submission from the Australian Muslim Community (2019) also emphasises the frequency of attacks against Muslims and emphasise the need for better protections in the bill.

The Forum of Islamic Relations Inc. (2019) recounts cases from the report on *Islamophobia in Australia* (Iner 2019). These include physical assaults such as 'throwing eggs, abuse, screaming (Case 230), grabbing the breast of a young Australian Muslim woman and repeatedly saying "we are going to bomb you all" (Case 226) and grabbing the victim by the neck and hair, forcing her head into the wall of the train carriage several times (Case 199)' (Forum of Islamic Relations Inc 2019: 4). They also list cases of verbal abuse and threats such as 'calling the victim "evil and violent" for wearing the hijab and ranting vitriol for 13 minutes (Case 151) and threats like "we bury you in pig bits to match your gutless yellow spines. ..." (Case 22)' (Forum of Islamic Relations Inc 2019: 4). Finally, they note cases of non-verbal abuse such as 'mocking gestures, stalking, negative stares and use of inappropriate images' and 'placing an innocent woman under scrutiny by making a false report to the police (Case 232)' (Forum of Islamic Relations Inc 2019: 4).

Some Concerned Minorities raise specific concerns regarding how the bill would impact their ability to live out their religious identity. For example, the submission by the Australian Sikh Association and United Sikhs (2019) said that the bill needs to go further to protect their right to adorn their articles of faith, such as a turban and kirpan, in the workplace, school and in everyday life. They describe several experiences of events in which Sikhs have been subject to discrimination due to a lack of accommodation for their articles of faith. For example, they describe being made to remove their turban at construction sites and not being allowed to ride a bike without a helmet. They argue that the bill may be used to discriminate by allowing employers to impose rules of conduct that are claimed to be 'inherent requirements' of the work.

Some larger Christian groups express views that are supportive of the Concerned Minorities. The Uniting Church in Australia (2019: 2), for example, convey a concern that the Bill 'leans too heavily in favour of religious freedom over other rights'. They argue for legislation that creates a society that encourages 'mutual respect and is free from discrimination for everyone'. There are a group of similar submissions from Christian groups and individuals, and these are quite different to the submissions made by the Privileged Conservatives.

The concrete, often violent, and harmful nature of the experiences recounted in the submissions by the Concerned Minorities underline the importance of effective religious anti-discrimination and anti-vilification legislation. Their hopes are oriented towards the future, forming a more egalitarian, inclusive and respectful multifaith Australian society. Their experiences are in stark contrast to the concerns of the Privileged Conservatives, who rarely recount evidence of similar concrete harms, and are mainly concerned with their desire to themselves engage in practices that may harm others, as is demonstrated below. Their concerns are more oriented towards preserving past traditions and heritage, often paying little attention to the harms these cause (see Beaman 2020). We turn now to the Victorian religious anti-discrimination and anti-vilification legislation to examine how members of religious minorities can be effectively protected by legislation.

The law and transformative self-reflection

The Victorian religious anti-discrimination and anti-vilification legislation effectively protect members of religious minorities from some aspects of discrimination and vilification. First, we examine how the Victorian legislation enables transformative self-reflection, typically by privileged Christian organisations, to either make explicit, or to remove, discriminatory practices. Second, we examine how the legislation constrains the expression of harmful attitudes and behaviours through 'legal agonism'.

Some of the cases that go before VCAT involve making visible or explicit previously hidden or latent discriminations, exclusions and othering. The case of *Rocca v St Columba's College Ltd & Rogers* is one in which previously hidden discrimination was made explicit. Here, the Catholic school St Columba's College denied enrolment to a Greek Orthodox eleven-year-old as a result of an enrolment policy prioritising the enrolment of Catholic students. As Catholic schools are legally permitted to prioritise Catholic students, the school was not required to change its discriminatory enrolment procedures. As a result of the case, however, this practice was made explicit, and St Columba's College was obliged to clarify their enrolment procedures (Ezzy, Banham and Beaman 2022).

Other cases result in Christian groups engaging in self-reflection leading to the removal of discriminatory practices. As tribunals have different procedures to judicial courts, transformative self-reflection is encouraged by VCAT through negotiated outcomes which emphasise mediation and conciliation (Ezzy, Banham and Beaman 2022). Tribunals are also more oriented towards a pragmatic resolution of an issue, with an orientation to constructive future action, rather than the more adversarial and punitive approach of judicial courts.

Arora v Melton Christian College provides an excellent example of this process that we have analysed in detail elsewhere (Ezzy, Banham and Beaman 2022). The Sikh Arora family sought to enrol their five-year-old son Sidhak at Melton Christian College (MCC), a non-denominational Christian school, in March 2016. We interviewed a Sikh from Melton, who was familiar with the details of the MCC case. He described it as follows:

> [A Sikh man] wanted his son to go to the Melton Christian College, or Christian school. He put the application in, and when they interviewed the child, they saw the patka, the head covering on child's head. The person who was [doing the] interview said, 'you won't be accepted in the school due to the head covering. So, either you cut your son's hair, and not wear the patka. Or if you want, we will refuse the admission'. So, [the Sikh man] asked them to put [it in writing]. And they put it in [writing] and sent a letter to him. And then the whole community was involved in the case at VCAT which went in the community's favour. Then the school allowed [the young boy] to go to [to the school].

Particularly notable in this case is 'the way in which MCC's internal processes, which had remained largely out of view, were rendered visible and thus subject to scrutiny' (Ezzy, Banham and Beaman 2022: 29). The case made clear that the discrimination towards the Sikh student occurred because of his clearly non-Christian appearance, rather than simply because he was a Sikh. This became apparent when a representative of the school explained the school's uniform policy, saying that 'it was ok for a student not [to] be Christian, so long as the student did not look like they were not a Christian' (para. 66.w.). This discriminatory uniform policy would not create a problem for most students – for example, Christian students, those with no religion or those from other religions who do not wear clothing that distinguished them as non-Christian – and so had escaped scrutiny. This VCAT case brought by a Sikh student made explicit the previously hidden discriminatory policy.

VCAT's approach to resolving this issue was oriented towards the future, addressing the discriminatory exclusion (that is to say 'future forming'; see

Beaman 2020), rather than adopting a punitive approach. J. Grainger stated that 'allowing Sidhak to wear a patka in the same colour of the school uniform is a … reasonable accommodation' (para. 102). As a result, the uniform policy of the school was changed and Sidhak was enrolled at the school. The school expressed 'regret [with] the difficulties that took place with respect to the enrolment' (Grewal 2021). This is an example of how a privileged Christian institution was prompted to engage in constructive reflection on its practices, resulting in a significantly more inclusive outcome (Ezzy, Banham and Beaman 2021).

The Sikh interviewee's comments on this are insightful. He highlights how the financial and institutional power and privilege of Christians serves to exclude Sikhs. He also points to the importance of the ability to be able to confront such discriminatory practices:

> We thought we would never win [the case] because [the Christians] were the owners of the school and what they said we had to follow. [The Sikhs] didn't have the knowledge that they could challenge that. But now [the Sikhs are] saying this is really good for the community. We can practice the way we are.

We also interviewed a Christian who was familiar with a similar case that went before the Tribunal involving a Christian organisation and the treatment of a member of a minority religion. That interviewee said:

> I think we did have two religious minorities, both feeling besieged, both feeling discriminated against. A Christian organization feeling discriminated against because [acceptance of religious difference] was an imposition on them. [And a religious minority] feeling like the exclusion … was discrimination against them and was hardship.

Note the structure of these comments from the Christian interviewee. The interviewee characterises the requirement to treat a member of a religious minority with respect as 'discrimination' against Christians. This is a surprising use of the term 'discrimination', when it is the member of the religious minority that was harmed by these actions, not the Christian. It is also surprising that the interviewee describes the experiences of both groups as 'feeling besieged'. This sense of 'feeling besieged' is a good indicator of the sorts of 'harm' that some Christians report. Treating members of religious minorities with equality makes some Christians feel very uncomfortable. This is at the heart of their sense of 'feeling besieged' and the 'harm' they experience. These Christians rarely report any concrete personal experience of violence or harm.

In contrast, the experiences of members of religious minorities are quite different. Their experiences of discrimination do not just cause them discomfort, they cause them serious harm and exclusion: a halal shop is vandalised, a Sikh is excluded from a school, people in power speak hateful things about them that result in them being vilified and violently attacked. Christians rarely describe experiences of this nature. Thus, the Christian characterisation of themselves as a besieged minority belies the privilege that undergirds their discriminatory practices of exclusion. What is at issue, we argue, is the threat to power and the right to discriminate associated with it. This is a classic move among privileged groups, whether the analysis is of privilege rooted in religion, race or gender.

It is hard to know how widely the MCC's changed uniform policy was accepted among the Christians involved in the MCC school. It is likely that some people's views were changed while others remained unconvinced that Sikh students should be allowed to wear clothing that publicly displays their non-Christian religious identities. This leads into a more detailed discussion of legal agonism.

Legal agonism: The constraint of harmful attitudes

Legal agonism *constrains* harmful attitudes and practices, restricting their public expression. This is clearly demonstrated in the case between the Islamic Council of Victoria and the evangelical Christian group Catch the Fire Ministries (*Islamic Council of Victoria Inc v Catch the Fire Ministries Inc*, and the subsequent appeal: *Catch the Fire Ministries Inc and Ors v Islamic Council of Victoria Inc and Anor*). It involved an allegation that Catch the Fire Ministries had vilified Islam at a public event (Brennan 2011; Deen 2008; Ezzy 2013, 2018; Gelber 2011). The consequence of this case was to effectively constrain the public expression of Islamophobia. This has been discussed extensively elsewhere (Ezzy, Banham and Beaman 2021, 2022).

A less discussed VCAT case illustrates that the same process can be found in the conflict between Olivia Watts and Councillor Rob Wilson from the Victorian council of Casey (Ezzy 2013). Watts, a Witch, made a complaint to VCAT against Wilson, a Christian. The issue began in June 2003 when 'the City of Casey's Rob Wilson … issued a press release claiming that a satanic cult was about to take over the city', naming Olivia Watts (Strong 2003: 2). In the six months after this Watts experienced considerable personal harm: 'Her business on the city's outer suburban fringe has collapsed; she has been physically attacked; and her home and car vandalised' (Strong 2003: 2). The case was resolved through negotiation and did not go to trial at VCAT, as 'Councillor Wilson agreed to "make no other comment on Ms Watt's faith" and acknowledged "all followers of lawful religions may practice their faith without vilification"' (Ezzy 2013: 205).

Witchcraft is a minority religion that began in the 1970s in Australia and grew rapidly in the 1990s. Paganism is an umbrella term that includes Witches, who make up the largest subgroup of Pagans, with other groups including Druids, Goddess Spirituality practitioners and a variety of other smaller traditions. At the 2016 Census 0.12 per cent Australians identified as Pagan and 0.15 per cent in the 2011 Census (ABS 2022). The beliefs and practices vary significantly but typically focus on a view of this earth as sacred and a celebration of the seasonal cycles through festivals and rituals (Berger and Ezzy 2007). Witchcraft remains a highly stigmatised religion in Australia, despite the positive media exposure it has received, particularly through positive portrayals in movies and TV series. Some Christians are particularly uncomfortable with Pagans and Witches.

This structure of power, privilege and harm is important in the Watts and Wilson case. Wilson is a Christian and was a member of a local council, both positions associated with considerable social power, resources and influence. Wilson did not describe any concrete experiences of harm he had experienced. Rather, he focused on Olivia Watts's desire to be elected to the local council which he saw as threatening to the traditional dominance of Christian values in society. In contrast, Watts comes from a stigmatised minority religion and reported experiencing considerable financial harm and physical violence as a result of the incident.

We interviewed a Pagan who lived in Casey at the time of this incident and was very familiar with the details of the case. He reported that fundamentalist Christianity had a strong presence in Casey. Two or three times a month Christians would knock on his door seeking to convert him: 'The Jehovah's Witnesses, obviously, the Seventh-day Adventists, various varieties of Baptist denominations.'

The incident and sensationalist media surrounding it had a broad negative impact on Pagans:

> I think it certainly made people more aware at the time of displaying [Pagan] religious insignia, pentacles around the neck, things like that. ... Certainly, those who are in a more vulnerable environment, such as schools for example, would have had to be a lot more careful. I stopped doing worship practices outside in the backyard in case neighbors were aware. I didn't want to draw any attention to myself.

This case ... was ... based on mistaken beliefs about [a] person's attributes, beliefs, and practices. The Racial and Religious Tolerance Act gave those of us who are affected by this a civilized method of redressing that victimization. (Casey Pagan)

Talking about the broader impact of the case, the Casey Pagan said that he observed a change in the way that Christians talked about Pagans:

The rhetoric changed very much in terms of what Christian communities were willing to say about Pagans. I think they understood that there is a Pagan community out there, and that there are people willing to stand up and refute the claims, which had up until that point gone pretty much unchallenged. I think it came as a big shock to a number of Christians who had been putting this stuff out there, appealing to their own base [... I'm not sure] whether they actually stopped that or [perhaps they were] just more picky about not being willing to express it in public forums, to the press, or go on the public record to talk about these things. (Casey Pagan)

The structure of this analysis by the Casey Pagan is insightful. Previously, there was an unchallenged conservative Christian narrative that imagined Pagans as a dangerous and threatening influence on society. As a result of the VCAT case, some conservative Christians have now understood that this way of talking about Pagans is not acceptable in public forums of a religiously diverse society. Wilson publicly acknowledged that 'all followers of lawful religions may practice their faith without vilification' (Ezzy 2013: 205). This is a clear example of a change in the public rhetoric similar to the change associated with the Christians involved in the Catch the Fire case (Ezzy, Banham and Beaman 2022). In both cases, a legal appeal using the Victorian legislation resulted in constraints on the expression of potentially harmful and derogatory views about Muslims and Pagans. In both cases public statements were made by conservative Christians that explicitly accept the rights of religious 'others' to freely practise their religion. However, while Christians such as Cr Wilson and the leaders of Catch the Fire have now constrained their public expression of derogatory views of Muslims and Pagans, it is also probable that many conservative Christians retain their distrustful and fearful views of Muslims and Pagans. That is precisely what we mean by 'legal agonism' that the legal negotiation of religious conflict has productive outcomes for *public* expressions that reduces discrimination and vilification experienced by members of religious minorities.

Privileged Conservatives

Finally, we turn to examine a group of submissions from the Privileged Conservatives to the first exposure draft of the federal Religious Discrimination Bill. These actors are typically Christian organisations who are powerful stakeholders in Australian culture and the service provision economy, or are minority religions whose goals align with these stakeholders. Submissions we examined in this category include the *Australian Catholic Bishops Conference*, *Australian Christian Lobby*, *NSW Ecumenical Council*, *Sydney Diocese of the Anglican Church*, *the Executive Council of Australian Jewry* and *Freedom for Faith*, which is endorsed by *Anglicare, Baptist Association of NSW & ACT, United Shia Islamic Foundation* and *The Presbyterian Church in Australia*.

In these submissions, the Privileged Conservatives argue that religious voices are at risk of being suppressed in the Australian public sphere. For example, the NSW Ecumenical Council quotes David Gill: 'Most churches are suffering from a sort of institutional post-traumatic stress disorder. In recent times, they have experienced a loss of prestige ... a loss of power ... a loss of privilege' (Gill, quoted in NSW Ecumenical Council 2019: 2). This loss of power and privilege concerns the Privileged Conservatives who want their conservative values to be adhered to by the broader Australian society. The NSW Ecumenical Council go on to identify multiple reasons for their loss of power and prestige, including 'secularization, consumerism, and militant atheism' alongside 'the aftermath of the Royal Commission into Institutional Responses to Child Sexual Abuses' and 'The Safe Schools Programme'. Their comment on 'The Safe Schools Programme' is instructive. The NSW Ecumenical Council recognise that 'this was introduced to create safer and more inclusive environments for same sex attracted, intersex and gender diverse students, staff, and families,' but go on to say that it was 'perceived by many as actively advocating promiscuity' (NSW Ecumenical Council 2019: 2). The claim that it advocates promiscuity is debatable. However, leaving that aside, the Council is arguing that the Safe Schools Programme is problematic because they claim it encourages sexual behaviours that make them feel uncomfortable and are inconsistent with their conservative Christian morality, whilst simultaneously recognising that the program is designed to prevent harm to young people in government-funded education provided to the general public. That is to say, the 'harm' identified by Privileged Conservatives is minimal, in this case, arguably, increased acceptance of promiscuity. In contrast, the activities they object to are designed to prevent significant harm, including higher rates of suicide and mental health issues experienced by same-sex attracted, intersex and gender diverse students, staff and families.

There is also a demographic dimension to this. Bouma and Halafoff (2017: 133) observe that the increasingly multicultural, multifaith and nonreligious landscape of Australian society is challenging the 'once privileged social and economic positions and values' of conservative Christians. These demographic changes are increasingly in tension with conservative Christians' influence on Australian society through their participation in the provision of education, healthcare, aged care and social welfare services.

Submissions from Privileged Conservatives often highlight their size and importance. The comments from the Australian Catholic Bishops Conference were noted earlier in the chapter. Here we recount the comments made by the Sydney Diocese of the Anglican Church:

> The Diocese is an unincorporated voluntary association comprising 270 parishes and various bodies ... These bodies include 40 Anglican schools, Anglicare Sydney (a large social welfare institution, which includes aged care), Anglican Youthworks and Anglican Aid (which focusses on overseas aid and development). ... The Diocese, through its various component bodies and through its congregational life, makes a rich contribution to the social capital of our nation, through programs involving social welfare, education, health and aged care, overseas aid, youth work and not least the proclamation of the Christian message of hope for all people. (Anglican Church Diocese of Sydney 2019: 1)

The intention of the Anglican Church Diocese of Sydney in this listing of activities is to highlight its 'rich contribution to the social capital of our nation'. However, it also highlights the extraordinary privilege and power of this organisation in both the receipt of government funds and the influence it has on society. Anglicare Sydney alone received more than A$240 million in government subsidies in both 2020 and 2021 (Anglican Community Services 2021). The Anglican Church Diocese of Sydney say that the aim of this work is 'the proclamation of the Christian message'. Perhaps they mean this to apply only to their explicitly religious activities, but it seems reasonable to assume that they see their involvement in government-funded education, social welfare, healthcare and aged care that provide services to the general population as at least partly motivated by the desire to proclaim the 'Christian message'.

The primary concern of Privileged Conservatives is to ensure their ability to express their religious identity in all facets of their activities with minimal intervention. The Presbyterian Church in Australia (2019: 2) express this point clearly, writing: 'Christianity is not simply a private matter that can be left at the door of the home, or of the church, but a view of the world that shapes public life.' That is to say, the Privileged Conservatives express a desire to not only practise their religion but to have their religious ideas and norms shape the public life of all Australians, and they want to be allowed to do this in the context of government-funded services they provide to the general Australian population.

The evidence used in submissions by Privileged Conservatives is distinctive. They often rely on hypothetical examples. They do not provide concrete cases of experiences of harm. For example, when discussing the importance of selecting all staff (including beyond chaplaincy roles) according to religious adherence, the Australian Catholic Bishops Conference suggests that in a Victorian aged care facility 'cleaners may be the first people approached by residents to discuss the state's Voluntary Assisted Dying (VAD) scheme' (Australian Catholic Bishops Conference 2019: 12). They want to be able to discriminate against cleaners who do not share Catholic views on voluntary assisted dying. This discrimination is justified, they argue, because of the hypothetical possibility that the cleaner might have a discussion about voluntary assisted dying with a resident, both of whom are quite likely to not be Catholics themselves.

One noticeable difference between the submissions to the federal government's exposure draft and the cases drawing on the Victorian legislation is that in the submissions relating to the federal legislation we examined, the Privileged Conservatives rarely, if ever, discuss their desire to discriminate against members of religious minorities (such as Muslims, Buddhists, Hindus or Sikhs). Simon Rice (2020) points out that vilification towards Muslims, Buddhists, Hindus or Sikhs would be made legal in the second exposure draft of the bill. Many of the cases involving religion brought before VCAT in Victoria involve minority religious groups defending themselves against discrimination by privileged conservative Christians. The federal Religious Discrimination Bill has not become law, but if it had, it would have allowed, rather than prevented, some forms of discrimination and vilification against members of minority religions.

The arguments of the Privileged Conservatives are primarily driven by conservative Christians. A small number of Islamic and Jewish groups do make similar arguments to those of the conservative Christians. For example, the Australian Federation of Islamic Councils (2019: 6) argues for the legislation to go beyond the protection of individuals from discrimination to allow 'a positive right to religious freedom'. However, the situations of Muslims and Jews are significantly different, due to their minority status, and the nature of the religious practices they seek to protect. Further, Islamic and Jewish organisations do not have the privilege and broad social impact of government-funded conservative Christian organisations. This creates a different set of issues and potential harms (see Ezzy et al. 2022; Evans and Gaze 2010).

Many Christians do not agree with the arguments of the Privileged Conservatives. For example, as noted earlier, The Uniting Church in Australia (2019: 2) 'are concerned that the Exposure Draft leans too heavily in favour of religious freedom over other rights'. Similarly, the Religious Society of Friends provide a succinct summary of their central concern with the legislation: 'It would be regressive if anti-discrimination laws already put in place were undermined by favouring the anxieties of religious groups that are challenged by the "progressive" trends in secular society' (Religious Society of Friends 2019: 5).

Conservative Christians are disturbed, and even distressed, by challenges to their institutionalised power and prestige. This can be observed both in their submissions to the first exposure draft of the federal Religious Discrimination Bill and in the cases involving conservative Christians brought before VCAT in Victoria. Submissions by Privileged Conservatives argue for a broad right to engage in practices that would harm people from religious and other minorities. In contrast, the Victorian legislation has constrained conservative Christians' ability to engage in such harmful practices. While some have changed their behaviours, as illustrated by the case of the Sikh student at Melton Christian College, others remain less enthusiastic about treating members of religious and other minorities with equality and respect.

Discussion and conclusion

Concerned Minorities want to live their lives while expressing the religious dimensions of their identities. Privileged Conservatives want to be similarly protected, but they also want to impose their conservative Christian religious norms and values on Australian society. Concerned Minorities express strong support for diversity. Privileged Conservatives give grudging acknowledgement to diversity. To be clear, not all Christians are Privileged Conservatives, and numerically Privileged Conservatives are a minority in Australian society (Ezzy et al. 2022). But they are a vocal and powerful minority with considerable institutional power and financial resources. Privileged Conservatives are mobilizing a particular version of the past and seeking a continued state endorsement of their practices that would allow discrimination against members of religious and other minorities.

Beaman (2021: 206) provides a succinct analysis of how majoritarian Christian assumptions enter legal cases through claims that their views and symbols are 'cultural'. Analysing cases that involve challenges to, for example, the use of the Christian Cross in public settings, she invites the reader to 'think about how challenges to such symbols and practices are in fact challenges to privilege and power and, further, to consider the possibility that a refusal to acknowledge those power relations puts the reputation of democracy and human rights at risk'. We make a similar argument in this chapter. The legal challenges from members of minority religions to the practices of privileged conservative Christian groups represent challenges to their privilege and power, which is why they are passionately resisted by conservative Christians. Effective religious anti-discrimination and anti-vilification legislation, such as the Victorian legislation, encourages democratic participation and protects the human rights of members of minority religious groups who experience considerable harms, often in the contexts controlled by privileged conservative Christians.

The issue of school uniforms at Melton Christian college and the submissions to the first exposure draft of the federal bill typically represent the views of people in privileged positions *within* their religious organisations. As already noted, it is unclear what other people associated with the Melton Christian College community thought about the visual presence of a Sikh boy in their school. Submissions made by the Privileged Conservatives to the first exposure draft were produced by the leadership class of the religious organisations they represent. They do not tell us about what laypeople from these traditions think. Méadhbh McIvor (2020) makes a similar point in her observation that conservative Christian legal bodies in the UK are more concerned about some issues than people who attend conservative Christian churches. She suggests the latter are more resigned, reluctantly accepting the reality of diversity and progressive values in the public sphere, rather than passionately resisting it.

The concept of an organisation's 'religious purpose' is central to the argument of religious bodies to their desire to discriminate. What does it mean to say that an organisation has a 'religious purpose'? More specifically, what does it means to say that a school, hospital, aged care facility or social welfare organisation has a 'religious purpose' when it is primarily government-funded and many or most of the people who use the service do not belong to the religion to which it is affiliated? For example, in the Australian Catholic Bishops Conference submission (2019: 2) they argue that it 'is necessary in religious schools, Catholic health and welfare agencies need to be able to hire staff who support their religious mission and to set employee conduct standards'. This requires more discussion and debate. A first step, following Sider and Unruh (2004), might be to develop a more complex typology of non-profit religious organisations. However, the analysis also needs to take account of the size and impact of the organisation.

Some Christian groups engage with religious minorities in complex ways. For example, the Catholic Archdiocese of Melbourne supported the Islamic Council of Victoria in the case against Catch the Fire Ministries (Ezzy 2013) whilst also supporting the Federal Religious Discrimination Bill that would have allowed Catholic service providers to discriminate against members of religious minorities in their hiring policies (Beck 2021). We are not aware of any studies of the discrimination experienced by Muslims, Hindus, Buddhists or Sikhs who work as teachers, social workers, nurses or other similar occupations. How would discriminatory hiring policies affect religious minorities, given that a substantial section of the employment opportunities for such occupations are in Christian-affiliated organisations? This also requires further research.

Deep equality and cosmopolitanism are interwoven with the issues discussed in this chapter. Beaman's concept of deep quality emphasises that it is 'a process enacted and owned by so-called ordinary people in everyday life. Deep equality is a vision of equality that transcends law, politics, and social policy, and that relocates equality as a process rather than a definition, and as lived rather than prescribed' (Beaman 2017: 13). In everyday interactions it is often the case that religious differences are unproblematically negotiated, without the need for legal interventions. How do laws, such as the Victorian legislation or the proposed federal Religious Discrimination Bill, impact everyday negotiations on religious difference? On the one hand, this chapter has shown how legal mechanisms such as VCAT require religious organisations to reflect on potential harms of their practices, and also provide minority religions with a means to challenge discrimination, both of which can lead to positive change. On the other, the exposure drafts of the federal Religious Discrimination Bill differ in that they raise the stakes of the game and turns religious differences into a liability for members of religious minorities. If enacted as law, the federal bill would create institutional contexts in which religious discrimination is not challenged, removing the everyday mechanisms that make deep equality and cosmopolitanism possible. The bill gives religious institutions greater power, and it allows them to bypass the interpersonal elements of deep equality such as, 'agonistic respect, recognition of similarity, and a concomitant acceptance of difference, creation of community, and neighbourliness' (Beaman 2017: 12).

Effective anti-discrimination legislation, such as the Victorian legislation, and the concerns of members of minority religions are oriented towards future-forming narratives. They express a social imaginary rooted in complex diversity characterised by equality and inclusivity. In contrast, conservative Christians advocate practices that represent a past-preserving approach that seeks to re-invigorate vertical power relations that privilege discriminatory values, norms and practices. Anti-discrimination legislation can encourage greater self-reflection among Christian organisations and facilitate practices of respect and equality.

References

ABS (Australian Bureau of Statistics). 2022. 'Census' https://www.abs.gov.au/census. Accessed 1 March 2023.

Anglican Community Services. 2021. *Financial Report*. https://www.anglicare.org.au/media/8470/anglican-community-services-financial-report-2021.pdf. Accessed 1 March 2023.

Australian Government, Attorney General's Department. 2019. Religious Discrimination Bills – First Exposure Drafts. https://www.ag.gov.au/rights-and-protections/consultations/religious-discrimination-bills-first-exposure-drafts. Accessed 12 February 2021.

Beaman, Lori G. 2017. *Deep Equality in an Era of Religious Diversity*. Oxford: Oxford University Press.

Beaman, Lori G. 2020. *The Transition of Religion to Culture in Law and Public Discourse*. New York: Routledge.

Beaman, Lori G. 2021. 'Our Culture, Our Heritage, Our Values: Whose Culture, Whose Heritage, Whose Values?' *Canadian Journal of Law and Society/La Revue Canadienne Droit et Société* 36(2): 203–23.

Beck, Luke. 2021. 'Third Time Lucky? What Has Changed in the Latest Draft of the Religious Discrimination Bill?' *The Conversation*. 23 November 2021. https://theconversation.com/third-time-lucky-what-has-changed-in-the-latest-draft-of-the-religious-discrimination-bill-172386. Accessed 1 March 2023.

Berger, Helen, and Ezzy, Douglas. 2007. *Teenage Witches*. New Brunswick, NJ: Rutgers University Press.

Bouma, Gary, and Halafoff, Anna. 2017. 'Australia's Changing Religious Profile – Rising Nones and Pentecostals, Declining British Protestants in Superdiversity: Views from the 2016 Census'. *Journal for the Academic Study of Religion* 30(2): 129–43.

Brennan, F. 2011. 'Religion, Multiculturalism and Legal Pluralism'. In N. Hosen and R. Mohr (eds), *Law and Religion in Public Life*. London: Routledge, 69–95.

Deen, H. 2008. *The Jihad Seminar.* Crawley, WA: University of Western Australia Press.

Elphick, Liam, Amy Maguire, and Anja Hilkemeijer. 2019. 'The Government Has Released Its Draft Religious Discrimination Bill. How Will It Work?' *The Conversation*, 29 August 2019. https://theconversation.com/the-government-has-released-its-draft-religious-discrimination-bill-how-will-it-work-122618. Accessed 1 March 2023.

Evans, Carolyn, and Gaze, Beth. 2010. Discrimination by Religious Schools: Views from the Coal Face. *Melbourne University Law Review* 34: 392–424.

Ezzy, D. 2013. 'Minimising Religious Conflict and the Racial Religious Tolerance Act in Victoria, Australia'. *Journal for the Academic Study of Religion* 26(2): 198–215.

Ezzy, D. 2018. 'Minority Religions, Litigation, and the Prevention of Harm'. *Journal of Contemporary Religion* 33(2): 277–89. DOI: 10.1080/13537903.2018.1469272.

Ezzy, D., Banham, R., and Beaman, L. 2021. 'Religious Diversity, Legislation, and Christian Privilege'. *Journal of Sociology* 59(1): 70–86.

Ezzy, D., Banham, R., and Beaman, L. 2022. 'Religious Anti-discrimination Legislation and the Negotiation of Difference in Victoria, Australia'. *Religion, State & Society* 50(1): 22–39. DOI: 10.1080/09637494.2021.2010906.

Ezzy, D., Fielder, B., Dwyer, A., and Richardson-Self, L. 2022. 'LGBT+ Equality, Religious Freedom and Government-Funded Faith-Based Religiously Affiliated Educational Workplaces'. *Australian Journal of Social Issues* 57(1): 185–201.

Galanter, M. 1983. 'The Radiating Effects of Courts'. In K. Boyum and L. Mathe (eds), *Empirical Theories about Courts.* New York: Longman, 117–42.

Gelber, K. 2011. 'Religion and Freedom of Speech in Australia'. In N. Hosen and R. Mohr (eds), *Law and Religion in Public Life.* London: Routledge, 95–112.

Halafoff, Anna. 2013. *The Multifaith Movement: Global Risks and Cosmopolitan Solutions.* Dordrecht: Springer.

Halafoff, Anna. 2016. 'Governance and Religious Diversity in Australia: Multifaith Relations and Religious Instruction in the State of Victoria'. In Andrew Dawson (ed.), *The Politics and Practice of Religious Diversity.* New York: Routledge, 101–17.

Iner, Derya. 2019. *Islamophobia in Australia (2016–2017).* https://www.islamophobia.com.au/wp-content/uploads/2019/12/Islamophobia-Report-2019-2.pdf. Accessed 1 March 2023.

Karp, Paul. 2022. 'Anthony Albanese Warns Religious Discrimination Bill Could "Drive Us Apart" as Labor Pushes for Amendments'. *The Guardian*, 9 February 2022. https://www.theguardian.com/australia-news/2022/feb/09/labor-to-seek-protections-for-lgbtq-students-but-will-pass-religious-discrimination-bill-in-lower-house. Accessed 1 March 2023.

Mahmood, Saba. 2015. 'Religious Freedom, Minority Rights, and Geopolitics'. In Winnifred Sullivan, Elizabeth Hurd, Saba Mahmood and Peter G. Danchin (eds), *Politics of Religious Freedom.* Chicago: University of Chicago Press, 142–8.

McIvor, Méadhbh, 2020. *Representing God: Christian Legal Activism in Contemporary England.* Princeton: Princeton University Press.

Mouffe, Chantal. 1999. 'Deliberative Democracy or Agonistic Pluralism?' *Social Research* 66(3): 745–58.

Rees, N., Rice, S., and Allen, D. 2018. *Australian Anti-discrimination and Equal Opportunity Law,* 3rd edition. Sydney: Federation Press.

Rice, Simon 2020. 'Government's Religious Discrimination Bill Enshrines the Right to Harm Others in the Name of Faith'. *The Conversation.* 10 February 2020. https://theconversation.com/governments-religious-discrimination-bill-enshri nes-the-right-to-harm-others-in-the-name-of-faith-131206. Accessed 1 March 2023.

Sider, R. J., and Unruh, H. R. 2004. 'Typology of Religious Characteristics of Social Service and Educational Organizations and Programs'. *Nonprofit and Voluntary Sector Quarterly* 33(1): 109–34.

Strong, Geoff. 2003. The Councillor, the Witch, and the Tribunal. *The Age*, 27 December 2003. https://www.theage.com.au/national/the-councillor-the-witch-and-the-tribu nal-20031227-gdx0cx.html. Accessed 1 March 2023.

All the following submissions are found at

https://www.ag.gov.au/rights-and-protections/publications/submissions-received-religi ous-discrimination-bills-first-exposure-drafts-consultation Accessed 1 March 2020.

Anglican Church Diocese of Sydney. 2019. Submission.

Australian Catholic Bishops Conference. 2019. 'Exposure Drafts of the Religious Discrimination Bills'.

Australian Federation of Islamic Councils. 2019. 'Religious Discrimination Reform Package'.

Australian Sikh Association and United Sikhs. 2019. 'Submission on Religious Discrimination Bills & the Impact on Australian Sikhs'.

Forum on Australia's Islamic Relations Inc. (FAIR) 2019. 'Submission to the Attorney-General's Department with Respect to the Religious Discrimination Bill'.

Freedom for Faith. 2019. 'Religious Discrimination Bill 2019 – Exposure Draft'.

Joint Submission from the Australian Muslim Community. 2019. 'Exposure Draft: Religious Discrimination Bill'.

New South Wales Ecumenical Council. 2019. 'Position Paper on Religious Freedom'.

Rabbinical Council of Australia and New Zealand. 2019. 'Religious Discrimination Bill – Exposure Draft'.

Religious Society of Friends (Quakers) in Australia. 2019. 'Quaker Peace and Legislation Committee Submission on Religious Freedom Legislation'.

The Presbyterian Church in Australia. 2019. 'Religious Discrimination Bill – Exposure Draft'.

Uniting Church in Australia. 2019. 'Religious Discrimination Submission'.

8

Policing and Religious Diversity

Rebecca Banham, Angela Dwyer, Douglas Ezzy, Greg Barton and Danielle Campbell

[In Victoria] we worship over 130 different faiths. We speak well over 200 languages which don't include the original Indigenous languages ... we have very diverse areas and we always talk to police about understanding their local demographic ... just to understand that what applies in one group won't necessarily apply in the other.

Steven (Victoria Police)

Introduction

As Steven highlights above, policing in contemporary Australia is increasingly defined by how officers engage with diverse community members. In this context – marred by the deaths of people of colour at the hands of police, and marked by worldwide protest movements around how policing is done – it is vital that we examine the power of the state institution tasked with maintaining public order and protecting community safety. There are two key reasons for doing this work.

Firstly, it is imperative to interrogate how policing works in relation to religious diversity, as the global population increasingly and inescapably lives in the context of the volatile tensions around religious diversity and conservative politics emerging chiefly as a result of events including the 11 September 2001 terrorist attacks. In Australia, Muslim people (and visible presentations of Islamic faith) have been targeted with unprecedented violence and discrimination; while 'almost 70% of Australians [have] a very low level of Islamophobia ... 10% [are] highly Islamophobic' (Hassan 2018: 12). Tensions related to religious diversity have always existed in Australia but were perhaps less pronounced than they became after the Bali bombings in 2002; more recently, after the Christchurch shootings in New Zealand in 2019, the Islamophobia Register Australia recorded a 'fourfold increase in reports of in person incidents of anti-Muslim hate' (Convery 2022). Police are among first responders in acute situations arising from such disturbing attitudes (such as the Christchurch massacre), where they are thrust into managing negativity demonstrated towards Muslim people (Markus 2021; Poynting 2020).

Secondly, and perhaps unsurprisingly, such events – and the relevant discourses, prejudices and beliefs – can influence the actions of police officers. Police officers are drawn from the community generally, and as such are not immune to discriminatory behaviours and prejudicial attitudes. For instance, shortly following the Christchurch massacre, two police officers from New South Wales police engaged in racial abuse of Afghan women over their allegedly not wearing a seatbelt (Iner 2019). As indicated in the videos of the incident circulated in the media, the officers engaged in threats and humiliation clearly informed by significant racial bias.

Given that police are tasked with upholding community safety, it is vital that we unpack how policing practice *and/or* misconduct intersects with religious diversity. For example – in a contemporary context, what is the role of police when their 'mission' is creeping well beyond the scope of their original intended purpose (for instance, policing infringements related to the Covid-19 pandemic)? How do police balance community engagement whilst still maintaining law and order? Does the diversity of the police force reflect the diversity of the community that they serve? How does this reflect power dynamics between authority, police and diverse communities? What does a respectful engagement with diverse communities look like? What strategies do or could police employ to promote such engagement? Given the likely tensions between these complex and often contradictory concerns, this chapter specifically examines the perspectives of police participants around the strategies used by Victoria Police and Tasmania Police to respectfully engage with religiously, culturally and ethnically diverse people.

To begin addressing these questions, this chapter:

- Introduces key concepts relating to policing and diversity;
- Identifies national and international events, trends and movements impacting policing in Australia; and
- Illustrates how these events shape policing in Australia, and the strategies used by Tasmanian and Victorian police staff to respectfully engage with diversity.

Focused particularly on religiously diverse people, police participants' stories highlight attempts to build trust in, and visibility of, police amongst religious minority groups. The strategies used to do this are shaped, challenged and informed by political and cultural changes such as international migration, Islamophobia, mass media and concerns about right-wing extremism. Further, the geographical location of communities and officers markedly shapes policing resources and practices – as the differences between our Tasmanian and Victorian participants demonstrate. We draw on stories of interaction between officers and community members to illustrate complexities of contemporary policing practice. Through concepts such as 'reactive' and 'proactive' policing, community policing, diversity and reassurance, this chapter introduces core academic issues surrounding policing and religion in Australia.

Policing in a diverse world

Key concepts: Community policing, recruitment, reassurance and legislation

There is a small body of academic and policy-adjacent literature about policing and religious diversity in Australia, focusing primarily on four themes:

1. Countering violent extremism (CVE), and anti-terrorism/anti-radicalisation strategies (e.g. Mazerolle et al. 2020);
2. Crime and crime prevention in CALD (culturally and linguistically diverse) and refugee communities (e.g. Shepherd and Masuka 2021);
3. Police culture and patterns of police interactions with specific communities, including community perceptions of police (e.g. Knight 2017); and
4. Reporting and managing crimes committed against minorities, including experiences of discrimination and vilification (e.g. Wiedlitzka et al. 2018).

The stories included in this chapter extend this literature through the real-world experiences – positive and negative – of police officers and civilian staff. When police organisations were originally established, the activities that characterised policing work could be broadly described as 'community policing', a more proactive form of policing work grounded in engagement with communities. While definitions of community policing are highly contested (Cordner 2014), it has generally come to be considered as a 'philosophy' rather than a specific set of practices that police engage in (Cordner 2014). Community policing typically involves partnerships with communities, in order to ensure that policing activities are chiefly guided by the perspectives of community members, and that police are focused on proactive problem-solving and crime prevention rather than typical, reactive, 'call and response' models of doing policing (Skogan 2019). Proactive forms of policing work emerged out of the very earliest police organisation established in the United Kingdom by Sir Robert Peel (Levinson 2007); Peel was focused on how the public responded when the armed services were engaged to bring the public to order, and he therefore developed a form of policing that was grounded in support and trust from citizens (Levinson 2007). These police officers were dressed differently from the army, and they were unarmed so they were 'more citizen like than militaristic' (Levinson 2007: 270). For Peel, successful policing was evidenced by the absence of crime and disorder because officers engaged respectfully and worked proactively with diverse communities; that is to say, Peel's vision of policing was policing through consent. Most importantly here, harmonious, consensual relationships between diverse people and police was the measure of police integrity. In this vision of policing, effective police work happened through proactive negotiation and collaboration with communities, rather than through reactive responses wielding authoritative power and control, and these ideas fed into the development of the contemporary models of community policing (Levinson 2007; Skogan, 2019).

However, policing has shifted considerably from the idea of 'proactive policing by consent' developed by Peel. Increasingly, officers have conceptualised proactive engagement with diverse communities as antithetical to the (now more standardised) 'call and response' model of doing police work. Research with police officers tells us that while consensual proactive community policing measures are valued by some, they are also often perceived as 'soft' police work (Chan 1995; Innes 2007; Grossman et al. 2013) that most officers do not value because the policing profession venerates control of public order and safety through 'quick, decisive action' (Ratcliffe 2018: 52). Furthermore, police are contemporaneously working in fiscal, capitalistic environments where resources are tight, and community policing is devalued due to requiring the commitment of resources that police organisations do not necessarily have (Cordner 2014). It is important to note the extent to which successful policing is now measured by a neoliberal governance approach focused on counting policing activity itself – including the ingrained use of daily policing activity 'quotas' as a key accountability measure – and this is defined more clearly by metrics of control and regulation, rather than consent.

There are, however, many ways that Australian police organisations engage (and potentially engage effectively) with diverse communities. The diversification of the people recruited to police organisations is one area of focus. While police officers are drawn from the communities they seek to service, recruitment processes are often criticised for mainly recruiting people that are 'capital-T Typical': white, male, conservative, middle class and privileged. Recruitment generally filters out people of colour, religiously diverse people and people who have disabilities, mental health issues or who are gender diverse. However, some incidents have pushed police organisations to diversify their workforces (Bartkowiak-Theron and Asquith 2012; 2014). Cultural sensitivity and awareness training has also been implemented across most Australian police academies to some extent (Blumberg et al. 2019). However, this work does not necessarily equate to better overall relationships between diverse people and frontline general duties officers; entrenched racism within police culture means that ethnically diverse recruits will often not report their diversity or cultural skills, such as speaking another language, because they assume these characteristics are undervalued (Bartkowiak-Theron and Asquith 2014). Furthermore, 'cultural awareness training fails to broaden the scope of this awareness to an actual capacity to deal with diversity in the field' (Bartkowiak-Theron and Asquith 2014: 96).

The dissonance between what is *said* to be valued, and the empirical reality of contemporary Australian policing, is seismic. We argue that the profession of policing has come to devalue precisely the things that the first ever police organisation was established for: reducing crime using 'soft' proactive, community-focused policing by consent grounded in respectful engagement upholding the dignity of diverse people. Even more importantly, and perhaps most ironically, is how policing work is now focused almost solely on the reactivity of officers achieving 'quotas' with these diverse people, with this shift being largely driven by police organisational culture (Innes 2007). Increasingly, good, accountable policing is defined by officers reaching their daily quotas, and these moves stand in uncomfortable opposition with community policing initiatives. In this chapter, we seek to push forward this problematic context, both in parallel and contrast with the stories from the officers and staff we interviewed.

Emerging out of this context is a focus on what commentators have called 'reassurance policing'. This form of policing work was developed chiefly in the United Kingdom (Millie and Herrington 2005), in response to the significant lack of public knowledge about falling crime rates and escalating fear of crime. These practices included activities such as having more visible police presence in and around local areas, police clamping down on antisocial behaviour and disorderly conduct to improve how community members see the police, and to, in turn, better facilitate police intelligence gathering (Millie and Herrington, 2005). Ultimately, all these activities focused on the idea of reassuring the public that police were doing their job effectively, in addition to being able to measure this (Fielding and Innis 2006). Ideas about reassurance policing were still heavily bound up in similar ideas around community policing because typically the public work with police to identify 'signals' (physical and social) that crime is a risk in that area (Fielding and Innis 2006). Police then work to ameliorate these 'signals' to subjectively reassure the public that they are reducing the risk of crime: 'here, the "police officer acts as a "control signal"' (Millie 2007: 226). Reassurance policing therefore 'works through the enactment of signs and symbols of authority in order to exert influence over the perceptual field of citizens' by way of 'perceptual interventions' (Innes 2007: 133). As Millie (2007) indicates, these forms of policing rely explicitly on ideas about whose views count for police as those worthy of consultation. The middle-class 'worried well' are highly likely to be those informing police about 'signals' in their local, more gentrified areas, and those in their sights 'given a signal crime badge' (Millie 2007: 231) are people 'who cannot make it – the nonwhite and the nonmonogamous, the poor and the genderdeviant, the fat, the disabled, the unemployed, the infected, and a host of unmentionable others' (Love 2007: 10). The activities of reassurance policing are therefore in danger of bleeding into other zero tolerance, 'hard' policing approaches focused on control and regulation, and those 'who cannot make it' can be subject to unacceptable levels of police intervention (Millie 2007).

Various practical or structural elements shape how Australian police respond to diverse communities, such as national/state/territory legislation, organisational recruitment policies and the restrictions imposed by the rotation of policing roles. A good example of this relates to anti-discrimination legislation. As Fokas (2019) describes, legislation creates a 'shadow' whereby the boundaries of what is 'acceptable' in society are reflected in, and shaped by, the legal structures that govern the relevant behaviour. In the case of anti-discrimination legislation, the extent to which one can discriminate against a minority group without ramification is established by legislation. If a person breaches these parameters, the legislation establishes the consequences and, therefore, the seriousness of the breach. Here, the primary significance of the legislation is in its 'shadow', which defines the boundaries of acceptable behaviour, rather than viewing legislation (and sentencing) simply as a means for punishing those who breach these parameters.

However, different police organisations respond differently to legislation and incorporate legislation into their policies and everyday policing in different ways. It is often up to the individual police officer with whom the incident is raised, to use their discretionary decision-making around whether the incident does in fact represent a breach of anti-discrimination legislation. For instance, a transgender person might be subjected to transphobic harassment from a member of the public, in full view of many people, but the officer may refuse to act on this as they themselves may have anti-transgender attitudes and not recognise this as a crime. Further to this, the anti-discrimination legislation that officers are obligated to uphold is inconsistent across Australian jurisdictions. In the context of our participants, for example, Victoria is the only state to have a Racial and Religious Tolerance Act, which has been used to criminally prosecute one case of serious (religious) vilification (see Ezzy, Banham and Beaman 2022 for further details about the Act).

Rotational roles are another good example of how administrative structures shape policing and diversity. In Australia, policing policy most often requires officers to be rotated to different positions after a defined period of time. This practice emerged out of past inquiries into police corruption where investigations found that certain officers had developed strong, sustained connections with criminal networks, especially people providing information to police officers. Mandated rotation in police positions means that police officers are not provided with the opportunity to create these types of connections, and the benefit of this is more accountable police work. The challenges with mandated rotation of police roles stem precisely from the need to be able to create strong, ongoing relationships with members of diverse communities to be able to produce more supportive policing experiences for these diverse communities. Reflecting on the context of LGBTI police liaison officers, Dwyer (2019) explains how, after setting up extensive networked relationships between LGBTIQ community members, LGBTIQ service providers and LGBTI liaison officers, these liaison officers would be rotated out of their role; subsequently, the networked relationships would fall away. This meant that a community who had developed relationships with particular officers would then need to rebuild these relationships with another officer after they were rotated.

National and international context

As highlighted elsewhere in this volume (Chapters 1 and 4), Australia not only has a long history of ethnic and religious diversity, but this diversity is 'becoming more diverse – as new waves of immigrants and residential relocators compound and complicate existing patterns of religious difference in different parts of major cities' (Bouma et al. 2022: 7). Complicating this is the persistent and 'institutionalised nature of Christian privilege' (Ezzy, Banham and Beaman 2021: 3) in Australia, where the cultural practices of those who are not Christian – and particularly those who are part of non-Christian religious communities – are seen as 'other'. In Australia, Christians account for 43.9 per cent of the total population, while nonreligious Australians account for 38.9 per cent (ABS 2022). As such, Australians who are part of non-Christian religious communities – including Muslims, Hindus, Buddhists and Sikhs – comprise only a small proportion of the total population (around 10 per cent, as of 2021 (ABS 2022)). Despite popular claims of being 'proudly multicultural', discrimination against non-white Australians is still routine, and there remain persistent beliefs – with resultant cultural, political and legal implications – that those who do not fit within the normative practices of 'white Australia' are in some way problematic (a theme returned to consistently throughout this volume).

The geographic distribution of religious diversity has important implications for policing. Police in different jurisdictions face different challenges and have different opportunities as a product of this demographic diversity. In this chapter, we explore one example of these differences, between Victoria and Tasmania. Despite their geographical proximity, Tasmania and Victoria have strikingly different historical and present demographics – differences which profoundly shape each state's economies, legislative structures and cultural expectations and, in turn, shape how police respond to minority religious communities.

Policing practice in relation to ethnic diversity is also profoundly shaped by the national and international political context. This chapter does not consider these issues in detail, although we note their significance in framing many of the issues discussed. For example, Islamophobia remains a major issue in Australia (Iner 2019), as does the demonising of various migrant communities, led by politicians and media alike (Poynting and Briskman, 2018). That is to say, respectful community and policing engagement with diversity is sometimes undermined by political and media strategies that have goals that are not always aligned with those of police. For example, the extremely high rate of Indigenous deaths in custody in Australia (Klippmark and Crawley 2018) is both a problem for policing practice and a social policy issue which continues to be inadequately engaged in policy terms, and particularly in the context of policing organisations. On the other hand, The Faith Communities Council of Victoria (2022) resources relating to family violence are part of a coordinated response by state government, police and faith and migrant communities to address this issue.

As noted above, other international social and cultural issues shape the context of policing religiously diverse people, especially around collective trauma events (Harms, Kosta and Hickey 2022). Events like these feed into the increased experience of discrimination and vilification on an everyday basis, as evidenced by the anti-Asian sentiment that emerged during the Covid-19 pandemic (Tan, Lee and Ruppanner 2021). The political debate around refugees, migration and displacement fuels conservative government policies leading to mandated detention of traumatised asylum seekers. Often people from different parts of the world are exposed to severe trauma from police, including circumstances where they have witnessed police killings, and this leads to significant distrust of police. These circumstances are often ignored entirely when diverse people engage in serious criminal behaviour and the media stigmatises the diversity of these people by pairing it with understandings of inherent criminality and deviance (Warner 2004; Pittaway and Dantas 2021). These circumstances also coalesce with the rapid growth of right-wing extremism in Australia, as evidenced by the shootings in Christchurch discussed earlier. Further, these concerns are filtered through an Australian policing context increasingly influenced by global policing concerns, particularly the Black Lives Matter movement (Deemajnee et al. 2022; Gatwiri and Townsend-Cross 2022) in relation to increasing numbers of Aboriginal deaths in custody. All these global events reflect and shape how policing and diversity works in Australia (see Chapter 10).

Diversity in Tasmania and Victoria

The stories in this chapter come from interviews with Tasmania Police and Victoria Police, occurring within two very different contexts of ethnic and religious diversity. Victoria – and particularly Melbourne, as 'one of the world's most cosmopolitan cities' (Bouma et al. 2021: 1) – is highly diverse, both religiously and ethnically. The 2021 Census data (ABS 2022) shows that Victoria is extremely diverse with 32.8 per cent of the population speaking a language other than English at home, and 30.0 per cent born overseas in 2021, including people born in India (4.0 per cent), England (2.7 per cent), China (2.6 per cent) and New Zealand (1.5 per cent). In comparison, Tasmania is much less diverse with only 13.9 per cent of Tasmanians speaking a language other than English at home, and 15.3 per cent of Tasmanians being born overseas, including people born in England (3.5 per cent), China (1.2 per cent), Nepal (1.1 per cent) and

India (1.1 per cent). Reflecting this difference in ethnic diversity, Tasmania is also less religious in comparison to Victoria. Among Victorians, 40.9 per cent identified as Christians, 39.3 per cent said they had no religion, with 13.1 per cent of people affiliated with a non-Christian religion, including Islam (4.2 per cent), Hinduism (3.3 per cent) and Buddhism (3.1 per cent). In comparison, in Tasmania, 50.0 per cent said they had no religion, 38.4 per cent identified as Christians and 4.5 per cent were affiliated with a non-Christian religion, including Hinduism (1.7 per cent), Buddhism (1.0 per cent) and Islam (0.9 per cent) (ABS 2022).

Generally speaking, participants regularly referred to ethnic diversity, but these comments also often intertwined elements of religious diversity. The Tasmanian participants were more likely to discuss ethnic diversity (or unspecified 'diversity'), than they were to discuss religious diversity specifically. When religious diversity was discussed, it was very often related to threats to minority religious groups, as explored in greater detail in this chapter.

Methods

Interviews were conducted with four Tasmanian Police representatives and five Victoria Police representatives between September 2020 and February 2021, including police officers and civilian staff. Interviews in Tasmania were conducted in person. Interviews in Victoria were conducted remotely, due to restraints imposed by the Covid-19 pandemic. Interviews were transcribed by a secure transcribing service and thematically analysed using the qualitative analysis software NVivo. In order to protect anonymity, participants are referred to in this report by pseudonyms. The four Tasmanian participants were Greg, Cameron, John and Tracey. The five Victorian participants were Chris, Steven, Kim, Phil and Andrew. This project has approval from University of Tasmania Human Research Ethics Committee, Tasmania Police and Victoria Police Research Coordinating Committee.

Because the sample size is small, the views expressed by participants cannot be generalised to all members of these organisations. However, participants were chosen strategically for their ability to provide information about policing practice in dealing with religious diversity, and as such they provide key information about main trends in current policing practice and policy. The sample size also reflects the research team's obligation to respect the resource pressures experienced by police due to the Covid-19 pandemic.

Strategies for engaging with diversity

There are many strategies that police organisations and officers employ in engaging respectfully with diverse communities. These strategies often aim to build community trust in police, and have police be increasingly seen as 'embedded' within the wider community. This can be through activities such as uniformed officers attending community events in a civil capacity; developing policies that prioritise diversity in staff recruitment; and supporting training programs that bring police officers and community members together. 'Community policing' involves police engaging with members of the public in ways that do not centre on law and order, and most of the examples in this chapter come under the umbrella of community policing strategies.

Attending events is an important part of how police organisations can visibly engage with the wider community. For example, police representatives might attend events such as Diwali celebrations or cultural festivals, as a show of police support and community engagement. Event attendance has benefits both for officers and community members, but this also raises potentially complex issues of trust and communication. For example, describing police attendance at a lunch with the local Hazara community, Cameron (Tasmania Police) said:

> It was well-received and probably not what [the community members] expected would happen. As in, the police coming along, sitting there having lunch and being friendly and open to chatting to people … that [response] sort of indicated that [event attendance was not] happening enough, if it was such a surprise. [Police need to empower communities to] identify and implement solutions to local problems and influence strategic priorities and decisions … I just don't think we're at that point.

The benefits of this kind of community engagement can be difficult to realise due to role rotation, which sees officers moved between different positions within the organisation. Describing their current position, Kim (Victoria Police) said:

> This is a completely different role for me [than my previous role] … but we always need to stay educated. For an organisation where people rotate and move through roles a lot, it's difficult.

Attempts to connect with people is often further complicated by the apprehension, anger or fear that some community members (particularly those who have experienced abuse or trauma at the hands of authority figures) feel in response to police. This is an important consideration, especially for officers working in areas with particularly high populations of refugees, those seeking asylum and/or those with related trauma experiences. Chris's (Victoria Police) remarks reflect this:

> One of the common messages coming back to me was there was a fear of police and based on experiences that people had in [the countries] where they were born. So, [attending events] was a good opportunity for us, I guess, to make ourselves available to those communities in uniform, interact with them, just to provide them the confidence that, in Australia, police aren't like that.

Community policing is strongly intertwined with language around 'proactive' and 'reactive' policing. Here, 'reactivity' refers to responding to problems of order and safety as they occur, while 'proactivity' relates to actions that build a police organisation's capacity to foresee, prevent and insightfully respond to issues. Tasmanian and Victorian participants had quite different perspectives of how these approaches worked in their organisations.

All four Tasmanian participants referred to issues with funding and resourcing community policing methods that they saw as proactive and preventative. They attributed this in part to heavy workloads and competing priorities; as Cameron put it, 'I suppose, if you call it bang for buck, then you've got to work out where you're best-off spending your money.' Proactive policing work requires a high level of resourcing and funding, and Tasmanian participants described difficulties in resourcing and funding the role of Multicultural Liaison Officer,[1] particularly compared with other states. As John described:

> I mean there's ongoing dialogue from the counterterrorism world with both the federal police, attorney generals and our counterterrorism unit as well. [That] does build networks – but it's probably a bit more specific to threats only rather than broader understanding [of diversity]. Those three areas are probably much more prominent than the Multicultural Liaison Officer [role] in Tasmania Police.

Two participants further indicated that part of Tasmania Police's reactive approach stems from the concerns of the Police Association of Tasmania, who focus on 'keeping those resources on the frontline, in uniform, out, responding to jobs, [rather than] community engagement' (Greg).

For Victorian participants, proactive community policing responses include the work of liaison and community officers, including with particular cohorts (such as youth) and in particular regions (such as Dandenong in Melbourne's south-east). Participants referred to Victoria Police's involvement with interfaith organisations and events, including participation by officers of different ranks:

> I would attend [events] as much as I possibly could, myself, but also have constables, senior constables, sergeants, senior sergeants involved. So, right up and down the rank and file. The purpose for that was if there was a call for assistance, or if there was going to be an interaction out on the street, it was [likely to involve] our people that are out there working in the street, they will be the first responders. (Chris)

> [We] always want the grassroots copper on the van to go to the dinner to sit down and to just see what's going on and just to enjoy it, et cetera, et cetera. It's only through shared experience and through exposure and through engagement that things have improved. (Steven)

This is not to say that Victoria Police's community engagement is perfect (or perhaps even adequate), given the pressures of daily 'law and order' policing. As Phil argues,

> I think we could always look at different ways of enhancing how we connect with the community. Because that sort of connection sits in that proactive space whereas most of our resources are put into a reactive space, to meet service demands. It's really hard to measure.

Nonetheless, our interviews indicate a clear locational, or jurisdictional, difference between Australian states. In these examples, there is much more demand, and resourcing available, for proactive community policing practices in Victoria than in Tasmania.

Reassurance

'Reassurance activities' are policing practices designed to help minority groups feel safe and supported following events that make them feel targeted, such as terrorist events. This includes things like a police organisation contacting religious leaders and liaising with local officers, or officers providing a police presence during Friday prayers at a mosque. As both proactive and reactive practices, reassurance activities are clearly informed by global processes of violence, displacement, media and political power, and these types of police practices are most often conducted in times of collective trauma events (Harms, Kosta and Hickey 2022). Given Australia's serious problems with Islamophobia (Hassan 2018), Muslim communities feature prominently in the reassurance activities discussed by participants. Our interviews took place around 18–24 months after the Christchurch massacre in New Zealand and participants discussing reassurance policing mostly referred to the efforts made following this disturbing event, recognising the fear that Australian Muslims might feel for their community's safety.

> Look, when things like [Christchurch] happen we'll go and proactively just have a presence at the mosque … when something happens and when they have their big days, we'll make sure we've got a presence there … we'll connect with them through that and try and build relationships that way. (Phil)

> In those early days after the [Christchurch] shooting [it] was really evident that there was a lot of benefit in having [relationships with community/religious leaders] … I worked very closely [with a fellow officer who is Muslim]. Being a Muslim himself, he had that personal interaction. So, we found that that was absolutely a positive [after Christchurch]. (Kim)

Notably, Chris highlighted that it was also important for officers to account for other, non-Muslim religious communities as part of their reassurance activities:

> We set up security patrols around places of religion, not just mosques, also around synagogues, Sikh gurdwaras because [offenders won't necessarily] know a gurdwara from a mosque. In their eyes, they're just full of people who dress funny, et cetera, et cetera.

This misidentification – where non-Muslims are targeted due to being perceived as Muslim – is something noted in Chapters 4 and 9 and reflects important problems for the safety, respect and wellbeing of all Australians who do not fit the mould of 'White Australia'.

Reassurance activities have their limits, however. As Greg pointed out,

> I know there have been times, following like Christchurch and things like that … we reached out [to the Muslim community] at that time, but we also would have been better positioned had we have built those relationships more, earlier.

In this sense, it is reasonable to describe reassurance activities as more often falling within the domain of reactive policing practices, rather than proactive practices. Further, as noted above, reassurance policing in general risks becoming overly focused on control and regulation. As such, while reassurance activities acknowledge the unique experiences and needs of minority communities, it is important that these practices are not solely performed in response to significant incidents such as terrorist events but are part of a broader response of respect and reciprocal dialogue.

Recruitment and training

Recruitment and training of officers and civilian staff – who applies and is employed by police organisations, the training they receive, the resources they have access to and the facilities and services prioritised – have important implications for the ways in which a police organisation is equipped to engage with diverse communities. Rob and John discussed the importance of having a police force that represents the ethnic, linguistic and religious diversity of Australian communities. As Rob noted, this does come with challenges and the need to be adaptable:

> It's difficult, to be honest, because [our] standards are our standards, and we only have one point of entry. [But we can] build [potential recruits] up to that entry point … for instance, we've now got a [CALD] group [that] come to fitness testing. [At first, not] many passed. So we now have them coming back to the academy every Friday to do some training, getting them to the standard … Normally, we wouldn't do that. Normally, if you don't pass the fitness test we say go away, you can't do it.

Both Rob and John were clear on the benefits of such efforts:

> It's that 'lightbulb' moment … of realising we're going to be a lot more effective, from sitting next to someone in one police car that actually thinks very differently to me … [it's important to] recruit more people from greater religious diversity so they're actually within the organisation so we can learn from them as well … really making that change, letting the people from the mosque [see] that that person is also, that afternoon, he's on duty as a police officer. (Rob)
>
> As you are probably aware we're trying to recruit from different cultures … we've got people who are Muslims now, in the organisation. It's no big deal. In fact we use their strengths. We've got [an officer who speaks] three different languages and he's got a name tag that has those languages on it. We've got another six people who do that. (John)

Here, participants highlight how recruiting for greater diversity – whether ethnic, linguistic, religious or LGBT+ – results in greater resources for police organisations to draw on. This is a proactive process and may come with challenges but, as Rob put it, recruiting for greater diversity is 'longer, and it's slower, but we could put resources into it and start getting some wins'.

While participants described Victoria Police as having invested considerable effort in diversifying their organisation, these efforts to recruit more staff from more diverse backgrounds highlight the current *lack* of diversity within Australian police organisations. Here, investment in training resources is particularly important, ensuring that police recruits have at least some level of diversity knowledge and connection with community members before they begin work on the frontline. It is significant that those recruited to policing organisations may often be not only white and male, but might have little experience interacting with ethnically and religiously diverse Australians. As Steven put it,

> Picture this: you've got a group of recruits … at a rough demographic guess I'm saying average age about 32 … 60 per cent male, probably not a very diverse group, pretty much Anglo-Celtic background … volunteers came in [and] spend 10 to 15 minutes talking with these recruits. It's a mind-blowing experience because it will be the first time that many of these people have actually met a Muslim woman in a hijab, will be the first time that many of them have every actually sat down with a Jew, or met an Aboriginal, and they will discuss their preconceived notions.

Participants in Victoria highlighted these efforts more than Tasmanian participants did, likely reflecting the relative disparity in funding and resourcing between the two organisations. Nevertheless, both Victoria Police and Tasmania Police provide new recruits, current officers and civilian staff with a range of resources that encourage relationships, knowledge and personal interaction with diverse community members. This includes volunteer programmes, engagement with interfaith networks, place of worship tours, local council resources and access to specialist divisions and expert advice. Steven praised the Community Encounters program, where officers hear stories from people different to themselves; similarly, Chris commended the Cultural Diversity Resource Hub, describing it as 'a great resource for police now that's available to us, that never used to exist'. Phil described the importance of activities such as place of worship tours and speaking with people in the community, acknowledging that it is important that all officers engage in these activities, not only those in community engagement portfolios.

However, while police organisations might make efforts towards diverse recruitment and training in community engagement, this alone says little about the extent to which these programmes and policies are truly valued and prioritised (whether by leadership staff or on-the-ground staff). The ability for police organisations to implement effective, systematic outcomes from such processes also requires further consideration and research.

Flexibility, listening and discretion

In many ways, interactions between Australian police and community members are deeply shaped by the formal practices and procedures described above. However, meaningfully respectful engagement with members of the public – particularly people who may be scared, marginalised or lacking social supports – is complex, and often requires careful and individualised judgement. To this end, participants shared many anecdotes showing how flexibility and respect can lead to good outcomes, through creative and empathetic responses to challenging situations.

Steven, for example, described a situation following a suicide in the local Islamic community, in which a sergeant negotiated to allow the deceased's brother to lie in the back of a coroner's van with the body. In the Islamic faith it is often preferred that burials take place as soon as possible after death and as such, the legislative need to transport the body was challenging for the grieving family. As Steven said, this small change in protocol 'meant the world to the family and it meant the world obviously to the brother of the deceased, but it also evidenced nous, it evidenced compassion'. Steven also told a story of providing guidance to Sudanese community members who wished to hold a protest, advising the group how to hold a safe, dignified and effective demonstration:

> This guy couldn't believe it. He said, 'in Sudan you'd be lining me up on a wall and here you're actually telling us how to have a good protest'.

Chris described engaging with right-wing groups holding Islamophobic protests, ensuring that they had 'eyes' on the situation to mitigate increasing tensions:

> [Victoria Police] could actually put in place a plan to make sure that things didn't escalate and get hijacked by others with different agendas.

Participants provided other examples of flexibility and innovation that helped them to respond to diverse needs across their community. To address callouts related to mental health, Phil described a Victoria Police partnership between officers and health workers where, 'instead of then tying ourselves up with hospitals and other things, we try and deal with the person there and then'. Part of understanding and responding respectfully to community members also lies in having diverse staff members whose needs are also respected. To this end, Cameron described how

> [There was] a Muslim lady employed by the department and, for her prayer times, [she] would go to the filing room in the records department and sit on

the floor amongst all the files ... for an organisation that was arguably trying to embrace multiculturalism and community engagement, we didn't even provide our own employees with prayer facilities.

Some of the examples described above – such as providing extra fitness training for potential recruits, promotion of language skills and encouraging all officers (regardless of rank) to attend community events – provide further evidence of the benefits of creative, flexible and equity-centred thinking for police engagement with the wider community. These stories illustrate key examples of how, as Steven put it, 'discretion coupled with understanding is a powerful tool', allowing officers to compassionately respond to difficult situations.

Discussion

Our findings highlight three key themes of policing in religiously diverse Australia:

- The presence of clear differences in the responses between Victoria Police and Tasmania Police;
- The complex role of 'respect' in how police engage with minority communities; and
- The ongoing nature of improving these engagements.

Participants' responses showed clear differences in how Tasmania Police and Victoria Police engage with diversity in their communities, at the levels of both organisational structure and everyday practice. As indicated above, a clear example of this lies in differences between resourcing and funding. Working with far larger and more diverse population, it is clear that Victoria Police staff had far greater access to support and educational resources than Tasmania Police staff did, with a greater emphasis placed on targeted and informed response to issues of religious and cultural diversity (e.g. through the Priority Communities Division, a group of roles that exist in Victoria but not in Tasmania). Tasmanian participants, on the other hand, consistently identified shortfalls in resourcing roles such as a Multicultural Liaison Officer – but did praise the educational resources available to them, such as their collaboration with the University of Tasmania. It is also important to note that compared to Tasmania, officers and civilian staff in Victoria are engaging with the very different situations, opportunities and challenges presented by a highly religiously diverse population.

Tasmanian and Victorian participants also described the different ethical frameworks guiding their policing practices. Victorian Police participants largely emphasised the significance of knowledge and relationship with the community. For these participants, knowing who lives in their communities, the specificities of local diversity and community members' religious and cultural needs helped foster good policing work.

> I think [it's important to encourage] our members not to be afraid to ask questions around religion. It's all well and good to be politically correct but be inquisitive and ask questions and educate yourself around it. If you go to some incident and there's an obvious religious impact behind it, ask questions. Ask why that might have been part of it. (Kim)

> [The place of worship tours] take you to a mosque and a temple and other things and talk about different religions ... it's about building capability at the start to understand it ... [it's important to include] frontline police officers [in interfaith tours]. Really, if you're going to work in this area and deal with the community, you need to understand it. (Phil)

As participants' stories demonstrate, this approach is heavily influenced by community policing paradigms grounded in community partnerships between police and members of the public; as Andrew put it, 'I'm confident that we know who our stakeholders are fairly well.' Participants' responses also demonstrate that this has been an effective approach for Victoria Police for some time. Engagement is at the core of this approach, but this may mean the approach is subject to certain limitations, particularly in terms of resourcing. As the participants themselves note, this form of policing require far more investment and resources than just 'showing up' to cultural events and gatherings. It requires a sustained, multi-level and multi-rank approach – an approach that likely sits outside police organisational role-rotation requirements.

By contrast, Tasmanian participants were instead more likely to emphasise a general model of respect and an underlying 'code of conduct', which would ideally see all encounters between police and the public performed according to the pledge taken by new recruits:

> You won't find a black and white document that says 'when you go and deal with a person of that background, here's what you do'. I think that's appropriate. We take an oath ... The constable's oath is about fairness, impartiality, it's got words like performing our duties without favour or fear ... and we have a code of ethics. (John)

> We don't have formal policies and procedures as such. We have like a diversity framework which is more like a guideline, like a code of conduct type thing. Which, the essence of it is, be respectful, be accepting. Try and understand where appropriate, make the allowances or the changes that you need to without compromising an investigation or legislation. (Tracey)

These differences also carried into how participants described legislation. Victorian participants were far more likely than Tasmanian Police participants to reference specific legislation, strategic policies and intra-organisation advisory roles. This reflects – as discussed elsewhere in this volume – the unique position of Victoria within Australia's 'tapestry' of legislation relating to ethnic and religious discrimination and vilification. Despite this, Victorian participants also reflected upon their reliance on a general ethos of rights and respect. Recent, troubling examples of public displays of Nazi ideology in Australia also provide a clear example of how police are required to operate within the overarching bounds of legislation (ABC News 2023) which, again, vary between Australia's states and territories and raise serious questions about the 'real world' impact of legal frameworks upon policing practices.[2]

As the examples discussed above show, engaging respectfully with diversity requires more than the bare basics of police interacting with members of the public. Rather, these examples show the complex meanings and processes of respect, representation, visibility and accountability embedded within this work. In this way, a police officer attending a community event has multiple 'layers'. On one hand, it is a simple act of ensuring police presence at an event to which they have been invited. On the other, attending this event is a complex process shaped by factors such as the officer's identity, cultural knowledge and rank; the characteristics, needs and experiences of the community whose event is being attended; the policies and legislation informing the relevant police organisation; and wider geopolitical forces including globalisation, migration, discrimination and political violence.

Many of the examples provided by participants relate to 'respect'. This raises the question of identifying what being 'respectful' entails in practice – for example, how might a commitment to fairness and impartiality counteract unconscious bias or systemic discrimination? Further to this, research indicates the importance of procedural justice in positively shaping relationships between police and community members. Implicit in this is a broader process that engages with practices of respect as these relate to the constable's oath and commitments to fairness and impartiality. Also important is coherence between respect and visibility of the internal diversity of staff, and the external diversity of the communities being served. That is to say, an important aspect of how community members respond to police lies in whether – and how – they see themselves being represented within police organisations. While education, training and resources go some way to ensuring that police staff understand and value the diversity of the community they serve, these processes are not a complete substitute for the lived experiences and relationships made possible by a diverse workforce.

Finally, a consistent theme across all interviews was the idea that respectful engagement with diversity is a 'work in progress' – something that is not only imperfect, but could (or should) always be worked on. This seems particularly true in Tasmania, but it is perhaps equally important to acknowledge the ongoing nature of improvement in the Victorian context. From research, it's clear that there are issues with police engagement with minorities (Asquith and Bartkowiak-Théron 2021). The resourcing of policing organisations means that there will always be room to improve community policing approaches that sustain strongly functioning partnerships and relationships with ethnically and religiously diverse populations. Victorian (and increasingly, Tasmanian) communities are highly diverse and very complex and we argue that even with ongoing, immersive training experiences for recruits and in-service officers, this still may not be enough. Consideration could also be given to shifting organisational structures and practices to ensure that this load does not just fall to a few dedicated police officers (Staines, Scott and Morton 2021). We argue that deep, respectful communication between officers and community members requires comprehensive localised knowledge and long-term relationships. Improving the productive collaborative partnerships between Victoria Police and ethnically and religiously diverse people requires continued creative, innovative ways of rethinking policing training and practice.

This chapter has introduced the social, cultural and political issues informing the broader context of policing religiously diverse people in the contemporary moment. It has explored the unique viewpoints of police officers and the strategies they use to engage respectfully with religiously diverse people. Grounded in a complex social, cultural and political terrain, police narratives indicate how they seek to build trust with religious minority groups, and the broader cultural and political movements that trigger tensions within these forms of engagement. Moreover, their perspectives highlight the significant influence of financial and other resourcing, in addition to location, and how these factors shape the types of relationships these officers can build and sustain over time. Moving in and out of reactive and proactive responses, and cycling through modes of policing reflective of reassurance and community models of policing, police officers' narratives provide examples about how these engagements happen, and provide considerations of how they could happen in the future.

Notes

1 Multicultural Liaison Officers (MLOs) are officers with a responsibility to interact closely with ethnically and linguistically diverse communities to deliver culturally sensitive services. Andrew (Victoria Police) describes MLOs as ' "proactives" [who] are the frontline of engagement with the community'.

2 During an anti-transgender rights protest in Melbourne in March 2023, a group of men performed the Sieg Heil (Nazi salute) outside the Victorian Parliament. While the use of the Nazi swastika is banned in Victoria, the Sieg Heil is not. As such, police officers present at the scene were unable to intervene in the men's actions, prompting calls for the strengthening of relevant legislation (ABC News 2023).

References

ABC News. 2023. 'Victorian Government May Consider Amending Laws after Nazi Salutes at Parliament Rallies'. *ABC News*, 19 March. https://www.abc.net.au/news/2023-03-19/victoria-nazi-salute-peformed-parliament-government-respo nse/102116672. Accessed 2 April 2023.

Asquith and Bartkowiak-Théron. 2021. *The Guardian*. https://www.theguardian.com/uk-news/2022/feb/28/england-and-wales-police-bosses-will-not-admit-to-institutio nal-racism-in-their-forces. Accessed 1 December 2022.

ABS (Australian Bureau of Statistics). 2022. 'Religious Affiliation in Australia'. https://www.abs.gov.au/articles/religious-affiliation-australia. Accessed 1 December 2022.

Bartkowiak-Théron, I., and Asquith, N. 2012. 'The Extraordinary Intracacies of Policing Vulnerability'. *Australasian Policing: A Journal of Professional Practice and Research* 4(2): 43–9.

Bartkowiak-Théron, I., and Asquith, N. 2014. 'Policing Diversity and Vulnerability in the Post-Macpherson Era: Unintended Consequences and Missed Opportunities. *Policing* 9(1): 89–100.

Blumberg, D. M., Schlosser, M. D., Papazoglou, K., Creighton, S., and Kaye, C. C. 2019. 'New Directions in Police Academy Training: A Call to Action'. *International Journal of Environmental Research and Public Health* 16: 4941.

Bouma, G., Arunachalam, D., Gamlen, A. and Healy, E., 2022. 'Religious Diversity through a Super-Diversity Lens: National, Sub-regional and Socio-economic Religious Diversities in Melbourne. *Journal of Sociology* 58(1): 7–25.

Chan, J. 1995. 'Police Accountability in a Multicultural Society'. *Crime Australia* 2–6 May. https://search.informit.org/doi/pdf/10.3316/ielapa.951110776. Accessed 17 March 2022.

Convery, S. 2022. 'Muslims in Australia Experienced Surge of Hate after Christchurch Massacre, Report Reveals'. *The Guardian*. https://www.theguardian.com/austra lia-news/2022/mar/15/muslims-in-australia-experienced-surge-of-hate-after-chris tchurch-massacre-report-reveals. Accessed 1 December 2022.

Cordner, G. 2014. 'Community Policing'. In M. D. Reisig and R. J. Kane (eds), *The Oxford Handbook of Police and Policing*. Oxford: Oxford University Press.

Dejmanee, T., Millar, J., Lorenz, M., Weber, K., and Zaher, Z. 2022. '#Aboriginallivesmatter: Mapping Black Lives Matter Discourse in Australia'. *Media International Australia* 184(1): 6–20.

Dwyer, A. 2019. 'Queering Police Administration: How Policing Administration Complicates LGBTIQ–Police Relations'. *Administrative Theory & Praxis* 42(2): 172–90.

Ezzy, D., Banham, R., and Beaman, L. 2021. 'Religious Diversity, Legislation, and Christian Privilege'. *Journal of Sociology* 59(1): 70–86.

Ezzy, D., Banham, R., and Beaman, L. 2022. Religious Anti-discrimination Legislation and the Negotiation of Difference in Victoria, Australia'. *Religion, State & Society* 50(1): 22–39, DOI: 10.1080/09637494.2021.2010906.

The Faith Communities Council of Victoria. 2022. 'Faith Communities Preventing Family Violence'. https://www.faithvictoria.org.au/programs/family violence. Accessed 1 Feb 2023.

Fielding, N., and Innes, M. 2006. Reassurance Policing, Community Policing and Measuring Police Performance'. *Policing & Society* 16(2): 127–45.

Fokas, E. 2019. 'Religion and Education in the Shadow of the European Court of Human Rights', *Politics and Religion* 12(S1): S1–S8.

Gatwiri, K., and Townsend-Cross, M. 2022. 'Block, Unfollow, Delete': The Impacts of the #BlackLivesMatter Movement on Interracial Relationships in Australia'. *British Journal of Social Work* 52: 3721–39.

Grossman, M., Brack, D., Stephenson, P., Dwyer, R., and Roose, J. 2013. *Learning to Engage: A Review of Victoria Police Cross-Cultural Training Practices*. Melbourne: Centre for Cultural Diversity and Wellbeing, Victoria University. https://www.vu.edu.au/sites/default/files/ccdw/pdfs/learning-to-engage-cross-cultural-train ing-practice-review-victoria-police-2013.pdf. Accessed 17 March 2023.

Harms, L., Kosta, L., and Hickey, L. 2022. 'Effective Reassurance Policing after Collective Trauma Events: Perceptions of Australian Police'. *Police Practice and Research* https://doi.org/10.1080/15614263.2022.2117178. Accessed 1 December 2022.

Hassan, R. 2018. *Australian Muslims: The Challenge of Islamophobia and Social Distance.* International Centre for Muslim and Non-Muslim Understanding. https://www. unisa.edu.au/contentassets/4f85e84d01014997a99bb4f89ba32488/australian-musl ims-final-report-web-nov-26.pdf. Accessed 14 March 2023.

Iner, Derya. 2019. *Islamophobia in Australia (2016–2017).* https://www.islamophobia. com.au/wp-content/uploads/2019/12/Islamophobia-Report-2019-2.pdf. Accessed 1 December 2022.

Innes, M. 2007. 'The Reassurance Function'. *Policing* 1(2): 132–41.

Klippmark, P., and Crawley, K. 2018. 'Justice for Ms Dhu: Accounting for Indigenous Deaths in Custody in Australia'. *Social & Legal Studies* 27(6): 695–715.

Knight, L. 2017. 'Police-Faith Relations: Perceptions, Experiences and Challenges'. Doctoral Thesis, University of Leicester. https://pure.northampton.ac.uk/en/publi cations/police-faith-relations-perceptions-experiences-and-challenges. Accessed 19 March 2023.

Levinson, D. 2007. 'Community Policing'. In D. Levinson (ed.), *Encyclopedia of Crime and Punishment.* London: Sage Publications.

Love, H. 2007) *Feeling Backward: Loss and the Politics of Queer History.* Cambridge, MA: Harvard University Press.

Markus, A. 2021. *Mapping Social Cohesion 2020: The Scanlon Foundation Surveys. Scanlon Institute.* https://scanloninstitute.org.au/report2020. Accessed 12 March 2023.

Mazerolle, L., Eggins, E., Cherney, A., Hine, L., Higginson, A., and Belton, E. 2020. 'Police Programmes That Seek to Increase Community Connectedness for Reducing Violent Extremism Behaviour, Attitudes and Beliefs'. *Campbell Systematic Reviews* 16: e1111. https://onlinelibrary.wiley.com/doi/epdf/10.1002/cl2.1111. Accessed 18 March 2023.

Millie, A. 2007. 'Whatever Happened to Reassurance Policing?' *Policing* 4(3): 225–32.

Millie, A., and Herrington, V. 2005. 'Bridging the Gap: Understanding Reassurance Policing'. *Howard Journal* 44(1): 41–56.

Pittaway, T., and Dantas, J. A. 2021. African Youth Gangs: The Marginalization of South Sudanese Young People in Melbourne, Australia'. *Journal of Immigrant & Refugee Studies* 1–17. DOI: 10.1080/15562948.2021.2017534.

Poynting, S. 2020. '"Islamophobia Kills". But Where Does It Come From?' *International Journal for Crime, Justice and Social Democracy* 9(2): 74–87. https://doi.org/10.5204/ ijcjsd.v9i2.1258.

Poynting, S., and Briskman, L. 2018. 'Islamophobia in Australia: From Far-Right Deplorables to Respectable Liberals'. *Social Sciences* 7: 213.

Ratcliffe, J. 2018. *Reducing Crime: A Companion for Police Leaders.* New York: Routledge.

Shepherd, S. M., and Masuka, G. 2021. 'Working with At-Risk Culturally and Linguistically Diverse Young People in Australia: Risk Factors, Programming, and Service Delivery'. *Criminal Justice Policy Review* 32(5): 469–83.

Skogan, W. G. 2019. 'Advocate: Community Policing'. In D. Weisburg and A. A. Braga (eds), *Police Innovation: Contrasting Perspectives*. Cambridge: Cambridge University Press.

Staines, Z., Scott, J., and Morton, J.(2021. 'Without Uniform I Am a Community Member, Uncle, Brother, Granddad': Community Policing in Australia's Torres Strait Region'. Journal of Criminology 54(3): 265–82.

Tan, X., Lee, R., and Ruppanner, L. 2021. 'Profiling Racial Prejudice during COVID-19: Who Exhibits Anti-Asian Sentiment in Australia and the United States?' *Australian Journal of Social Issues* 56(4): 464–84.

Warner, K. 2004. 'Gang Rape in Sydney: Crime, the Media, Politics, Race and Sentencing'. *Australian & New Zealand Journal of Criminology* 37(3): 344–61.

Wiedlitzka, S., Mazerolle, L., Fay-Ramirez, S., and& Miles-Johnson, T. 2018. 'Perceptions of Police Legitimacy and Citizen Decisions to Report Hate Crime Incidents in Australia'. *International Journal for Crime, Justice and Social Democracy* 7(2): 91–106. doi: 10.5204/ijcjsd.v7i2.489.

9

The Evolution of Preventing and Countering Violent Extremism (P/CVE) Policy and Programmes in Australia

Greg Barton and Anna Halafoff

Introduction – the aftermath of 9/11

This chapter charts the evolution of preventing and countering violent extremism (P/CVE) programmes in Australia with a particular focus on the state of Victoria. P/CVE programmes complement and overlap with counterterrorism (CT) programmes. P/CVE programmes are more holistic than CT programmes. And whereas CT programmes, which focus on the detection and disruption of terrorist threats, remain firmly under the control of police and security agencies, P/CVE programmes are generally community-led. They seek to work well upstream of CT interventions, to prevent the need for arrest and prosecution, as well as working downstream to facilitate disengagement from extremist networks, rehabilitation and reintegration into mainstream communities. They are commonly understood using the conceptual framing of public health as involving primary interventions across society intended to reduce risk and build resilience, secondary interventions aimed at at-risk individuals and groups, and tertiary interventions directed at rehabilitation. In some countries the terminology of PVE (preventing violent extremism) is preferred to CVE, and there has been a general shift globally towards using P/CVE to better capture the full spectrum of preventative measures. In Australia, until recently at least, the standard terminology has been CVE, and that is reflected in the usage in the historical programmes discussed in this chapter.

Up until 2015 the majority of CVE programmes in Australia were focused at the primary intervention level. The rise of the Islamic State (IS) caliphate, out of the rapid advance of ISIS (Islamic State in Iraq and Syria) from northern Syria across northern Iraq, in mid-2014, revealed that hundreds of young Australians were being groomed, recruited and radicalised to travel to support IS and other violent extremist groups in Syria and Iraq. This precipitated renewed efforts to foster collaboration between police, agencies and community groups to protect at-risk individuals. This required building deeper engagement and trust between police and community at a time when the Muslim community was feeling more stigmatised than ever.

Of all the social policies that impact on multicultural communities in highly diverse societies, policies intended to prevent and counter violent extremism are some of the least understood and most controversial. There are many factors involved in this, but broadly the problem has to do with the perception and practice, whether intentional or not, of placing a securitising lens on the Muslim community in particular, and on religion more broadly, in the wake of the al-Qaeda terrorist attacks of 11 September 2001. Muslims in Australia, as in other diaspora communities across the Western world, report that the 9/11 attacks were a pivotal moment in perceptions of Islam and Muslims. Prior to 9/11 there had been relatively little suspicion of Muslims. These events, and the 7 July 2005 (7/7) London transport bombings, also saw well-documented negative impacts on members of the Sikh community, who were mistaken as Muslims, and other communities of so-called Middle Eastern appearance, a highly problematic term and phenomenon that contributed to the violent 2005 Cronulla race riots in Sydney, at the height of the Australian values debate (Bouma et al. 2007; Bouma 2011; Halafoff 2006).

Al-Qaeda had, of course, been responsible for a series of significant terrorist attacks prior to 9/11 and 7/7. These included the bombing attacks on US embassies in Kenya and Tanzania in 1998, and the ramming of the USS Cole at harbour in Aden, Yemen, with an explosive-packed boat in 2000. Al-Qaeda had been a growing concern since its emergence in 1988 out of the resistance to the Soviet military occupation of Afghanistan in the 1980s. In hindsight, the seeds of future problems were sown in the US and allied support for the *mujahideen* fighters' military action in Afghanistan in the 1980s and 1990s, combined with failing to follow through with assisting in the rebuilding of Afghan society. But it was direct military action in Afghanistan, and then in the Middle East and Africa, that was to have devastating unintended consequences in compounding, amplifying and expanding the threat posed by al-Qaeda and its spin-offs like IS (Barton 2004, 2018; Cockburn 2015; Gerges 2016).

While Muslims living in the West and Islam were generally not seen as posing a serious security threat before the 9/11 attacks, this unfortunately changed in multiple ways in the wake of them. Tragically, some of the main casualties of the poorly framed 'global war on terror' were innocent Muslim families and communities across Afghanistan and the Middle East, and the sense of peace and trust that had previously marked successful and productive Muslim migration to Western democracies (Kenney 2018).

The 'global war on terror' exacerbated the existing problems, shifted the balance of power and set in motion a cascade of unintended consequences which led to decades of violent insurgency in Afghanistan and Iraq, contributed to the collapse of order in Syria and Libya, and indirectly compounded problems across Africa. One of the consequences was that millions of people were forced from their homes, fleeing to 'internally displaced people' camps, getting caught up in insurgent conflict and being forced to join vast streams of refugees (Cockburn 2015; Gerges 2016).

Many of these asylum seekers came to Australia, successfully started new lives from nothing, in a country which, for all its missteps and long history of racism, as documented in previous chapters in this volume, had previously been largely welcoming of refugees. Unfortunately, beginning in 2001 attitudes to asylum seekers and refugees changed significantly, under the conservative leadership of Prime Minister John Howard. Australia's commitment to multiculturalism and respect for cultural and religious diversity was eroded during the Howard years, which were characterised instead by Islamophobia, xenophobia and a confected moral panic about asylum seekers arriving by boat (Bouma et al. 2007; Halafoff 2006). This was reflected in national rhetoric and policies for countering terrorism at that time, which placed an emphasis on a narrow nationalism founded on 'Australian Judeo-Christian values'. By contrast, the state of Victoria maintained its commitment to multiculturalism, which provided the foundation for policies and practices to counter violent extremism (CVE), including community policing. The Victorian Department of Premier and Cabinet (DPC) also invested heavily in CVE research, funding Monash University's Global Terrorism Research Centre (GTReC). Victoria's DPC and GTReC were among the pioneers in a community resilience model of preventing and countering violent extremism (P/CVE), which gradually spread to the national Australian level and internationally (Barelle 2015; Halafoff 2013; Halafoff and Wright-Neville 2009; Ilardi 2008; Lentini 2013).

Interest in CVE once again increased with the rise to prominence of Islamic State (IS) in 2014. By late 2014, and through into 2015 and 2016, hundreds of young Australians were stopped from travelling to join the Islamic State caliphate in Syria and Iraq (Harris-Hogan and Barrelle 2020. The significant success in halting would-be foreign fighters was a direct result of not just police working counterterrorism intelligence but also close collaboration with the communities being targeted by recruiters. The lives of many young Australian Muslims were saved because of the intervention of their friends and family members who spoke up, raised the alarm, and shared their concerns (Zammit 2015).

Not only did Muslim families and community groups contribute to countering loved ones being at risk of radicalisation and travelling to become foreign fighters in the Middle East, but their contribution was also significant to police counterterrorism operations that stopped two dozen attempted attacks in the years that followed. This chapter argues that cooperative P/CVE strategies involving communities and security agencies are the most effective and need to be implemented across multiple levels aiming to prevent and counter hate and extremist violence. There are inherent tensions between community, security and political objectives that require careful negotiation, and require the building and maintaining of relationships based on trust and open channels of communication. Lessons learned in Australia, and Victoria specifically, can be instructive on this.

Terrorism and P/CVE in Australia since the 1978 Hilton bombing

In February 1978 a bomb placed in a rubbish bin outside the Sydney Hilton Hotel detonated, killing two workers, and a police officer, and injuring eleven others at the site of the blast. The blast occurred in the middle of the night when the workers loaded the bin into a garbage truck. It is thought that the target was a Commonwealth Heads of Government Regional Meeting being hosted at the Hilton and attended by twelve foreign leaders, including the Indian prime minister Morarji Desai, who claimed that he was the target of an assassination attempt by the Indian spiritual group Ananda Marga. The subsequent investigations, trials and inquiries failed to dispel doubt and accusations of cover-up (Landers 2016).

The Hilton bombing was regarded as the most serious act of terrorism in Australia up to that point. It triggered major investments in counterterrorism capacity, including the formation of the Australian Federal Police in 1979. It remained the most significant terrorism case in Australia up until the Islamic State-inspired Lindt Café siege of December 2014. But other significant incidents contributed to enduring concerns about terrorism.

In Yeppoon Queensland on the 29 November 1980, the day of the state elections, a Japanese-owned business, the Iwasaki resort, was bombed. And, in an unrelated incident, two weeks later Sarik Ariyak, the Turkish consul general in Sydney, and Engin Sever, his security attaché, were shot dead by gunmen on motorcycles. In the late 1980s, and then again in the early 2000s, the Western Australia-based neo-Nazi group led by Jack van Tongeren, The Australian Nationalist Movement, was responsible for multiple arson attacks on Asian restaurants and businesses, together with other acts of violence including the murder of a suspected informant. In 1982 the Israeli Consulate, and the Hakoah Club, in Sydney were bombed. In 1986 a bomb detonated prematurely in a basement car park under the Turkish Consulate in Melbourne, killing the bomber. In 1989 far-right extremists linked to the neo-Nazi National Action group attempted to assassinate African National Congress (ANC) representative Eddie Funde. Then in 1995 the French Consulate in Perth was hit with a firebomb. And in July 2001 an obsessive anti-abortionist attacked the East Melbourne Family Planning clinic, shooting dead a security guard.

Western CVE programmes first emerged in response to the challenge of home-grown radicalisation and the emergence of domestic extremist networks. And while it was the 9/11 attacks that marked the turning point for thinking about counterterrorism and the specific threat presented by al-Qaeda and related Salafi jihadist groups, it was home-grown attacks such as the 11 March 2004 Madrid commuter train bombings and the 7 July 2005 London tube and bus bombings that brought home the threat posed by home-grown extremist networks.

For Australia, however, it was the bombings in Bali on 12 October 2002 that killed 88 Australians, and took a total of 202 lives, which brought home the threat of terrorism. And while the attack did not take place on Australian soil, it involved a Southeast Asia group, Jemaah Islamiyah (JI), which had an active Australian branch operating in Sydney and Perth (Barton 2004). Subsequent cooperation between the Australian Federal Police and Indonesian police proved transformative for both police forces and nations as post-blast forensic investigations revealed an extensive home-grown threat in Indonesia. Similarly, the MV SuperFerry 14 bombing in Manila harbour that killed 116, which was carried out by JI partner, the Abu Sayyaf Group (ASG), reinforced the scale of the threat posed by home-grown terrorist groups in the Philippines. In the two decades that followed these attacks Australia was to become extensively involved in developing the first CT and then also P/CVE capacity in its Southeast Asian neighbours (Barton, Vergani and Wahid 2022). A productive programme of exchange and cooperation also benefited P/CVE programmes within Australia.

Operation Pendennis 2005

Prior to the AFP's involvement in the post-blast forensic investigation following the Bali bombings of 2002, the largest police CT operation in Australian history occurred in 2005–6 with Operation Pendennis. This was purely a police-led CT operation but it was to have a transformative impact on the development of CVE in Victoria because it contributed directly to the development of the Community Integration and Support Program (CISP), Australia's first rehabilitation CVE programme, discussed later in this chapter.

Operation Pendennis employed an undercover police officer and listening devices to monitor al-Qaeda inspired extremist cells in Victoria and New South Wales (Ilardi 2017; Moroney 2018; Schuurman et al. 2014). The surveillance operation ran through 2004 and 2005 and resulted in the arrests of seventeen men in Melbourne and Sydney in November 2005 and further arrests in March 2006. In October 2009, following what became the longest running and most expensive court trials of their kind in Australia, nine men in New South Wales were found guilty of terrorism offences, and they were sentenced in February 2010. It was argued that had they not been arrested they would have attempted to carry out a terrorist attack in 2006. The nature of the preparations undertaken by the nine men in New South Wales meant that most were sentenced to lengthy prison sentences of up to twenty-eight years. Twelve men appeared in court in a separate trial in Victoria including the spiritual leader of both the Melbourne and Sydney cells, Abdul Nacer Benbrika. Benbrika was found guilty in September 2008 and in February 2009 was sentenced to fifteen years in jail. Eight others were also found guilty. The prison sentences given in Victoria were shorter, on average, but most were still very substantial.

Operation Neath 2009

In 2007 the AFP, in partnership with Victoria Police, launched Operation Rochester to investigate the recruitment of Somali-Australians from Melbourne to fight with the terrorist group al-Shabab in Somalia. After struggling to collect sufficient evidence to file charges, Operation Rochester was called off. But concerns remained and Operation Neath was commenced in February to investigate fresh evidence of al-Shabab support in Australia. Through the course of investigations by the AFP, Victoria Police, ASIO and the Defence Security Division, twenty Somali-Australians were suspected of supporting al-Shabab, and by 2009 investigations had broadened to include people from non-Somali backgrounds. On 4 August 2009 four men suspected of supporting al-Shabab were arrested and charged with making preparations for an act of terror; a fifth man was charged several days later. It was alleged that the men, realising that their path to joining al-Shabab in Somalia was blocked, were planning to attack Holsworthy Barracks, an Australian Army training centre in Sydney's outer Southwest. In December 2011 three of the men were sentenced to eighteen years in prison. Although this was a police-led CT operation, important lessons about working with communities were learnt from the Operation Pendennis arrests in 2005, and Victoria Police community liaison teams made extensive preparations to reduce the impact on the families of those arrested. This laid a foundation for the further development of community liaison and CVE teams within Victoria Police.

Brighton Siege 2017

The CISP rehabilitation programme has been evaluated multiple times as it has evolved and has been assessed as being effective and necessary. But no rehabilitation can have perfect results, as is seen in the case of Yacqub Khayre. Khayre was one of the five men arrested in Operation Neath, but terrorism charges were later dropped. He had travelled to Somalia in April 2009 and allegedly undertaken training with al-Shabab, and obtained a fatwa, or religious judgement, allegedly to authorise a terrorist attack in Australia. He was acquitted in December 2010 after spending sixteen months in prison on remand. But he was later arrested and in 2011 sentenced for other criminal offences; while in jail he was engaged in the CISP CVE rehabilitation programme. On 5 June 2017, apparently following instructions set out in the IS e-magazine *Rumiyah*, Khayre, then twenty-nine years old, set up a siege situation at the Buckingham International Serviced Apartments in the wealthy Melbourne bayside suburb of Brighton. After checking in he made a telephone booking for a sex worker, taking her hostage after she met him in his room at 4 pm. She managed to momentarily free herself and alert the police. Kharye shot dead Kai Hao, a receptionist working in the foyer. Kharye called the police and Seven News, saying 'This is for IS, this is for al-Qaeda'. Shortly after 6 pm, Kharye ran from the apartment and fired at the police with a sawed-off double-barrel shotgun, injuring three officers. He was shot dead in the exchange of fire.

Endeavour Hills stabbings 2014

The first person to die in Australia as a consequence of IS radicalisation was a Hazara teenager, Numan Haider. Tragically, even though his family had fled Afghanistan because of violence directed against the Shia Hazara by Sunni Islamist extremists he fell under the influence of a self-proclaimed fundamentalist sheikh and an IS-inspired extremist group at the al-Furqan centre in Springvale in the south-east of Melbourne. On 23 September 2014 this influence led him to launch an attack on two CT police officers who had come to speak to him outside the Endeavour Hills police station. In what appears to have been a martyrdom attack, he slashed a Victoria Police officer and then stabbed an AFP agent in the head and torso before the Victoria Police officer pulled out his pistol and shot dead Haider as he continued to attack his AFP colleague. The tragic case of Haider points to a potential missed opportunity for CVE interventions with the community of youth associated with the al-Furqan centre, which had first come to the attention of Victoria Police in September 2012 because of extremist posts on Facebook.

Numan Haider may have been the first person to die in Australia as a result of radicalisation by IS, but other Australians died before him overseas. Although it was only just becoming clear at the time of the September 2014 attack in Endeavour Hills, many dozens of Australians had begun to travel to Syria to join IS, or al-Qaeda linked groups, in the two years preceding this event.

In total it was thought that more than 150 Australians travelled to Syria and Iraq. In 2012 and 2013 around three dozen had returned home, but dozens of others died fighting in the Middle East, and many more including women and children remain detained in camps or prisons in Syria and Iraq. A much larger number, however, in the order of 300 to 500 people, were successfully stopped from flying out of Sydney or Melbourne airports (Barton 2015).

Lindt Café siege 2014

Three months after Numan Haider's stabbing attack in Melbourne a second man, without prior links to IS, launched a terrorist attack in the name of IS. This attack took the form of a long-drawn-out hostage siege in a city café. Shortly after 8.30 am, on 15 December 2014, an Iranian-born, self-proclaimed Shia cleric, Man Haron Monis, entered the Lindt Café in Martin Place, in the Sydney CBD. Monis was notorious for his hateful campaign of sending threatening letters to families of soldiers who had died fighting in Afghanistan. On 12 December 2014, three days before he entered the Lindt Café, Monis had lost an appeal against his conviction for criminal use of the postal service. Separately, he had been charged with being an accessory to murder in relation to the death of his former wife in April 2013, but had been granted bail in December 2013. He had a long list of charges of sexual assault and common assault, some of which related to his time as a spiritual healer. On 10 October 2014 he was charged with forty addition sexual assault offences against six women, but remained free on bail. Days before the siege he had used his website to proclaim that he had turned his back on Shia Islam and sworn an oath of allegiance (*bayat*) to 'the caliph of the Muslims', apparently referring to IS leader Abu Bakr al-Baghdadi.

At 9:44 am, Monis opened a bag and pulled out a sawed-off shotgun. He ordered the doors of the café to be locked, taking hostage ten customers and eight café employees. Monis declared that he was acting in the name of IS. Monis attempted to negotiate to be allowed to talk to the prime minister on ABC radio, saying that he would release half of his hostages in exchange. During the afternoon, five hostages managed to escape, angering Monis, who was frustrated with his lack of access to media. Throughout the day and into the night, police followed a 'contain and negotiate' strategy. The forward commander was never properly briefed on Monis's background and criminal history and was operating on poorly informed advice from a consultant psychiatrist that, as a narcissist, Monis was engaged in attention-seeking behaviour, and that he would calm down during the night. At 1.43 am, Tori Johnson, the café manager, texted his family to say that Monis was becoming increasingly agitated. At 2.03 am, six more hostages escaped. At 2.13 am, Monis executed Johnson and the police launched a clumsy breach operation, storming the café from two opposite sets of doors. Monis was shot dead, but fragments from twenty-two high-velocity rounds, fired from M4A1 carbines, ricocheted from the granite walls wounding four and killing Katrina Dawson. Two weeks later, in the following edition of *Dabiq* magazine in a multi-page spread, IS praised Numan Haider and Man Haron Monis, declaring them to be martyrs (Barton 2015, 2018).

Broader acceptance of P/CVE in Australia

Following the above tragic events, and by the time that the federal Attorney General's Department was hosting a regional international CVE summit in Sydney in 2015, it had become clear that CVE could be a vital counterpart to CT (Barker 2015). Despite the earlier decade of community-policing and GTReC research on CVE in Victoria, it wasn't until Australia began to feel the direct impact of IS radicalisation and recruitment that the concept of CVE became more concrete and sharply defined, and its contribution widely recognised.

By the 2020s the concept of P/CVE became widely accepted both in Australia and around the world. For a long while, however, the concept of P/CVE drew sharply divided opinions, both within general society, including particularly the communities that were generally the focus of CVE initiatives, such as the Muslim community in particular, and within police circles.

Within police forces CT is regarded as an essential aspect of modern policing, with a focus on detecting and disrupting would-be attackers and plots. In contrast, P/CVE is often dismissed as a soft measure of uncertain utility. Within communities targeted by P/CVE programmes, there is a long history of suspicion, not without considerable justification, that P/CVE is a securitising approach that taints the target community and frames community members as being somehow untrustworthy.

Up until recently, the majority of community-led P/CVE programmes suffered not just from short-term funding and inadequate support, but also from the perception that they were contributing to securitising the problem and framing it as the responsibility of the Muslim community (Akbarzadeh 2013; Aly 2013). Even when operating at arm's length from police and intelligence agencies they bore the burden of suspicion (Aly 2014). And while attempting to design and implement programmes that lacked the support and direction to target those most at risk, they were open to the criticism of being ineffectual (Harris-Hogan, Barrelle and Zammitt 2015).

While these problems are not completely resolved, it is now more generally accepted within policing that there is a limit to what can be achieved with hard measures alone, and that CT needs to be augmented with interventions both upstream of CT operations, and downstream in the domain of disengagement and rehabilitation. It is now widely recognised that while police forces cannot run P/CVE programmes by themselves, and need to work with communities and civil society organisations, their role and contribution cannot be completely separated from an effective approach to P/CVE. This is because to work at the level of focusing on individuals and groups at risk of radicalisation to violent extremism, as well as attempting to effect rehabilitation, police counterterrorism units are uniquely equipped with respect to intelligence analysis to identify those in need of P/CVE interventions.

Without the assistance of police, community groups struggle to direct P/CVE initiatives where they are most needed. At the same time, however, with appropriate training it is families and communities that are often the first to see signs of radicalisation and recruitment. To achieve optimal results in a sustained fashion there needs to be a high degree of trust between police counterterrorism forces and community groups and civil society. Operationally, this requires not just trust and mutual respect but also discretion. Families and other members of communities will not have the confidence to speak up and raise concerns about loved ones if this information is leaked into the community in a manner that generates stigma and prejudice.

P/CVE and Australian politics

Another factor that impeded the acceptance of a P/CVE approach is that, over the past two decades, P/CVE programmes have been particularly susceptible to the vicissitudes of politics. While national security in Australia, at least as much as in other Western democracies, has generally enjoyed broad non-partisan support, P/CVE has been one area that has been especially vulnerable to political contestation and what has been described as cultural wars. In the United States, where there has been a growing awareness of the problem of far-right extremism, the reactionary administration of Donald Trump not only applied the brakes to P/CVE programmes, it especially singled out research and policy initiatives to engage with the threat of far-right extremism. In Australia the conservative government of Prime Minister John Howard was praised for the timely response in the wake of the Bali bombings of 2002 to the threat of terrorism in the region, but its domestic response to CT and CVE suffered from perceptions of bias towards the Muslim community. In September 2005, in the wake of the July 2005 '7/7' attacks in London, the state governments and Australian federal government, under the rubric of the Council of Australian governments (COAG) established a National Action Plan to build on social cohesion, harmony and security under the direction of the National Counterterrorism Committee (NCTC). A month prior, the Howard government had established a Muslim community reference group (MCRG) to tackle the problem of home-grown extremism and radicalisation. It was an initiative that was, arguably, sound in principle but clumsy in its implementation and led to perceptions that the conservative federal government was backing moderate Islam and moderate Muslims while singling out Salafi and other conservative communities as being part of the problem.

In September 2005 the Victorian government also launched a major initiative in the P/CVE space, marking the beginning of proactive engagement by state governments, particularly in the two key states of Victoria and New South Wales, home to the largest Muslim communities. The Victorian government published a paper entitled 'Protecting Our Community: Attacking the Causes of Terrorism'. While not explicitly using the terminology of CVE it focused on preventative, noncoercive, measures conducted in partnership with community groups, founded on its commitment to multiculturalism. This vision was further detailed the following year in a paper entitled 'A Safer Victoria: Protecting Our Community – New Initiatives to Combat Terrorism'. This 2006 Victorian government paper outlines a plan for interfaith dialogue, community engagement and the sponsorship of academic research into radicalisation. This started the process in which Victorian government initiatives fed into federal government thinking and P/CVE programmes and in turn to responses in New South Wales.

The Victorian approach to P/CVE was also informed by, and had an impact on, other P/CVE programmes that were being developed internationally, such as the UK Prevent programme and Dutch CT and CVE programmes. Even before the 7/7 attacks in London in 2005, the UK had begun thinking about what role preventing violent extremism should play in its national counterterrorism strategy. In 2003 the Labour government of Tony Blair launched its CT strategy under the title of Contest. Contest was composed of several distinct strands, one of which was called Prevent, which was intended to 'prevent people from becoming terrorists or supporting terrorism' (HM Government 2011; O'Toole, DeHanas and Modood 2012). Two weeks after the Madrid train attacks, the European Union (EU) adopted a declaration on combating terrorism and later followed it up with the EU plan of action on combating terrorism. The UK prevent programme was almost entirely focused on the Muslim community, a reality that was to cause considerable resentment and distrust (Thomas 2010). In particular, efforts to engage schoolteachers in detecting and reporting on alleged early signs of radicalisation caused much harm, in no small measure because of the unrealistic expectations placed upon schools and schoolteachers and the propensity for false alarms (Busher, Choudhury and Thomas 2017). It generally seems to have become even worse when David Cameron replaced Gordon Brown in May 2010 with the UK moving into a long period of conservative governments that were seen as sceptical of multiculturalism, prone to blaming migrant communities for social problems and to tolerating, or even on occasion advocating, Islamophobic views.

In December 2007 the Australian Labor federal government of Kevin Rudd was sworn in, after almost twelve years of conservative government under John Howard. Labor, under Kevin Rudd and Jullia Gillard, was to be in power for a little over six years before Tony Abbott and his conservative coalition government came to office in September 2013 marking nearly a decade of conservative governments that only concluded in May 2022 with the arrival of the Labor government of Anthony Albanese.

In Victoria differences in policy and outlook between Labor and conservative Liberal governments on matters of security have been much less sharply drawn than has been the case at the federal level. Over the past two decades Labor governments have predominated, being in power from October 1999 through until December 2010, and then again from December 2014 through until the present. And whether in government or in opposition, Liberal leaders have tended to work closely with Labor leaders on issues of security including CT and CVE. This political context is significant because it tends to colour both the perception and implementation of policy with respect to P/CVE, and developments in Victoria have tended to lead in framing, developing and implementing policy at the federal level (Victorian Government 2005, 2006).

The change to a Labor national government in December 2007 saw an explicit pivot towards actively developing CVE programmes at the national level. The new Rudd government held a series of community roundtables which resulted in policy on CVE been assigned to the NCTC. The NCTC in turn moved to set up a permanent Subcommittee for Countering Violent Extremism (CVESC). The NCTC and CVESC developed a national framework on CVE that outlined four key aims: (1) identify and divert violent extremists and provide them with disengagement options; (2) Identify and support at-risk individuals; (3) Support community resilience and build cohesion; and (4) Achieve effective communications which challenge extremist messages and support alternatives.

A more fully developed CVE policy framework was set out in the 2010 Counterterrorism white paper that was entitled 'Securing Australia: Protecting Our Future' (Australian Government 2010a). This marked the beginning of a shift towards a whole of government approach to CVE at the federal level, involving multiple departments. The contentious Muslim Community Reference Group was disbanded in favour of a decentralised approach to engaging with individual elements of the Muslim community. A key 2010 development by the Attorney General's Department, which was assigned leadership of policy on CVE, was establishing a CVE unit tasked with identifying and diverting at-risk individuals, challenging extremist ideologies and strengthening community cohesion (Australian Government 2010b).

In 2011 a programme of community grants was introduced, which was called the Building Community Resilient Grants programme. The emphasis on resilience was intended to build capacity within communities to resist violent extremism and specifically to support vulnerable youth (Duckworth 2015). This programme funded fifty-nine initiatives over the next two years out of a total budget of $5.3 million AUD, before the programme was wound up in 2013.

In 2011 the Obama administration released its own national P/CVE strategy publishing a paper entitled 'Empowering Local Partners to Prevent Violent Extremism in the United States' that articulated the vision for cooperation and capacity building through community partnerships (The White House 2011). The P/CVE paper and associated strategy for the United States was the work of a leading American expert on Salafi Jihadi thought, Quintan Wiktorowicz, who was chair on the interagency intelligence subcommittee in radicalisation from 2005 to 2009 and then was sent to London to study the UK approach to CVE. Exchanges of insights on P/CVE strategies also took place between Victorian, Monash GTReC scholars and those informing US policies.

This period marked a significant turn in which, under more progressive leadership, P/CVE strategies that emphasised community partnership and resilience became mainstreamed. An international conference of international experts working in this field on Building Community Resilience and P/CVE was convened in Singapore in 2013, which resulted in an edited collection of chapters that evidence this shift (Gunaratna et al. 2013).

Immediately after the conservative coalition Liberal government of Tony Abbott came to office in 2014 it introduced a revised CVE programme. The government had announced a new grants programme under the rubric of the Living Safe Together, specifically set up as part of the government's CVE strategy (Living Safe Together 2015). The programme design work commenced in November 2014 and concluded in March 2015 (Attorney-General's Department 2016). In August 2014 it announced that it would set aside as much as $13.4 million AUD for community programmes as part of a new $630 million CT package. By the end of 2015, however, only $1.8 million had been provided to organisations that met the government's criteria.

The 2017 National Framework to Counter Violent Extremism

The conceptual framing and policy implementation of P/CVE reached a point of maturity in 2017 with the National Counterterrorism Plan. The National Framework to Counter Violent Extremism defines CVE in Australia as being activities that seek to achieve either of the following aims:

1. To prevent individuals becoming or remaining violent extremists (by supporting diversion, rehabilitation and reintegration programmes).
2. To address the social impacts of violent extremism (by supporting programmes to build community resilience).

These two aims can be described as: reducing the likelihood of violent extremism through effective early intervention; and reducing the consequences of violent extremism through effective preparedness and response.

Building upon earlier iterations of CVE policy but with a more sharply focused and concrete articulation the National Counter-Terrorism Plan spelled out that:

> The aim of countering violent extremism (CVE) is to reduce the risk of individuals becoming or remaining violent extremists, and to address the social impacts of violent extremism.
>
> Australia's approach to countering violent extremism is set out in the National Counter-Terrorism Plan (2017). The National C-T Plan provides three strategic objectives:
>
> 1. Build the resilience of communities to violent extremism.
> 2. Support the diversion of individuals at risk of becoming violent extremists when possible.
> 3. Rehabilitate and reintegrate violent extremists when possible.

The key elements of this are incorporated, with very little change, in the ANZCTC 2022 National Counter-Terrorism Plan (Attorney General's Department 2022). This conceptualization of P/CVE remains broadly influential. It echoes, without specifically referencing, the popular framing of P/CVE programmes around the world using the analogy of public health programmes (Weine et al. 2017). The broadly influential public health model, which has its origins in the 1957 classification of disease prevention by the Commission on Chronic Illness, articulates interventions in terms of three tiers (Simeonsson 1991). The first tier is that of primary intervention, which is aimed at the general population and intended to decrease the number of new cases of illness. The second tier of interventions is aimed at at-risk communities and is designed to decrease the prevalence of existing illnesses through targeted interventions. The third, or tertiary, tier of interventions is intended to encompass therapeutic interventions designed to decrease the amount of disability associated with existing illness. Primary interventions typically take the form of awareness campaigns designed to educate the general public. Secondary interventions target those particularly at risk or showing specific signs or symptoms of incipient illness. Tertiary interventions encompass treatments and therapies.

The public health model is commonly referred to as the PST model after the three levels of Primary, Secondary and Tertiary interventions. Primary CVE interventions are intended to educate the general public about violent extremism, in order to lessen the overall risk of society being susceptible to the influences of extremism. Secondary CVE interventions focus on individuals and groups at particular risk of being radicalised into violent extremism. And tertiary interventions refer to programmes intended to deradicalise, disengage and rehabilitate. Because tertiary interventions target those who have already been impacted by radicalisation and recruitment, they often commence in a penal setting but may then continue post the release of prisoners detained on charges of terrorism.

Radar: Assessing and addressing those at risk

One of the key lessons learnt is that if P/CVE programmes are to effectively address individuals and groups at risk, or to effect rehabilitation, they will need to be conducted in partnership with police and other agencies. One of the central challenges remains detecting early warning signs of radicalisation and recruitment. As it happens, by the time attention turned to working with families and communities to stop young Australians flying out of the country to travel to Syria to join the caliphate, new conceptual and practical tools were at hand to help. This was a direct result of earlier investment in research into radicalisation and responding to violent extremism.

One of the most useful practical tools available to practitioners and community groups in detecting possible early signs of radicalisation and recruitment is a risks-and-needs tool based on observable behavioural changes called Radar. Radar emerged out of research at the Global Terrorism Research Centre (GTReC) at Monash University between 2007 and 2014 (where the authors also worked). The Radar tool was developed out of PhD research conducted by Kate Barrelle into why people disengaged from violent extremism. Barrelle is a clinical and forensic psychologist who for almost a decade worked in the counterterrorism branch of the Department of Foreign Affairs and Trade in the Australian federal government. Her 2014 doctoral thesis was entitled 'Pro-integration: Disengagement and Life after Extremism'. From this research she developed a model of disengagement from extremism known as the pro-integration model (Barrelle 2015). And building on this research, and in conjunction with other colleagues at GTReC including Shandon Harris-Hogan, Barrelle developed a tool to be used with structured professional judgement (SPJ), that is to say, by suitably trained professional practitioners (and in an attenuated form by members of the community who have received training) that looks at simultaneous change in observable behaviour across three key domains: social relations, ideology and criminal action orientation. It is used to identify individuals who are likely to benefit from interventions designed to reduce or mitigate the risk of radicalisation into violent extremism by identifying warning signs that an individual is experiencing malign influence by those who would seek to recruit or radicalise them.

In the form used by trained police and other practitioners, Radar works with a set of twenty-seven indicators set out in a matrix across three domains of social relations, ideology, and criminal action orientation, and across three levels of severity. Within this three-column-by-three-row matrix, each of the nine fields contains three indicators using precise and concrete descriptors readily understood by practitioners. The tool is designed so that different practitioners at different points in time can reliably code observable behaviour, in order that change over time can be reliably documented and shared between practitioners. The details of these twenty-seven indicators and related matters are restricted in circulation and only available to police and other practitioners. A more attenuated version of the tool, however, has been developed, to be used by community groups and by general professionals dealing with young people.

Radar was initially used by Victoria Police but is now widely used by state police forces across Australia and by the Australian Federal Police (AFP) and other practitioners (Van der Heide, Van der Zwan and Van Leyenhorst 2019). The simplified version of the tool is used by the Australian Multicultural Foundation (AMF) to build awareness and to train community members to pay attention to early warning signs of possible radicalisation and recruitment. Harris-Hogan and others have also used this tool to train school leadership teams in programmes across Australia. Following consultation with education authorities, they were involved in developing a train-the-trainer model. This training was deliberately not directed towards schoolteachers, who are regarded as being already overloaded and otherwise not ideally positioned to be tasked with paying attention to possible signs of radicalisation, but rather to professional leadership teams in schools (Harris-Hogan, Barrelle and Smith 2019).

The result of extensive community awareness and training programmes conducted by the AMF and train-the-trainer programmes conducted with school leadership teams, alongside specialist training to police and other security practitioners, is that over the past eight years thousands of professionals and community leaders, whose work brings them into regular contact with young people, have been trained to identify the warning signs of possible radicalisation and recruitment.

It is difficult to quantify the extent to which this has made a concrete contribution to CVE and CT interventions, but it is reasonable to assume that some of the success in stopping would-be supporters of the Islamic State caliphate, or similar Salafi jihadi groups, from travelling abroad is due to the impact of such programmes.

The doctoral research that Barrelle was involved with at GTReC Monash University was part of a larger Australian Research Council linkage project conducted in conjunction with the Victoria police. The police officer who was seconded on a part-time basis to contribute to the research project was Gaetano (Joe) Ilardi. Ilardi had earlier earned a PhD at Monash working with GTReC director Peter Lentini (Ilardi 2008). Ilardi was one of the key pioneering research-oriented police officers who helped develop the CT and CVE programmes within Victoria police. He was closely associated with the key police counterterrorism operation Operation Pendennis discussed earlier. The fact that Victoria was suddenly faced with a much larger cohort of terrorism detainees than ever previously experienced, Ilardi successfully argued, warranted the development of a disengagement and rehabilitation programme.

The Community Integration Support Program (CISP)

In 2010, Ilardi led a Victoria Police team, working in partnership with the Islamic Council of Victoria (ICV), to develop a programme that they called the Community Integration Support Program (CISP). This programme was initially focused on terrorism detainees and other inmates judged to be at risk of radicalisation and willing to participate. It was built around a programme of one-on-one counselling and mentoring using professional *imams*, or Islamic clerics working in a pastoral role, to spend time working with clients intensively over a prolonged period. The *imam* who was selected to be assigned to the client was carefully chosen based on compatibility with the particular religious, cultural and social background of the client. In practice while some of the conversations that developed focused on grappling with religious issues, religious conversations were only one component of the programme. The programme was designed to encourage clients to disengage from, or refuse to engage in, malign social networks involved with violent extremist behaviour, and instead to reengage with mainstream Muslim community.

The programme leveraged the considerable social and cultural capital of *imams* to build engagement from clients. This required a considerable investment of time on the part of an already overworked cohort of *imams*. Ilardi successfully argued for government funds to be used to compensate *imams* for their time spent on the programme in order for other *imams* to be employed to do the pastoral work that they otherwise would have been doing. At that time, this was a major innovation in government policy, involving as it did a degree of cooperation with religious professionals that was previously unknown.

In time CISP expanded from its original brief and began to incorporate a larger range of clients and community members. In 2018 CISP made the significant step towards also working with clients outside of prison, whether in post-release programmes or other contexts, and engaging with their families and community networks (Victoria Police 2022). The lead partner shifted from the ICV to the Board of Imams Victoria (BOIV), the professional body tasked with the accreditation oversight of *imams* in Victoria. The BOIV is the state representative of the Australian National Imams Council (ANIC). The involvement of the BOIV has contributed significantly to minimising social stigma and building acceptance of working with law enforcement agencies.

CISP is currently led by the chair of the BOIV, Sheikh Moustapha Sarakibi. He reports that the opportunity for clients to work one-on-one with *imams* is a key motivating element in engaging with the programme. In addition to regular conversations with *imams* CISP also offers other lines of support for participants in the form of clinical social and family support. These elements are often critical in overcoming community suspicion towards participants. The programme is built around elements of the pro-integration model and focuses on improving outcomes with respect to social relations, identity, coping, ideology and action orientation.

The programme focuses on early intervention, where possible, to prevent deeper involvement violent extremism. It addresses not only the religious arguments used to justify violence but also other aspects of social cohesion and integration. The *imams* working as mentors make extensive use of classical and contemporary religious texts, as appropriate, but much of their conversations relate to matters that are not of the strictly religious nature. They work with case managers to identify problems and provide support for issues such as anxiety, depression personality disorders, trauma/PTSD, substance addiction, cognitive dysfunction, autism, ADD and learning difficulties. With the help of their *imam* mentors, most participants willingly engage in clinical sessions with professionals who can help them with their mental health and other clinical needs.

For those who are in detention and preparing for release a Reintegration Officer (RIO) helps the participants with necessary community support and practical matters necessary for social integration. The RIO is generally a respected community member, and their involvement is a practical way of modelling community engagement. They provide vital support to prisoners transitioning into community release, and then generally engage with prisoners towards the end of their sentences ahead of their release date. Participants can discuss a range of practical matters with the RIO in a manner that they might not have previously done with their *imam* mentor. The RIO provides practical support with things such as accessing welfare support and employment services, education opportunities, housing and even gym membership. After their release from prison they accompany the participant to appointments and help organise visits to local community centres and mosques.

In addition to the *imam*s and the RIO, CISP employs Family Support Officers (FSO) to act as gateways to the participants' immediate families. Due to cultural sensitivities the FSOs are often women. They sometimes help channel welfare support from CISP to families experiencing difficulties. They frequently also engage in a range of practical activities such as arranging social outings with families and children and assistance in enrolling in educational and training programmes, finding housing and suitable employment. Like the *imam*s working with participants the FSOs are often involved in counselling families, providing family therapy, personal development and career coaching. All CISP staff and *imam*s undertake regular programmes of professional development. These include practical programmes such as training in the Radar risk-and-needs tool, writing case notes and working in custodial settings. These personal development sessions regularly call on external professionals with appropriate skills and experience.

CISP has implemented a programme of community outreach to expand the scope of services beyond custodial settings. An outreach officer has been hired to help build better relations between the board of *imam*s in Victoria and the community groups and to develop community programmes. These outreach services involve things such as leadership camps, youth events, empowerment programmes, engagement with campus university Islamic groups and media training. This broader engagement has helped overcome misunderstanding and stigma towards being engaged with CV programmes, dispelling some of the myths and prejudicial understandings about what the BOIV and CISP do.

Proactive Integrated Support Model (PRISM)

For six years following its inception in 2010, CISP was the sole prison-based rehabilitation programme of its kind in Australia. But in 2016 Corrective Services New South Wales implemented a custody-based programme entitled the Proactive Integrated Support Model (PRISM), focused on inmates convicted of terrorism-related offences or identified as being at risk of radicalisation (Cherney and Belton 2021). As is typically the case with P/CVE intervention programmes working with at-risk individuals, or those involving rehabilitation, a case management approach is taken that is built around individually tailored intervention plans. PRISM was launched in February 2016 as a pilot programme and then expanded into a regular programme working with Corrections New South Wales. As of 2021 PRISM was working with thirty-one inmates charged with terrorism-related offences. New South Wales and Victoria have by far the largest cohorts of such inmates, with New South Wales generally having slightly more than Victoria. Consequently, the inception of PRISM addressed a major need in the national CVE space. A key element of the case management process with PRISM is client progress notes, based on need and risk assessments using the Radar tool.

Both the CISP programme in Victoria and PRISM in New South Wales are initiatives under the auspices CVESC. CISP and PRISM remain the two key tertiary CVE intervention programmes in Australia, and the only programmes operating within custodial settings. Given the fact that they were established in the first instance to work with inmates sentenced on terrorism-related offences the primary orientation of these programmes is towards rehabilitation. Nevertheless, given the fact that both programmes also decided early on to work with those at risk of radicalisation as well as those detained on terrorism-related offences there is a sense that these programmes work in both the tertiary intervention space and the secondary intervention space with at-risk individuals.

The National Intervention Program

Up until 2015 Australia had lacked any systematic approach to secondary CVE interventions identifying and addressing individuals and groups at particular risk of radicalisation to violent extremism. The knife attack by Numan Haider in September 2014, and the hostage-taking siege at the Lindt Café in Martin Place in the Sydney CBD three months later, led to extensive coronial inquests and a rethinking of managing individuals at risk of radicalisation to violent extremism (Australian Government 2015; Coroner's Court of Victoria 2017).

A National Intervention Program (NIP) was established under ANZCTC to focus on diversion and disengagement, coordinating with AFP disruption teams. Most of the activities of NIP, however, are managed by state and territory police, with New South Wales Police and Victoria Police managing the largest caseloads (Acil Allen Consulting 2019). The 2022 ANZCTC National Counter-Terrorism Plan (Attorney-General's Department 2022) describes the operation of the NIP in terms of disengagement and reconnection, in Paragraph 114: 'The intervention program relies on a network of government and community partners to implement individualised, early intervention and violence disengagement strategies. Their purpose is to bring together the necessary support so that people can disengage from violence and reconnect with their family and community before they harm themselves or others.'

The NIP teams use the Radar case management tool to map progress in conjunction with a case officer who works with psychologists and behavioural scientists (Barracosa and March 2022). Although the assessment can be conducted under the auspices of the AFP, interventions are generally implemented by state-based intervention teams working in coordination with state police.

Shortly after discussing the NIP the National Counter-Terrorism Plan set out four paragraphs on 'building community resilience and social cohesion'. Paragraph 119 discusses the funded social programmes: "Australian governments' activities include funding and conducting social policy programs that support community harmony and address barriers to social and economic participation. While these programs are not funded for security purposes they may indirectly contribute to security by developing protective factors in individuals and groups that can act as buffers against violent extremist influences."

It is significant that the plan speaks of governments in the plural. This is because, while there is coordination with the CT and CVE centre in the Department of Home Affairs, much of the programmatic work is conducted by state government CVE units. In Victoria the CVE unit is responsible for all state government coordination of CVE and supports the Minister for Police. This involves working regularly with the Departments of Education, Premier and Cabinet, Department of Families, Fairness and Housing, Youth Justice and

Corrections Victoria, Victoria Police and the Federal Department of Home Affairs.

CVE early intervention programs and community support groups in Victoria

In Victoria the implementation of early intervention programmes, together with a multitude of other community engagements, are largely conducted through one of four Community Support Groups (CSGs). These Community Support Groups work geographically across Melbourne and are also aligned with the predominant ethnic and cultural groups in each region. The largest and most complete programme in Melbourne is the Northern Community Support Group. This group works with Muslim migrant communities, of which the largest are the Turkish and Lebanese communities, but also significant South Asian communities in conjunction with Preston Mosque and the multicultural youth centre. Although the Northern CSG along with the other CSGs is occasionally tasked with cooperating on early intervention programmes, the majority of its work has to do with education employment and training, delivering culturally and religiously appropriate social services, assisting with programmes focusing on community resilience and religious identity designed to overcome intolerance and antisocial behaviour, and promoting social participation and community cohesion through practical measures such as sport recreation and leisure.

The work of these four CSGs in Victoria fits well with the work of building resilience and social cohesion set out in Paragraph 119 quoted earlier. But, in an organically integrated fashion, the CSGs also home the specialist NIP early intervention initiatives described in Paragraph 114 quoted earlier.

The Community Support Groups work with the AMF on programmes designed to build resilience, but at the same time they also engage in programmes employing the Radar tool to assess risk and needs model (Australian Multicultural Foundation 2013). Training and support in this equip them to engage in case management and referral processes as required to support early intervention initiatives.

When there are concerns about an individual in the North, for whatever reason, a referral is made to the Northern CSG staff who then arranges assessments in coordination with religious advisors, including *imams* from the BOIV and CISP, mental health and support services, employment services, family violence support services and Victoria police, as appropriate. Most of the problems that end up being referred do not relate to violent extremism but where there are concerns that an individual might be at risk of radicalisation and recruitment the referral organically interfaces with a larger set of community services.

A critical element in establishing a coordinated national approach to early interventions is the Community Diversion and Monitoring Team located within the Australian Federal Police National Disruption Group (NDG). The community diversion and monitoring team was established in late 2014 to work with CVE early intervention programs (CVE IEPs) in identifying potential clients. The team represents a mix of sworn AFP agents working with unsworn AFP personnel, including those involved in intelligence, and behavioural scientists. The team uses the Radar tool to assess the suitability of individuals for early intervention programmes. A Radar risk and needs tool assessment is conducted to determine whether an individual is too low a risk to warrant the investment of time and resources in the early intervention, or too high a risk for such an early intervention programme. The Community Diversion and Monitoring Team also works to manage possible confliction issues to ensure that the individuals involved are also not involved in concurrent police investigations (Harris-Hogan 2020). Once the Radar risk and needs assessment has been conducted, the individual is then managed by a multiagency panel to consider individual needs and to tailor an individual support plan.

In Victoria a second CSG works particularly with the South Sudanese community located in Melton/Brimbank on Melbourne's western fringe and in Dandenong/Casey in the south-east of Melbourne. A third CSG is located in the inner-city suburb of North Melbourne and has a particular focus on the Somali community associated with the high-rise public housing towers in the neighbourhood. And a fourth CSG is located in Dandenong and particularly supports the Afghan community in Melbourne's south-east. The four CSGs in Victoria represent an organic, community-led process of addressing P/CVE needs and priorities in the context of meeting broader community needs.

The formulation of P/CVE in this manner represents an evolution of thinking about CVE and community involvement. It allows room for recognising that primary intervention programmes should be understood, and evaluated, primarily in terms of their contribution to developing social cohesion and resilience (Urbis 2018). This does not discount the possibility that work in this area might also have positive benefit in contributing to reducing the risk of some individuals and communities being radicalised into violent extremism. At the same time, it allows space for initiatives such as Victoria's CSGs to meet basic social needs and look out for the wellbeing and welfare of individuals and communities across a wide range of social challenges and risks, with the support and assistance of police and other government agencies. This provides for effective points of contact for CVE Early Intervention Programs on the rare but critically important occasions that they are required.

Discussion and conclusions

P/CVE programmes in Victoria, and across Australia, reached a level of maturity between 2015 and 2017 after a period of accelerated development precipitated by the demands of sharply increased threat associated with the rise of the IS caliphate. The urgent need for targeted secondary interventions for individuals at risk saw P/CVE and CT come together to prevent people from leaving Australia to travel to the caliphate in Syria-Iraq. At the same time the CISP and PRISM tertiary level rehabilitation programmes in Victoria and New South Wales developed a broader range of programmes, extending in the case of CISP to programmes outside of prison setting. The leadership of the Board of Imams Victoria has contributed significantly to building trust across Victoria's Muslim community.

Debate continues around the role and place of primary level intervention programmes, given the difficulties in evaluating their effectiveness in preventing radicalisation into violent extremism. Nevertheless, the approach taken of framing such programmes in terms of building social cohesion and social resilience, rather than attempting to make a case for prevention, offers a more constructive path to programme development and evaluation (Victorian Government 2015). There are some who would argue that P/CVE is best managed by taking a focused approach to secondary and tertiary interventions and leaving primary level interventions to other areas of government. Against this view, however, is the growing realisation that the domains of both P/CVE and CT need to be understood holistically. This is seen in the fact that in 2022 the key federal departments of the Department of Home Affairs and the Department of Foreign Affairs and Trade (DFAT) reorganised to bring P/CVE and CT sections together. The same shift to connecting P/CVE and CT is also occurring at the state level, as is reflected in recent organisational changes in Victoria.

The conclusion is that P/CVE is best done consciously as a whole-of-government and whole-of-nation endeavour. There will always be legal, privacy and operational reasons for restricting the flow of information but building relationships of trust in which information flows between police, government agencies and community groups is recognised as being essential to healthy and effective P/CVE programmes. Initiatives like CISP and the Community Support Groups in Melbourne illustrate that, with trust, respect and understanding, civil society actors can take a holistic approach to the welfare of individuals that facilitates, without being dominated by, appropriate and discrete P/CVE interventions.

References

Acil Allen Consulting. 2019. *NSW Countering Violent Extremism Program Evaluation: Final Report*. Report to the Department of Communities and Justice. Sydney. October 2019.

Akbarzadeh, S. 2013. 'Investing in Mentoring and Educational Initiatives: The Limits of De-Radicalisation Programmes in Australia'. *Journal of Muslim Minority Affairs* 33: 451–63.

Aly, A. 2013. 'The Policy Response to Home-Grown Terrorism: Reconceptualising Prevent and Resilience as Collective Resistance'. *Journal of Policing, Intelligence and Counter Terrorism* 8: 2–18.

Aly, A. 2014. Illegitimate: When Moderate Muslims Speak Out'. *M/C Journal* 17. https://doi.org/10.5204/mcj.890

Attorney-General's Department. 2022. *National Counter-Terrorism Plan*, 4th Edition 2022 (v1.1), Australia-New Zealand Counter-Terrorism Committee. Barton ACT: Commonwealth of Australia.

Attorney-General's Department. 2016. *The Design of, and Award of Funding under, the Living Safe Together Grants Programme*. The Auditor-General ANAO Report No.12 2016–17 Performance Audit.

Australian Government. (2010a). *Counter-Terrorism White Paper – Securing Australia, Protecting Our Community*. Canberra: Department of the Prime Minister and Cabinet.

Australian Government. 2010b. *National Action Plan to Build on Social Cohesion, Harmony and Security: Final Evaluation Report*. Canberra: Department of Immigration and Citizenship.

Australian Government. 2015. *Review of the Commonwealth's Counter Terrorism Arrangements*. Canberra: Department of the Prime Minister and Cabinet.

Australian Multicultural Foundation. 2013. *Community Awareness Training Manual: Building Resilience in the Community*. Melbourne: Counter Terrorism Coordination Unit, Victoria Police.

Barker, C. 2015. *Australian Government Measures to Counter Violent Extremism: A Quick Guide*. Canberra: Department of Parliamentary Services.

Barracosa, S., and March, J. 2022. 'Dealing with Radicalised Youth Offenders: The Development Implementation of a Youth-Specific Framework. Perspective Article'. *Frontiers in Psychiatry*. Volume 12–2021 | https://doi.org/10.3389/fpsyt.2021.773545.

Barrelle, K. 2015. 'Pro-integration: Disengagement from and Life after Extremism'. *Behavioural Sciences of Terrorism and Political Aggression* 7: 129–42.

Barton, Greg. 2004. *Indonesia's Struggle: Jemaah Islamiyah and radical Islamism*. Sydney: UNSW Press.

Barton, Greg. 2015. 'Islamic State, Radicalisation and the Recruitment of Foreign Fighters in Australia: Making Hijrah from Lucky Country to God's Nation'. In Wilhelm Hofmeister (ed.), *From the Desert to World Cities – The New Terrorism*. Panorama. Singapore: Konrad-Adenauer-Stiftung.

Barton, Greg. 2018. 'Jihadi-Salafi Terrorism and Violent Extremism in the Era of al-Qaeda and the Islamic State'. In Jane Ireland (ed.), *The Routledge International Handbook on Human Aggression*. London: Routledge, 376–8.

Barton, Greg; Vergani, Matteo, and Wahid, Yenny (eds). 2022. *Countering Violent and Hateful Extremism in Indonesia: Islam, Gender and Civil Society*. Singapore: Palgrave Macmillan. https://doi.org/10.1007/978-981-16-2032-4.

Bouma, G., Pickering, S., Halafoff, Anna, Dellal, H. 2007. *Managing the Impact of Global Crisis Events on Community Relations in Multicultural Australia*. Deakin University, Australia. Report. https://hdl.handle.net/10536/DRO/DU:30043775.

Bouma, Gary D. 2011. 'Islamophobia as a Constraint to World Peace: The Case of Australia'. *Islam and Christian–Muslim Relations* 22(4): 433–41. DOI: 10.1080/09596410.2011.606189.

Busher, J., Choudhury, T., and Thomas, P. 2017. *The Prevent Duty Is Two Years Old. What's Really Going On in Schools and Colleges?* Democratic audit UK. Retrieved from http://www.democraticaudit.com/2017/07/04/the-prevent-duty-is-two-years-old-whats-really-going-on-in-schools-and-colleges/. Accessed 14 November 2023.

Cherney, A., and Belton, E. 2021. 'Evaluating Case-Managed Approaches to Counter Radicalization and Violent Extremism: An Example of the Proactive Integrated Support Model (PRISM) Intervention'. *Studies in Conflict and Terrorism* 44(8): 625–45. https://doi.org/10.1080/1057610X.2019.1577016.

Coroners Court of Victoria. 2017. Ahmad Numan Haider: Finding into Death with Inquest. (2017, July 31). COR 2014 4917 (The Coroners Court of Victoria), Victoria.

Cockburn, Patrick. 2015. *The Rise of the Islamic State: ISIS and the New Sunni Revolution*. London: Verso.

Duckworth, M. 2015. 'The Idea of Resilience and Shared Responsibility in Australia'. In R. Bach (ed.), *Strategies for Supporting Community Resilience*. Stockholm: Multinational Resilience Policy Group, 83–119.

Gerges, Fawaz. 2016. *A History of ISIS*. Princeton: Princeton University Press.

Gunaratna, Rohan, Jerard, Jolene, and Nasir, S. M. (eds). 2013. *Countering Extremism: Building Social Resilience through Community Engagement.* London: Imperial College Press.

Halafoff, Anna. 2006. 'UnAustralian Values, in UNAustralia: Cultural Studies Association of Australasia Annual Conference'. Cultural Studies Association of Australasia, Canberra, ACT. pp. 1–18.

Halafoff, Anna. 2013. 'Encounter as Conflict: Interfaith Peace-Building'. In Cheetham, D. et al. (eds) *Understanding Interreligious Relations.* Oxford: Oxford University Press, 262–80.

Halafoff, Anna, and Wright-Neville, David. 2009. 'A Missing Peace? The Role of Religious Actors in Countering Terrorism'. *Studies in Conflict & Terrorism* 32(11): 921–32. DOI: 10.1080/10576100903262740.

Harris-Hogan, S. 2020. 'How to Evaluate a Program Working with Terrorists? Understanding Australia's Countering Violent Extremism Early Intervention Program'. *Journal of Policing, Intelligence and Counter Terrorism* 15(2): 97–116. DOI: 10.1080/18335330.2020.1769852.

Harris-Hogan, S., Barrelle, K., and Smith, D. 2019. 'The Role of Schools and Education in Countering Violent Extremism (CVE): Applying Lessons from Western Countries to Australian CVE Policy'. *Oxford Review of Education* 45(6): 731–48. DOI:10.1080/0 3054985.2019.1612343.

Harris-Hogan, S., and Barrelle, K. 2020. 'Young Blood: Understanding the Emergence of a New Cohort of Australian Jihadists'. *Terrorism and Political Violence* 32(7): 1391– 412 DOI:10.1080/09546553.2018.1473858.

Harris-Hogan, S., Baralle, K., and Zammit, A. 2015. 'What Is Countering Violent Extremism? Exploring CVE Policy and Practice in Australia'. *Behavioral Sciences of Political Aggression.* 4. http://dx.doi.org/10.1080/19434472.2015.1104710

HM Government. 2011. *Prevent strategy.* London: Stationary Office.

Ilardi, Gaetano. 2008. 'Al Qaeda's Operational Intelligence – a Key Prerequisite to Actiion'. *Studies in Conflict & Terrorism* 31: 1072–102.

Ilardi, Gaetano. 2017. 'A Homegrown Terrorist Cell: Observations of a Police Undercover Operative'. *Studies in Conflict & Terrorism* 41(6): 474–90.

Kenney, Michael. 2018. *The Islamic State in Britain: Radicalization and Resilience in an Activist Network.* Cambridge: Cambridge University Press.

Landers, Rachel. 2016. *Who Bombed the Hilton?.* Sydney: NewSouth Books.

Lentini, Peter. 2013. *Neojihadism: Towards a New Understanding of Terrorism and Extremism.* London: Edward Elgar.

Living Safe Together. 2015. *New Countering Violent Extremism Programme.* Canberra: Attorney-General's Department.

Moroney, Peter. 2018. *Terrorism in Australia: The Story of Operation Pendennis,* London: New Holland.

O'Toole, T., DeHanas, D., and Modood, T. 2012. Balancing Tolerance, Security and Muslim Engagement in the United Kingdom: The Impact of the 'Prevent' Agenda'. *Critical Studies on Terrorism* 5: 373–89.

Schuurman, B., Harris-Hogan, S., Lentini, P., and Zammit, A. 2014. 'Operation Pendennis: A Case Study of an Australian Terrorist Plot'. *Perspectives on Terrorism* 8: 91–9.

Simeonsson, R. 1991. 'Primary, Secondary, and Tertiary Prevention in Early Intervention'. *Journal of Early Intervention* 15: 124–34.

Thomas, P. 2010. 'Failed and Friendless: The UK's "Preventing Violent Extremism" Programme'. *British Journal of Politics & International Relations* 12: 442–58.

Urbis. 2018. *Evaluation of the COMPACT Program*. Prepared for NSW Department of Premier and Cabinet. Final Report 28 November 2018.

van der Heide, L., van der Zwan, M., and van Leyenhorst, M. 2019. *The Practitioner's Guide to the Galaxy – A Comparison of Risk Assessment Tools for Violent Extremism*. International Centre for Counter-Terrorism. https://www.jstor.org/stable/resrep29 450. DOI: 10.19165/2019.1.07.

Victorian Government. 2005. *Protecting Our Community: Attacking the Causes of Terrorism*. Melbourne: Victorian Government Premier's Department.

Victorian Government. 2006. *A Safer Victoria: Protecting Our Community: New Initiatives to Combat Terrorism*. Melbourne: Victorian Government Premier's Department.

Victorian Government. 2015. *Strategic Framework to Strengthen Victoria's Social Cohesion and the Resilience of its Communities*. Version 1 December 2015. Melbourne: Victorian Governement.

Victoria Police. 2022. 'Counter Terrorism Strategy 2022–2025'.

Weine, S., Eisenman, D. P., Kinsler, J., Gilk, D. C., and Polutnik, C. 2017. 'Addressing Violent Extremism as Public Health Policy and Practice'. *Behavioural Sciences of Terrorism and Political Aggression* 9: 208–21.

The White House. 2011. *Empowering Local Partners To Prevent Violent Extremism in the United States*. Washington, DC: Office of the President of the United States.

Zammit, A. 2015. *Australian Foreign Fighters: Risks and Responses*. Sydney: Lowy Institute for International Policy.

10

Australian Religious Diversity in an International Context

Lori G. Beaman

Introduction

As a number of chapters in this book illustrate, religious diversity in Australia is increasing even as the number of people who identify as nonreligious is also rising. In Canada I have argued that the religious landscape can be described as a 'new diversity' that includes a decline in Christianity, the traditional majoritarian religion since colonisation; a rise in the number of people who identify as nonreligious; an increase in non-Christian religions through migration and a renewed attention to Indigenous knowledge (Beaman 2017b). This new diversity maps on to the Australian situation rather well. Other Western countries have somewhat similar trajectories, although the specifics in each context are important to explicate, including the role of colonialism in a country's history, the presence of Indigenous peoples, the nature and shape of religious majorities, the form of government (e.g. democracy or dictatorship) and constitutional regimes.

What Bouma et al. (Chapter 1) make clear is that understanding this 'super-diversity' is a vital step in building inclusive societies. They highlight a number of dimensions of diversity that require attention. First is that diversity within diversity is an often overlooked fact of religious description. Thus 'Muslims' or 'Christians' are sweeping categories that offer little analytical purchase. The variability within these categories is significant (see, e.g. Selby, Barras, Beaman 2018) and has implications for understanding diversity at theoretical, empirical and policy levels.

Scholars elsewhere have also identified diversity within diversity as an important element of super-diversity. In other words, religion is practised in multiple ways that do not always fit the prescribed orthodoxies. This lived religion lends complexity to the multiple ways that people live out their religious identities. Moreover, religion is intertwined with other identities that can be equally or more important in living one's life. Further, religious identities and affiliations frequently change over the lifecourse. And finally, interactions among (non)religious people in day-to-day life produces multiple modes of finding common ground (Selby et al. 2018; Beaman 2017a)

Hearing discourses of othering and inclusion is essential to creating inclusive policy responses. This point is repeatedly made in a range of studies of diversities. For example, Martin Stringer (2016) explores the theme of common ground in his *Discourses on Diversity*, which has itself become a major contribution to discussions about religion in urban area. Stringer draws on the groundbreaking research of Gerd Baumann (1996) conducted in Southall, England (which did not focus on religion but included it in the analysis of community and diversity). Like Bouma and others, Stringer identifies specific configurations of diversity and the social relations that accompany them. For Stringer a key to understanding diversity and its navigation is to spend time listening to people who live in and use urban neighbourhoods.

The second dimension of diversity identified by Bouma and others is geographies. They point out that geographies matter. The content of diversity shifts between rural, urban and suburban areas and is not static. This is not unique to Australia. The importance of the spatial location of religious diversity is an observation that has been made elsewhere including by Knott (2015), Becci et al. (2013), Berking et al. (2018), Garbin and Strhan (2017) and of course by the originator of the term super-diversity, Steven Vertovec (2007). Central to Bouma et al.'s argument is the point that residential mobility imports a dynamic process of religious change and religious diversity in neighbourhoods.

Dejean and Germain's (2022) rich collection of the study of the 'religious laboratory' of the city (they include Paris and Vancouver, for example, but focus on Montreal) begins with the observation that as societies increasingly urbanise so too does religion in all of its diversity. Religion that accompanies migration, new forms of religion and spirituality and new ways of 'living' religion are part of the story of religion in the city. Dejean points out that cities can and do regulate religious diversity through zoning and other means of municipal control, including the building of places of workshop and the creation of cemeteries (Dabby and Beaman 2019). The close proximity of diverse people means that navigation and negotiation occur at other levels too, as Monica Grigore-Dovlete and I discovered in our study of a shared Catholic/Orthodox church space

(Grigore-Dovlete and Beaman 2020). Not only geographies but materialities are also important considerations in thinking about religious diversity in urban spaces (Knott, Krech and Meyer 2016).

Religious spaces are reflections of their neighbourhoods: Maltais and Koussens (2022) study a Catholic parish church in the heart of a gay village in Montreal. Their work underscores the fact that religion is only part of the diversity story: funerals for victims of AIDs and their communities shaped the relationship of the community with the church. This relationship has blossomed in multifaceted ways that model inclusive and respectful interactions that include the provision by the church of blessings of love for same-sex couples and welcoming of gay and lesbian godparents. The addition of a chapel of hope dedicated to victims of AIDS is a material reminder of the relationship. It is this layered, intersectional configuration of identities and commitments that makes the study of diversity so complex and so important.

The changing religious landscape raises a common question about how to live well together. There are overlapping approaches to this challenge, some of them legal and rooted in constitutions and human rights regimes, guiding policy commitments (such as multiculturalism) and some of them emerging from grassroots initiatives and interactions.

As the typologies developed by Bouma et al. demonstrate, religion, while important to some people, is not the only driving identity marker for people. Commonalities across lifestances (Beaman, Cragun and Ezzy In Press) – as in the 'Cosmopolitan Hipster Villages' – may rest on factors other than religion, creating a dynamic community that includes religious and nonreligious identities and their negotiation and navigation in day-to-day life. Bouma et al. note that it is thus important to pay close attention to re-homogenisation or reconstructed boundaries.

Tim Stacey's (2022) study of the Metro Vancouver Alliance (MVA) is a case in point. Reflecting on the church-state separation as the beginning assumption about the nation, Stacey explores the messy boundaries between so-called separate spheres, asking 'what if we're already living under a kind of all-encompassing ideology?' (Stacey 2022: 91). Stacey explains the social imaginary of his interlocutors as one which draws on an idealised past of social cohesion, a present which is in disarray and a future in which social relations are rebuilt around justice. This is the ideal of nation and citizenship that drives the MVA activists, who work 'with people you otherwise never would' to address poverty and homelessness, among other social justice issues. Stacey opens with a scene in an Anglican Church where both religious and nonreligious people talk about their shared world-repairing work. This work connects to convictions about good citizenship, an 'ultimate meaning of practice' located in relationships but also a vision that displaces colonial capitalism. Although local communities are arguably more salient for people as they live their everyday lives, they often also reference a broader understanding of how they fit in the nation and who they are as citizens.

Nationalism – Who Is 'We'?

Often at the core of these processes is a question about who 'we' are as a nation. Benedict Anderson argues that nations are imagined communities that create a horizontal comradeship. Anderson notes that this imagined community exists apart from actual inequalities and discrimination. Belonging, as Halafoff et al. (Chapter 5) point out, is a basic need, and so being excluded from the imagined community of the nation has a powerful impact. Multiple belongings, as is often the case for migrants, does not erase the need to feel at home in each of those communities.

In countries experiencing super-diversity there are often two competing imagined communities that speak to the question of 'who are we' in a diverse reality. One of those narratives is what we might understand as past preserving, reflecting a longing to preserve a 'past glory' that can be understood in terms of power and hegemony. The 'Privileged Christians' referenced by Ezzy et al. (Chapter 7) are an example of a group arguing for a vision of a 'we' that is past preserving. To be clear, Christianity needs to be understood as Christianities, with great variability in practice, belief and privilege. For example, Bouma et al. (Chapter 1) note the dramatic changes in the once dominant Anglican Church of Australia. Nonetheless, some forms of Christianity continue to wield significant institutional and financial power and seek to use that power 'to shape Australian responses to religious diversity in ways that maintain their power and privilege' (Chapter 7, p. 150). This power struggle between conservative Christian groups and those who have a more inclusive vision of society is taking place internationally, often in the political arena, in countries like the United States, Brazil and Italy.

Preserving existing power relations and privilege can exacerbate inequality, create hierarchies of belonging and obstruct positive social change. In this vision the 'we' is static, homogenous and often associated with narratives about a nation's culture and heritage (Beaman 2020). Again, this narrative of culture and heritage is not unique to Australia. In many Western countries in which the majoritarian religion has been Christianity the justification of Christian symbols and practices has been built around a claim that they are part of 'our culture and heritage'.

In Spain, for example, what Griera et al. (2021) call 'banal Catholicism' permeates everyday life. They argue that temporality and social space are key variables in the analysis of religious privilege and that religion is mobilised in different ways at different times. Thus, the role of the Catholic Church in Spain is complex in that its direct influence in morality issues such as abortion, same-sex marriage and assisted dying is weak in comparison with its role in welfare, education, health and heritage. Influenced by the multiple modernities and multiple secularities approach of Wohlrab-Sahr and Burchardt (2012), Griera et al. (2021: 2.1) link events with contingency and agency. Their notion of banal Catholicism 'helps to capture the many non-problematized Catholic references that prevail in Spanish state institutions and explain the persistence of traces of historical religious monopolies in public contexts'. We can transpose their identification of banal religion to other contexts, most especially, I would argue those in which an identifiable religion or configuration of religions (Christianities) has dominated at a particular point in time. We can then identify traces of that dominance through, for example, the 'our culture and heritage' argument.

A second version of the national imaginary also exists in tandem with the exclusionary one described above. It, in contrast, imagines the 'we' as diverse and equal. In this narrative, inclusion plays an important role. Multiculturalism can be one vehicle by which diversity is framed in an inclusive way, although not the only one. Canada and Australia share a similar trajectory. In Australia, early regulation (i.e. restriction) of migration through the Australian Immigration Restriction Act aimed primarily at Chinese and South Pacific migrants and effectively preserving white colonial power. These laws were gradually repealed, and a new Australian imaginary based on multiculturalism took hold in the 1970s. To be sure, this inclusive imaginary of a multicultural nation is threatened by an alternative one that in some measure reverts to an imaginary of a white Australia (Bouma and Halafoff 2017; Ezzy et al. 2020).

A similar trajectory has unfolded in Canada, with significant shifts in migration policy occurring in the same period and a turn to multiculturalism as central to the Canadian national imaginary in the 1970s and 1980s. Multiculturalism has remained a valid framework for understanding the navigation of diversity. The Supreme Court of Canada frequently references section 27 of the *Charter of Rights and Freedoms*, which states 'This Charter shall be interpreted in a manner consistent with the preservation and enhancement of the multicultural heritage of Canadians.' Canada and Australia are somewhat exceptional in the continued articulation of multiculturalism as a guiding policy, although elsewhere strong advocates such as Tariq Modood (2010) continue to advocate for a version of multiculturalism that is inclusive and non-pillarizing. Modood positions multiculturalism as part of the social imaginary that shapes who 'we' are:

> Multiculturalism is yet another response based not just on the equal dignity of individuals but also on the political accommodation of group identities as a means of challenging exclusionary racisms and practices and fostering respect and inclusion for demeaned groups. Moving beyond a focus on exclusion and minorities is a third level of multiculturalism, which is not just about positive minority identities but a positive vision of society as a whole – but remade so as to include the previously excluded or marginalized on the basis of equality and belonging. (Modood 2010: 6)

Modood here highlights multiculturalism both as an individual practice that encourages respect between diverse individuals and as a political practice that challenges exclusion and power. This point is developed below. Even in these supportive contexts multiculturalism has not been without its critics, and certainly is often accused as creating silos of identity or, worse, of masking discrimination and inequality (see Day 2010; Macdonald 2010; Fleras 2019; Winter 2014, 2011). However, one of the weaknesses of this body of literature is that there is little agreement on what, exactly, constitutes multiculturalism. Jedwab (2014) has reviewed the stages of multiculturalism in the Canadian context. There is little research that explores the use of multiculturalism in everyday life or in social relations.

For those countries in which multiculturalism lost or never had purchase, we might understand super-diversity, as Vertovec (2007) has articulated it, as a conceptual solution to the rejection of multiculturalism. In other words, super-diversity is a vehicle for acknowledging diversity and the need to create pathways to equality. However, super-diversity is primarily an academic analytical term rather than a guiding concept for living well together. Thus diversity, inclusion and equality are more likely to be the policy buzz words that shape public discourse about diversity.

Embedded in discussions of the 'we' are often debates about the secular nature of society. Here it is useful to consider the concept of secularity as defined by Kleine and Wohlrab-Sahr as: "*institutionally as well as symbolically embedded forms and arrangements for distinguishing between religion and other societal areas*" (2016: 3; emphasis in original). Accusations and declarations about the secular nature of society are deployed by social actors speaking from a number of vantage points. For example, as Ezzy et al. (Chapter 7) note, the New South Wales Ecumenical Council identifies multiple reasons for their 'exclusion' or loss of power, including 'secularization, consumerism, and militant atheism'. However, the term 'secular' is also deployed positively by other groups, including religious groups. For example, in arguing against the proposed Australian Religious Discrimination Bill, the Religious Society of Friends stated: 'It would be regressive if anti-discrimination laws already put in place were undermined by favouring the anxieties of religious groups that are challenged by the "progressive" trends in secular society' (Religious Society of Friends 2019: 5). It is important to pay attention to the use of the secular in public discourse to better understand public contests over religious and nonreligious diversity.

Finally, extraordinary events, either local or global, can be important vehicles for understanding the dynamics of diversity and the effectiveness of national policies for inclusion and equality. Halafoff et al. (2021) demonstrate convincingly that events like the global Covid-19 pandemic often lay bare the fissures that expose the 'us' and 'them' particularly around religion and ethnicity. It also demonstrates that traditional majoritarian religion, despite increased diversity, has considerable voice in public discussions during such events. The variable impact of the pandemic on religious communities and their ability to transform in-person rituals, practices and relationships into online format has been the focus of a number of studies (Parish 2020); see Lee et al. (2021) for a review of religious communities and their roles in mitigation and spread of Covid-19). Many of the fissures found expression in legal challenges, which is where we turn our attention now.

Law

One of the most powerful institutional and social tools for regulating and managing religious diversity is the law. While this language might seem to be negative, at their best legal regimes can promote inclusion and equality by offering guidelines that both enable and constrain. For instance, in one of the early decisions by the Canadian Supreme Court on the meaning of religious freedom in the then newly enacted *Canadian Charter of Rights and Freedoms*, the Court stated:

> What may appear good and true to a majoritarian religious group, or to the state acting at their behest, may not, for religious reasons, be imposed upon

citizens who take a contrary view. The *Charter* safeguards religious minorities from the threat of 'the tyranny of the majority'. (*Big M Drug Mart,* at para. 96)

The *Canadian Charter of Rights and Freedoms* contains a number of provisions relating to religion, including section 2(a) Freedom of religion and conscience and the section 15 equality provision, which states: 'Every individual is equal before and under the law and has the right to the equal protection and equal benefit of the law without discrimination and, in particular, without discrimination based on race, national or ethnic origin, colour, religion, sex, age or mental or physical disability.' These, or their provincial legislative counterparts, have been used to protect, among other things, a Sikh schoolboy's right to carry a kirpan to school, the right of orthodox Jews to put a succah on their balcony and an atheist's right to attend a municipal council meeting free of Christian prayers. As the Supreme Court of Canada stated in the latter case,

> By expressing no preference, the state ensures that it preserves a neutral public space that is free of discrimination and in which true freedom to believe or not to believe is enjoyed by everyone equally, given that everyone is valued equally .... The neutrality of the public space therefore helps preserve and promote the multicultural nature of Canadian society enshrined in s. 27 of the Canadian Charter. Section 27 requires that the state's duty of neutrality be interpreted not only in a manner consistent with the protective objectives of the Canadian Charter, but also with a view to promoting and enhancing diversity. (Saguenay SCC, at para. 74)

Here we see legal recognition of the entanglement of a neutral public space, the value of equality, the 'good' of multiculturalism and the promotion of diversity. In this example the law offers a robust support for a vision of an 'us' that is inclusive and diverse.

Each country has its own legal regime that sorts out the challenges of diversity. It is important to consider the ways that legal regimes translate in day-to-day life and provide protections for religious and nonreligious people. For example, a superficial analysis of the British regime might conclude that the fact that the Church of England is the official state church translates into embedded Christian privilege. To be sure, there are powerful vestiges of Christian privilege in Britain. But arguably there is greater protection for religious minorities and nonreligious people in Britain than there are in the United States, which prohibits 'establishment' or a state church. The religious history of a country, including the determination of which religion or religions have traditionally held power and privilege, is key to understanding its present-day approach to religious minorities, nonreligious people and Indigenous knowledge.

Law can also provide processual rather than content guidelines, as Ezzy et al. (2022) have argued, providing a moral etiquette for contests between individuals and groups. This is less a content-specific guide than a path for conflict resolution. In other words, law offers a process through which people can sort out conflicts and competing claims. Such a context can offer a controlled forum in which disagreement and dislike are contained within legal rules. It can offer participants a sense of being 'heard' even if the decision is contrary to their wishes.

The extent to which legal cases impact day-to-day life is a matter of debate. Do decisions about religious freedom or discrimination shape the decisions of social actors? In her study of minority religious groups in eight European countries, Effie Fokas measured the impact of decisions on religious liberty of the European Court of Human Rights on everyday decision-making. While such cases were important resources, Fokas found for the most part that the decisions had only a modest impact on social actors' decision-making processes around religious freedom issues (2017). However, as Ezzy et al. (2022) argue, legal agonism can constrain harmful attitudes and practices such as Islamophobia, restricting their public expression and facilitating equality and inclusion. Legal cases can establish norms of civility that make a real difference in the lives of marginalised groups such as Wiccans or Sikhs.

If we consider the two narratives of who 'we' are discussed above, law can play an important role in promoting and achieving a just, inclusive and equal society. On the other hand, law can also play a role in maintaining majoritarian religious privilege. The likely possibility of discrimination has been the basis of objection to the Australian Religious Discrimination Bill, which many argue would facilitate discrimination and vilification against religious and sexual minorities. At its worst, then, freedom of religion can be transformed into a right to discriminate or to force or coerce religious observance. The concerns expressed by those who objected to the bill are well grounded, as we need only look across the Pacific at developments in the United States.

A series of legal decisions in the Supreme Court of the United States illustrates the potential of law to enforce the religious beliefs of particular groups and to support discrimination. For example, in the 2022 *Kennedy* decision[1] a high school football coach lost his job after praying on the field after games. The Supreme Court ruled that the First Amendment protected the coach. It did not take into account power relations or potential coercion of the players. The 2014 *Hobby Lobby* decision[2] allowed a conservative Christian employer to deny birth control coverage to its employees; the *American Legion* decision[3] upheld the right of a municipality to maintain a 40-foot-tall Christian cross on state land; in *Masterpiece Cake Shop*[4] case the court supported a Christian cake shop owner in his refusal to make a wedding cake for a gay couple. The use of Christianity by conservative evangelical Christians to justify a particular vision of the nation, described in detail by Gorski and Perry (2022) as White Christian Nationalism, has infiltrated politics, law and civil society. The increasing use of religious freedom to support discrimination or to coerce religious observance has prompted the American Civil Liberties Association to turn its attention to fighting the use of religious freedom to effectively create a right to discriminate by conservative Christians.

In Canada, the right to discriminate was sidelined by the Supreme Court of Canada in its 2018 Trinity Western University decision.[5] In that case the university planned to open a law school. Accreditation was necessary from the various law societies and some of them objected because Trinity Western required students and staff to sign an agreement that they would not engage in sexual relations outside of marriage or with people of the same sex. The Community Covenant prohibited 'sexual intimacy that violates the sacredness of marriage between a man and a woman'. In balancing the harms to LGBTQ people and freedom of religion, the Supreme Court found that any infringement on religious freedom was outweighed by the potential harm to LGBTQ people. The university could not use a claim of religious freedom to create a right to discriminate.[6]

However, internationally there is a trend towards targeting particular religious groups for legal regulation. This is especially the case for Muslims, whose clothing, dietary needs and prayer practices have faced increasing scrutiny in the past two decades (Barras 2014, 2021; Selby 2011). In some cases 'general' laws impact Muslims disproportionately but not exclusively: for example the Quebec 'Act Respecting the Laicity of the State' bans public officials, including teachers, from wearing religious symbols while on the job (Meunier and Legault-Leclair 2021). Similar restrictive and discriminatory laws are in effect in many European countries, including Denmark, France, Austria and the Netherlands, although the specifics of each vary from country to country.[7] Public debates and state regulation have ventured into territory such as pork in school lunches and women's swimwear (the *burkini* ban).

Conclusion: Everyday navigation

In his book *Engines of Liberty: How Citizen Movements Succeed* (2017), David Cole, the director of the American Civil Liberties Union, maps the successful engagement by citizens to keep progressive civil liberties alive through the constitution. One of his case studies focuses on same-sex marriage. Cole argues that citizens can and do impact positive social change. Although written about the American context, Cole's book gives pause for thought and inspiration for optimism in this moment when regressive pressure seems to be greater than ever. (Non)religious diversity can support a freedom of religion side by side with other rights and responsibilities. And this is not only about law, but about the ways in which diverse people come together to find common ground to work for social change. Living well together is possible through deep equality, commonplace diversity and conviviality (Beaman 2017a; Wessendorf 2014; Wise and Noble 2016) as Bouma et al. (Chapter 1) argue. Common ground and everyday encounter and interaction can produce 'nonevents' in which people simply get along, enacting respect and recognition. The key is to dissolve the boundaries of otherness while maintaining space for difference. As Halafoff et al. so poignantly and pointedly asks, 'How can we belong together to something we are not really seen as part of, or that we chose not to be part of given its injustice, if the everyday racism and discrimination demonstrate that we are not one of the "us" but one of "them"'?

Everyday navigation and negotiation of difference takes place at many levels. Although technically 'state actors', the day-to-day interactions of police and citizens are an important site of the working out of difference. Community policing can facilitate the tone needed for respectful interpersonal interactions. Hiring practices for diversity within police forces can also create a sense that the police themselves diverse. This realisation has been part of conversations in many other countries and is a key point of conversation around racism and policing in the United States, for example. Not only police, but teachers, healthcare providers and other point-of-service social actors are key to the navigation of diversity and the achievement of equality. For example, Bertrand Lavoie (2022) found in his study of hospital emergency rooms in Quebec that medical staff often responded positively to religiously based needs. On the ground, responses were mostly positive, even in the face of contentious public debate and restrictive policies and laws around 'reasonable accommodation'. This was the case despite the fact that the Quebec government had banned the wearing of religious symbols by state service providers.

The 'global' nature of multifaith initiatives is also a site for the navigation of religious difference, as Smith and Halafoff (Chapter 6) point out. The Sacred Conversations group in Tasmania is one such forum for supporting positive relationships between people with different lifestances. As Smith and Halafoff demonstrate, a key to successful navigation of difference is respect. But beyond respect, there is something more in their description of the facilitator's approach: *His approach to these meetings signals a high regard for people's emotional, inner and personal experiences of encountering people who are different from one another.* This high regard is part of the shift from mere tolerance or living together to living *well* together. Halafoff's work on cosmopolitanism and Netpeace situates such local initiatives in the broader global framework that emphasises interconnectedness and the ability of multi-actor networks to facilitate living well together.

In addition to countless interfaith initiatives internationally, there are many examples of initiatives that bring people into contact who are, in one way or another, different from one another. Gordon Allport's (1954) contact theory proposes that interpersonal contact can reduce prejudice, especially if conditions support equal status, cooperation and common goals. The Human Library Project, the Cook a Pot of Curry Initiative and many others facilitate contact that can positively impact social relations. Such initiatives create a space in which super-diversity and diversity within diversity can be expressed and navigated. We might speculate that a commitment to a particular imaginary of the nation and how a good citizen participates in that nation is a critical, though perhaps often unarticulated, framework within which people see themselves in interaction with others who do not share their lifestances.

A final but foundational consideration of the successful navigation of diversity bears mention: Australia was built on Aboriginal land and using Aboriginal resources. The colonisation of Australia was devastating to Aboriginal peoples. This is also true of the United States, Canada, Brazil and many other religiously diverse nations. Indigenous knowledge has been and continues to be dismissed. States and Christianities collaborated extensively to ensure that this happened. Any prospect of living well together in super-diverse nations like Australia depends on the recognition by states, civil societies and religious groups of the harm done and a commitment to engaging in reconciliation on Indigenous terms.[8]

Notes

I would like to acknowledge the continued financial support of my research through my Canada Research Chair in Religious Diversity and Social Change. Thanks are owed to Lauren Strumos for editorial and research assistance. This chapter was written while I held the Leibniz Professorship at the University of Leipzig.

1 See *Kennedy v. Bremerton School District*, 597 U.S. ___ (2022).

2 See *Burwell v. Hobby Lobby Stores*, Inc., 573 U.S. 682 (2014).

3 See *American Legion v. American Humanist Association*, 588 U.S. ___ (2019).

4 See *Masterpiece Cakeshop v. Colorado Civil Rights Commission*, 584 U.S. ___ (2018).

5 See *Law Society of British Columbia v Trinity Western University*, 2018 SCC 32 and *Trinity Western University v Law Society of Upper Canada*, 2018 SCC 33.

6 In the 2019 case, *Christian Medical and Dental Society of Canada v. College of Physicians and Surgeons of Ontario* ONCA 393, the Court of Appeal for Ontario (Canada) weighed freedom of religion and patient needs, concluding that physicians have a duty to provide patients with effective referrals for services such as abortion and medical assistance in dying, even if such referrals violate a physician's freedom of religion.

7 Julia Martínez-Ariño (2020: 126) notes that 'when such local controversies reach national bodies, such as courts, they also tend to spark public debates, nationally and even internationally. This was the case with the *burkini* ban in 2016, when the debate expanded to other European countries, thereby setting the agenda internationally (at least temporarily).'

8 For a clear example of what this engagement can look like, see the 94 Calls to Action identified by the Truth and Reconciliation Commission of Canada (2015). Available at https://nctr.ca/records/reports/.

References

Allport, G. 1954. *The Nature of Prejudice*. Cambridge, MA: Addison-Wesley.

Barras, A. 2014. *Refashioning Secularisms in France and Turkey: The Case of the Headscarf Ban*. London: Routledge.

Barras, A. 2021. 'Formalizing Secularism as a Regime of Restrictions and Protections: The Case of Quebec (Canada) and Geneva (Switzerland)'. *Canadian Journal of Law and Society / La Revue Canadienne Droit Et Société* 36(2): 283–302.

Baumann, G. 1996. *Contesting Culture: Discourses of Identity in Multi-ethnic London*. Cambridge: Cambridge University Press.

Beaman, L. G. 2017a. *Deep Equality in an Era of Religious Diversity*. Oxford: Oxford University Press.

Beaman, L. G. 2017b. 'Religious Diversity in the Public Sphere: The Canadian Case'. *Religions* 8(12): 259.

Beaman, L. G., 2020. *The Transition of Religion to Culture in Law and Public Discourse*. London: Routledge.

Beaman, L. G., Cragun, R. T., and Ezzy, D. In Press. 'Lifestances: On the Positive Content of Nonreligion'.

Becci, I., Burchardt, M., and Casanova, J. 2013. *Topographies of Faith: Religion in Urban Spaces*. Leiden: Brill.

Berking, H., Steets, S., and Schwenk S. (eds.). 2018. *Religious Pluralism and the City: Inquiries into Postsecular Urbanism*. London: Bloomsbury.

Bouma, G., and Halafoff, A. 2017. 'Australia's Changing Religious Profile'. *Journal for the Academic Study of Religion* 30: 129–43.

Cole, D. 2017. *Engines of Liberty: How Citizen Movements Succeed*. New York: Basic Books.

Dabby, D., and Beaman, L. G. 2019. 'Diversity in Death: A Case Study of a Muslim Cemetery Project in Quebec'. In *Research Handbook on Interdisciplinary Approaches to Law and Religion*. Cheltenham: Edward Elgar, 420–37.

Day, A. 2010. 'Propositions and Performativity: Relocating Belief to the Social'. *Culture and Religion* 11(1): 9–30.

Dejean, F., and Germain, A. 2022. *Se faire une place dans la cite: la participation des groupes religieux à la vie urbaine*. Montréal: Les Presses de l'Université de Montréal.

Ezzy, D., Bouma, G., Barton, G., Halafoff, A., Banham, R., Jackson, R., and Beaman, L. G., 2020. 'Religious Diversity in Australia: Rethinking Social Cohesion'. *Religions* 11(2): 92.

Ezzy, D., Banham R., and Beaman, L. G. 2022. 'Religious Anti-discrimination Legislation and the Negotiation of Difference in Victoria, Australia'. *Religion, State & Society* 50(1): 22–39.

Fleras, A. 2019. '50 Years of Canadian Multiculturalism: Accounting for Its Durability, Theorizing the Crisis, Anticipating the Future'. *Canadian Ethnic Studies* 51(2): 19–59.

Garbin, D., and Strhan, A. (eds.). 2017. *Religion and the Global City*. London: Bloomsbury.

Gorski, P. S., and Perry, S. L. 2022. *The Flag and the Cross: White Christian Nationalism and the Threat to American Democracy*. New York: Oxford University Press.

Griera, M., Martínez-Ariño, J., and Clot-Garrell, A. 2021. 'Banal Catholicism, Morality Policies and the Politics of Belonging in Spain'. *Religions* 12(5): 293.

Grigore-Dovlete, M., and Beaman, L. G. 2020. 'The Nativity Scene in a Shared Religious Space: The Case Study of Saint-Pierre's Church in Montreal'. *Studies in Religion/ Sciences Religieuses* 49(3): 347–71.

Halafoff, A., Marriott, E., Smith, G., Weng, E., and Bouma, G. 2021. 'Worldviews Complexity in COVID-19 Times: Australian Media Representations of Religion, Spirituality and Non-religion in 2020'. *Religions* 12(9): 682.

Jedwab, J. 2014. 'Debating Multiculturalism in 21st Century Canada'. In J. Jedwab (ed.), *The Multiculturalism Question*. Queen's Policy Studies Series. Montreal: McGill-Queen's University Press, 1–29.

Kleine, C., and Wohlrab-Sahr, M. 2016. 'Research Programme of the HCAS "Multiple Secularities – Beyond the West, Beyond Modernities"'. *Working Paper Series of the CASHSS "Multiple Secularities – Beyond the West, Beyond Modernities"* 1(1). http://

www.multiple-secularities.de/media/multiple_secularities_research_programme. pdf. Accessed 27 March 2023.

Knott, K. 2015. *The Location of Religion: A Spatial Analysis*. London: Routledge.

Knott, K., Krech, V., and Meyer, B. 2016. 'Iconic Religion in Urban Space. *Material Religion* 12(2): 123–36.

Lavoie, B. 2022. La salle d'urgence comme lieu du droit: la liberté de religion dans le contexte pratique et clinique des soins critiques. *Revue de droit de l'Université de Sherbrooke* 51(2–3): 405–30.

Lee, M., Lim, H., Xavier, M.S., and Lee, E.Y. 2022. ' "A Divine Infection": A Systematic Review on the Roles of Religious Communities during the Early Stage of COVID-19'. *Journal of Religion and Health* 61(1): 866–919.

Meunier, E.-Martin, and Legault-Leclair, J. 2021. 'Nones and Catholics in Quebec'. *Secular Studies* 3(1): 93–117.

MacDonald, F. 2010. 'Relational Group Autonomy: Ethics of Care and the Multiculturalism Paradigm'. *Hypatia* 25(1): 196–212.

Maltais, A., and Koussens, D. 2022. 'L'église par-delà son village: Saint-Pierre-Apôtre de Montréal et l'extra-territorialisation de la paroisse en milieu urbain'. In F. Dejean and A. Germain (eds.), *Se faire une place dans la cité. La participation des groupes religieux à la vie urbaine*. Montréal: Presses de l'Université de Montréal, 71–84.

Martínez-Ariño, J. 2020. 'Urban Responses to Religious Pluralization in France'. In A. Körs, W. Weisse and JP Willaime (eds), *Religious Diversity and Interreligious Dialogue*. Cham: Springer, 117–30.

Modood, T. 2010. *Multiculturalism*. Chichester: John Wiley & Sons.

Parish, H. 2020. 'The Absence of Presence and the Presence of Absence: Social Distancing, Sacraments, and the Virtual Religious Community during the COVID-19 Pandemic'. *Religions* 11(6): 276–82.

Religious Society of Friends (Quakers) in Australia. 2019. 'Quaker Peace and Legislation Committee Submission on Religious Freedom Legislation'. https://www. ag.gov.au/rights-and-protections/publications/submissions-received-religious-dis crimination-bills-first-exposure-drafts-consultation Accessed 1 March 2020.

Selby, J. A. 2011. 'French Secularism as a "guarantor" of Women's Rights? Muslim Women and Gender Politics in a Parisian *Banlieue*'. *Culture and Religion* 12(3): 441–62.

Selby, J., Barras, A., and Beaman, L. G. 2018. *Beyond Accommodation: Everyday Narratives of Muslim Canadians*. Vancouver: UBC Press.

Stacey, T. 2022. *Saving Liberalism from Itself: The Spirit of Political Participation*. Oxford: Policy Press.

Stringer, M. 2016. *Discourses on Religious Diversity: Explorations in an Urban Ecology*. London: Routledge.

Truth and Reconciliation Commission of Canada. 2015. *Calls to Action*. trc.ca/websites/ trcinstitution/File/2015/Findings/Calls_to_Action_English2.pdf. Accessed 27 March 2023.

Vertovec, S. 2007. 'Super-Diversity and Its Implications'. *Ethnic and Racial Studies* 30(6): 1024–54.

Wessendorf, S. 2014. Commonplace diversity: Social relations in a super-diverse context. Cham: Springer.

Winter, E. 2011. '"Immigrants Don't Ask for Self-Government": How Multiculturalism is (De) legitimized in Multinational Societies'. *Ethnopolitics* 10(2): 187–204.

Winter, E. 2014. 'Us, Them, and Others: Reflections on Canadian Multiculturalism and National Identity at the Turn of the Twenty-First Century'. *Canadian Review of Sociology/Revue canadienne de sociologie* 51(2): 128–51.

Wise, A. and Noble, G. 2016. 'Convivialities: An Orientation'. *Journal of intercultural studies* 37(5): 423–31.

Wohlrab-Sahr, M., and Burchardt, M. 2012. 'Multiple Secularities: Toward a Cultural Sociology of Secular Modernities'. *Comparative Sociology* 11(6): 875–909.

Index

www.ingramcontent.com/pod-product-compliance
Lightning Source LLC
Chambersburg PA
CBHW071851270326
41929CB00013B/2180